THE
BRAIDED
RIVER

Praise for *The Braided River*

'Samrat Choudhury's tale of a journey on the Brahmaputra is a wonderful travelogue and history of a magnificent, often unjustly neglected, part of the country. Filled with rich imagery and speckled with deft touches of humour, Choudhury brings to life both the powerful river and those who made their lives along its banks.' —Dr Shashi Tharoor, Member of Parliament and author

'A scholarly and delightfully diverting journey of cultural and geographical exploration down one of the world's most important yet least-known rivers.' —Victor Mallet, author of *River of Life, River of Death*

'Meticulously researched yet very readable, this superb travelogue braids diverse experiences and observations together with vivid descriptions, reflections and humour, as the writer journeys through the waterways, valleys and mountains around one of the world's greatest river systems. A must-read.' —Mitra Phukan, novelist, translator and columnist

'Samrat Choudhury recounts the Brahmaputra's epic tale in a many-layered travel memoir that includes personal observations and encounters, history, geography, folklore and mythology. Each strand is deftly plaited into a compelling narrative that reveals the great river's vast breadth and length, as well as its hidden depths.' —Stephen Alter, author of *Wild Himalaya*

SAMRAT CHOUDHURY

THE BRAIDED RIVER

A JOURNEY ALONG THE
BRAHMAPUTRA

HarperCollins *Publishers* India

First published in India in 2021 by
HarperCollins *Publishers*
A-75, Sector 57, Noida, Uttar Pradesh 201301, India
www.harpercollins.co.in

2 4 6 8 10 9 7 5 3 1

Copyright © Samrat Choudhury 2021

P-ISBN: 978-93-9032-758-4
E-ISBN: 978-93-9032-759-1

Typeset in 11.5/15.2 Adobe Garamond at
Manipal Technologies Limited, Manipal

Printed and bound at
Thomson Press (India) Ltd

This book is dedicated to the last remaining free-flowing rivers of the world, and to all who love them

Contents

Preface   xi

Beginnings

1   The First Glimpse   3
2   Old Man River   6
3   The Guide   15
4   Who Moved My River?   21
5   Quicksand   28

Section I: Tributaries
Part 1: Lohit

6   Red River   37
7   Battle of Inner Line Permit   42
8   Oil, Opium, Apong   47
9   Parshuram's Bath   55

Part 2: Dibang

10 The River Damned   65
11 Temple of the Dread Goddess   75

Part 3: Siang

12	By Magic, Ferry, Winger and Tempo	83
13	Pasighat	88
14	Damn Dams	96
15	Two Kinds of People in This World	106
16	Funeral Bar	109
17	Into Terra Incognita	112
18	Test of Character	117
19	Dragon, Dragon!	120
20	Culture Shocks	129
21	Halted by the Army	134
22	Reincarnating Lamas and Evangelists	143
23	Breakdown	147
24	Yingkiong Again	150
25	The House with the Mithun Heads	153

Section II: Brahmaputra, Upper Assam

26	Dibrugarh	161
27	On Board the Akha	165
28	Chars and Chaporis	170
29	The Ahom Hardliner	179
30	ULFA	187
31	On the Tea Estate	198
32	Interview in a Dying Language	205
33	Sivasagar	210
34	Old Ahom Capitals All in a Row	214
35	The Pir from Baghdad	222
36	Spiritual Jorhat	225
37	A Dark Interlude	238
38	Onwards	242

39	Biswanath	247
40	What's in a Name?	251
41	Looking for the Xihu	256
42	Rhino Country	261
43	Wild Babies	270
44	Wild Grass	277

Section III: Lower Assam and Bangladesh

45	Saraighat	283
46	Guwahati	290
47	The Kamakhya Temple	296
48	Development?	304
49	Pilgrimage of Three Faiths	310
50	Language and Identity	317
51	Culture Wars to NRC and CAA	322
51	Vapour and Vigour	334
52	Guru Tegh Bahadur and the Sorceress	340
53	Citizenship Tensions	350
54	Into Bangladesh	357
55	River Pilot	364
	Epilogue	377
	Notes	383
	Index	387
	Acknowledgements	405
	About the Author	409

Map by Nitendra B. Srivastava

This map is for representational purposes only and does not purport to depict political boundaries.

Preface

IT WAS ALWAYS THERE, a near and distant reality. My first memories of it are of the chugging sound of the old train with its smoky diesel engine changing into a loud clanging as it crossed the old iron bridge near Guwahati. It was a thrill to look out and see the swirling waters below ... more water than I had ever seen in my brief life until then, because I had not seen the sea. The clanging went on for a marvellously long time. People would rush to the windows and even to the open doors, and thrillingly fling coins into the river. Sometimes I was given a ten- or twenty-paisa coin to throw in too. It was an offering to Brahmaputra the river god, the son of Brahma ... and meagre and mindless as it was, it was good sport; a grudging attempt at the appeasement of a force of nature whose might, even to a mere child of six or seven, was apparent.

As I grew older, I became aware of other things about the river, from my distant perch – because that was how it felt – 101 km away in the hill town of Shillong. There was the time a relative who owned a gramophone player got hold of an old vinyl record of songs by Bhupen Hazarika. The delight of the moment when I first heard his clear, mellifluous voice has stayed with me. It was a delight that brought confusion with it. I heard the classic '*Bistirno Duparer*', set to the tune of Old Man River, in Bengali, with the Ganga as the subject. A couple of years later, in Guwahati, where my father's elder brother who worked in the Brahmaputra Board lived, I heard the same song in Assamese in its avatar as '*Bistirno Parore*' with Burha Luit as the subject. I was confused. I didn't understand many of the words. And there was the Brahmaputra, and the Burha Luit, and the Ganga … were they all the same? Was the Burha Luit, perhaps, both Ganga *and* Brahmaputra?

Once I wandered along the riverside with an older neighbour. The river was right there, vast, swirling. Adventure beckoned. The neighbour, who was a college student at the time and had some pocket money, marched down to the ghat and struck a deal with a boatman. He would row us out in his motorless wooden boat towards the river island of Umananda, visible nearby.

It was only a short distance but it felt like an epic voyage. I had by then learnt to row, but rowing in the calm waters of Ward's Lake in Shillong was one thing and in the Brahmaputra was quite another. The wooden oar itself was too heavy for me. I still remember the boatman talking about underwater currents that sucked away unsuspecting people to their riverine graves.

Vague familiarity and a distant curiosity about the river were all I had when I left Shillong for college. Going off on quests was what people in books written by rich people with social security or trust funds did. I loved those stories, but staying alive and earning a living were the quests that I had been brought up to understand as real. India's Northeast in the 1980s and early 1990s was a troubled place. Insurgencies were everywhere, and riots were frequent. The army and paramilitary forces patrolled the streets in armoured vehicles. There were soldiers behind sandbags with machine guns at important places. The news was full of killing and dying.

I studied engineering. The plan was to get an MBA or take the GRE exam and escape to some place where there were no riots and insurgencies, things worked as they were supposed to, and people made a comfortable living. That's how it might have gone, but life had other plans. A series of events, some pure chance, saw me become a journalist instead. At first it was exciting enough, but in time the groove became a bit of a rut. It became a routine, which included in dollops the staples of office drudge work. In addition, there was the growing realization that my job was basically to ensure that the paper was run on a shoestring budget with minimal staff and resources, and came out on time with as few spelling and grammatical errors as possible. Not having the same stories as every other newspaper could get me into trouble; on the other hand, having an exclusive story that rocked the wrong boat could also do the same.

An old dream to live life as a writer came back. I had already written and published a novel in the midst of a demanding and stressful day job. I could not afford non-fiction. That required research, travel and free time, for which I had neither the budget nor the freedom. I might have continued with my comfortable Mumbai life if an invitation from Sanjoy Hazarika, who was then heading the Centre for North East Studies and Policy Research in Jamia Millia Islamia, hadn't landed in my inbox. On a whim, I bought a ticket, took two days off from work and went to Delhi to attend a conference where I was not even presenting a paper. During a tea break, a chance conversation led to the question: Would I like to write a book on the Brahmaputra?

It would involve going on an epic journey. The trouble was, I was living in Mumbai and had a job there. To go anywhere in the Brahmaputra Valley I would have to travel at the very least to

Guwahati, more than 2,000 km east. From there, I would have to make long and potentially difficult journeys by road and river. I could not afford to quit my salaried job, and getting a long sabbatical from work was out of the question. Nor could I afford the luxury of hiring cars and boats to go the entire, and quite considerable, length of the river. The sensible thing to do, it seemed, was to say no.

So I did what anyone in such a situation ought to do – I said yes without sweating the details, and plunged right in.

BEGINNINGS

BEGINNINGS

1

The First Glimpse

IT WAS AROUND 6 o'clock on a grey morning, crack of dawn by our standards, when my photographer friend Akshay Mahajan and I sleepily made our way to Mumbai's Chhatrapati Shivaji Maharaj International Airport for the flight to Dibrugarh in the eastern end of Assam to begin our journey. We had done a little homework, shopped for raincoats and hiking shoes, and stuffed sleeping bags into our backpacks, just in case. We were ready. The river was waiting, bright and clear on the map, a somewhat tasselled ribbon of blue winding its way down from… well, somewhere around Dibru Saikhowa in Assam where three other ribbons of blue, representing the Siang (also known as Dihang), Lohit and Dibang, meet untidily to become the Brahmaputra. Its origins, according to all authorities, lie in Tibet, near Mount Kailash, at an altitude of around 5,150 m, where it starts life as the Yarlung Tsangpo. From there, it flows from west to east before making a U-turn and entering Arunachal Pradesh. There its name changes to Siang. The Siang then gathers more streams and flows down through the Arunachal hills towards the plains of Assam. At the foothills, it meets the Lohit and Dibang. Downstream of this confluence, it is the Brahmaputra. The Brahmaputra in turn flows through Assam, gathering yet more streams, before entering Bangladesh. Upon entering that country it undergoes one more change in nomenclature, this time accompanied by a sex change – the 'male' Brahmaputra, for some reason, becomes the 'female' Jamuna. The Brahmaputra as Jamuna makes its way towards an eventual confluence with the Ganga, known in Bangladesh as the Padma. This great river of many great rivers finally flows into the Bay of Bengal, after undergoing yet another change of name as the Meghna. Its whole length is 2,880 km.

It had looked to my untrained eyes like the Brahmaputra existed only in Assam; though it is often identified as the Brahmaputra, the Tsangpo or Siang is, as far as I could tell from the map, only the longest tributary of that river – a part, not the whole. Beyond Assam, in Bangladesh, the Brahmaputra flows on until its confluence with the Ganga, but there is the matter of that inexplicable name and sex change.

Starting the journey further upriver than Dibrugarh was not practical; there was no airport with regular commercial flights anywhere near the remote hills of Arunachal through which the Siang, Lohit and Dibang flow, although some helipads exist. We would have to go to Dibrugarh and head upriver from there. I had no clue how we were going to do this, or what lay along the way. Google was not of much use and I didn't particularly want to find out that way in any case. We would find out as we went along; weren't serendipity and discovery what the adventure of travel used to be about before its soul was killed and its body came to be packaged and sold as mass tourism, the moneyed hordes being ferried to the ends of the world in cushioned, air-conditioned comfort for yet more selfies?

A rough plan, though, was necessary. The plan was that after pushing upriver some distance along the three formative tributaries – the Lohit, Dibang and Siang – we would drift downriver with the currents of the Brahmaputra, by boat where possible and by road where necessary, down to the last major town on the Indian side of the border. I wanted to see life in the places along the river as I drifted by, and to do it travelling like the locals did, because I wanted just a bit of an insider's view. The traveller is by definition an outsider in the lands he or she travels through; a visitor, not a local. I fit that description, but I was not a traveller from a foreign land. I was a traveller from next door.

I wanted to discover the history and cultures of the lands on the riverbanks with the fresh eyes of an outsider, and something of the knowledge of an insider. There are many ways of seeing. I wanted to see like someone who is a mix of both outsider and insider.

2

Old Man River

THE BRAHMAPUTRA IS A very old river. According to Arup Kumar Dutta in his book *The Brahmaputra*, it is older than the Himalayas. He writes:

> In the Cretaceous period of the Mesozoic era a sea called Tethys existed between the Tibetan and Indian land masses … which was later uplifted by a geological upheaval into the Himalayan mountain range. A corollary to this hypothesis is that in the prehistoric past the Tsangpo had actually flowed from east to west.

The Brahmaputra is called an antecedent river, and a paleo-Brahmaputra is generally accepted by experts to have flowed in what is now the Tibetan plateau before the Himalayas rose. The tributaries of the Tsangpo, even today, flow east to west, which is opposite to the Tsangpo's current flow.

The Cretaceous period lasted from approximately 145.5 million years ago to 65.5 million years ago. It followed the Jurassic period. Dinosaurs still roamed the earth; their extinction is believed to have occurred at the end of the Cretaceous period around the time when an asteroid hit the earth in the Yucatan peninsula in what is now Mexico, though it is not certain if the asteroid caused the extinction.

The Himalayas had not yet formed at that time. The mountains are estimated to have started forming around 20 million years ago. Geologists estimate they achieved their great heights less than a million years ago. Before they rose, a river flowing south of the watershed that became the Himalayas may have 'captured' a stream flowing to its north – the ancestor of the Tsangpo – thus giving rise to the Brahmaputra.

Anatomically modern human beings are believed to have emerged through evolution only around 200,000 years ago, but there is evidence that early human species were around as far as two million years back. According to the geologist Professor D.N. Wadia:

> There is a body of competent evidence, both physical and biological, to indicate that parts of the Himalayas have risen at least 5,000 feet since the Middle Pleistocene (780,000– 126,000 years ago). Early man thus witnessed the growth of this northern barrier interfering more and more with his migrations and intercourse across the Steppes of Asia.[1]

There are a number of ancient myths and legends surrounding the origins of the Brahmaputra. According to a Tibetan myth, there was once a great lake that existed in the area of the Chang Tan plateau through which the Tsangpo now flows. A Bodhisattva, Guru Padmasambhava, is believed to have cut a path through the mountains for the river to flow.

The real Guru Padmasambhava probably travelled from the area around what is now Odisha or Bengal to Tibet in the eighth century. There are legends that say he died in Hajo in Assam, a few kilometres downriver from Guwahati. Tibetan legends claim that the great guru converted the people from their animistic faith through a series of miracles, which included draining the waters of the great lake.

A similar myth exists in Hindu tradition as well. According to it, Brahma, the creator in the Hindu holy trinity, had a child with Amogha, wife of Sage Shantanu. The sage placed the child amidst four great mountains, of which one was Mount Kailash. The child turned into water and became a great lake bounded by the mountains, called Brahma Kund.

Sage Parshurama, who according to Hindu mythology had committed the horrific crime of axing his mother to death, arrived at this Brahmakund many years later, trying to wash away his sin. His axe had got stuck to his hand after the murder and all his efforts to get rid of it had failed. When he took a dip in Brahma Kund, the axe came loose. He threw it away with all his might. It cut a gap in the Himalayas, through which the Brahmaputra started to flow. The water turned red from the blood that washed off Parshuram's axe, and so the river came to be knows as Lauhitya, from 'lahu', which means blood. This is the river that we now call the Lohit.

There is a rational explanation that fits the myths, which were perhaps born of vague memories transmitted through stories from times long past. It is possible that the ancient Tsangpo may have been dammed by a natural barrier of ice and mud due to glaciation during the last Ice Age that ended around 12,000 years ago. As the ice age ended, the ice would have turned to water, creating a vast lake. At some point, the natural 'dam' that blocked the river's flow would have given way. The glacial lake would have burst out, giving reincarnation to the river.

The end of the Ice Age is the time when most of what we now call civilization was apparently coming to life. The thawing of the ice set free the frozen rivers. It also sparked off the beginnings of agriculture – and religion – and paved the way for the rise of kingdoms and empires. A new age of humankind began.

River valleys were the first cradles of ancient civilizations. There was the Indus Valley civilization, the civilizations of the Fertile Crescent around the rivers Tigris and Euphrates in what are now Iraq and Syria, the Yellow River civilization in China and the Nile Valley civilization in Egypt.

Thousands of years later, the Gangetic plains became the site of the first great Indian empire. This was the Mauryan Empire in fourth century BC.

They were not alone. Memories of the people who lived in that ancient past are lost in the mists of time. Some bits survive in mythical form – in the epic Mahabharata and in the Puranas, the collections of lore. These suggest that the Brahmaputra Valley, too, was home to kingdoms and empires that had close relations – friendly as well as hostile – with the kingdoms of 'mainland' India. The ties between India and its 'remote' Northeast are far from new.

Cultural, social and economic ties, however, do not equate to political union. The political maps of Bharat and Hindustan were different from those of modern India – not least because modern techniques of mapping and surveying were not invented until after 1569, when Flemish cartographer Gerardus Mercator created what is now called the Mercator projection. The present political map of India is one that took shape during the British colonial period. The mapping of rivers, and particularly the Brahmaputra, was crucial to this.

The Brahmaputra had already been identified, by the time Major James Rennell published his celebrated Bengal Atlas in 1779 and *Memoir of a Map of Hindoostan* in 1782, as one of the Indian subcontinent's major rivers. The recognition for the river owed much to the earlier efforts of Major Rennell himself. In 1765, according to a paper by John Ardussi on 'The Quest for the Brahmaputra River and its Course According to Tibetan Sources,' Rennell made an expedition to trace the course of the river 'from Goalpara in Bengal to the frontier of Assam, a distance ... of twenty-two miles by river'. He was surprised to discover that it was 'rather larger than the Ganges' and flowed from the east though 'all the former accounts represented it as from the north; and this unexpected discovery soon led to enquiries, which furnished me with an account of its general course, to within 100 miles of the place where Du Halde left the Sanpoo [Tsangpo]. I could no longer doubt that the Burrampooter and Sanpoo were one and the same river.'

Rennell was commissioned to map all such rivers in order to facilitate the smooth movement of the Company's boats. In his preface, he wrote:

> Whatever charges may be imputable to the Managers of the Company, the neglect of useful Science, however, is not among the number. The employing of Geographers, and surveying Pilots in India; and the providing of astronomical instruments, and the holding out of instruments to such as should use them indicate, at least, a spirit above the mere consideration of Gain.[2]

It was a task that Rennell undertook in the spirit of contribution to science. Though he was unable to enter the Ahom kingdom, he correctly concluded that the Tsangpo joined the Brahmaputra and not the Irrawaddy. He was, however, unable to trace the course of the river, and so a number of questions remained unanswered. If the Tsangpo was indeed the Brahmaputra, how did it turn from flowing west to east in Tibet to the exact opposite in Assam? By what means did it make the leap from the Himalayan heights of the Tibetan plateau, later found to be at an elevation of over 14,000 feet, down to the Brahmaputra plains which are less than 500 feet above the mean sea level? What mysteries lay in those blank areas on the map?

Finding answers was no easy task. The Himalayas were a formidable barrier, the Tibetan Plateau itself was desolate and inhospitable and the Tibetans were deeply suspicious of outsiders, particularly Europeans. Westerners were forbidden from entering Lhasa, and therefore knew it as the 'Forbidden City'. The mapping of India, which had become one of the grandest projects that would ever be undertaken by the British Raj – the Great Trigonometric Survey of India took seventy years from its beginning in 1802 and continued past the end of East India Company rule in 1857 when the crown took over the rule of its jewel – was proceeding apace, but the surveyors realized they knew little of what lay beyond their frontiers, and were not in a position to find out. Captain T.G. Montgomerie, an officer of the Trigonometric Survey in charge of mapping Kashmir, came up with a solution. In 1861, he proposed sending Indian spies on survey trips to fill the gaps in the map in Tibet and Central Asia. 'Asiatics, the subjects of the British Government, are known to travel freely without molestation in countries far beyond the British frontier; they constantly pass to and fro between India and Central Asia, and also between India and Tibet, for trading and other purposes, without exciting any suspicion,' he wrote in his 'Report of a route survey made by Pundit, from Nepal to Lhasa and thence through the upper valley of the Brahmaputra to its source'. Following his observation, a small group of Indian spies were recruited and trained in the methods of surveying; the report of 1868 was a result of their efforts. Through practice they learnt to walk 2,000 paces to the mile. To keep count, they were given Buddhist rosaries with 100 beads instead of 108. Their field notes, from which the reports were made, were hidden in scrolls in the heads of the prayer wheels. The compass was usually kept in a secret compartment in the head of the walking stick, whose hollow interiors would also hide gold and silver coins. Boxes with secret compartments hid thermometers to measure the boiling temperature of water, from which altitude could be calculated. Thus armed, the pundits – typically disguised as pilgrims or Buddhist lamas – undertook journeys of great danger and difficulty as players in what Rudyard Kipling called 'the Great Game' then on between the British, Russian and Chinese empires.

A village schoolmaster, Nain Singh from Pithoragarh, and a tailor from Darjeeling, Kinthup, were the pundits through whose efforts much of the course of the Tsangpo through Tibet was mapped. In 1880, Kinthup was despatched from Darjeeling and tasked with following the Tsangpo through Tibet into Assam. Being illiterate, he was sent along with a Chinese lama who unfortunately sold him into slavery and decamped with the survey equipment. However, after a series of adventures, Kinthup managed to reach the periphery of the Buddhist sacred zone known as the Pemako that lies in remote eastern Tibet. His observations, recounted from memory years later, were recorded and – perhaps owing to a later misinterpretation – became the source of the legend of the greatest waterfall on earth, believed for many years to exist on the Brahmaputra in its upper reaches.

Until the end of the nineteenth century, that part of the world was a place known mostly through myth and legend.

Even after 1900, there remained an unmapped territory extending south from Tibet's Kham region down to the foot of the Abor Hills of what is now Arunachal Pradesh. The foremost experts of the time gathered what information they could about the place, but the reports were not very encouraging. Lawrence Waddell, a controversial man of many parts who had a remarkable talent for being in every troubled spot in the East from China to Sumeria at just the wrong times, was an adviser to the Francis Younghusband expedition of 1903 that was the first Western force to reach Lhasa. He published a contemporary account on *Lhasa and its Mysteries: With a Record of the Expedition of 1903-04* soon after the event. Writing about the hills south of Tibet, he wrote, 'The country here is inhabited (if you can call a country inhabited which has only one person to the square mile) by a sprinkling of savage cannibal tribes called by the Tibetans "Lalo" (i.e. savages) and Chingmi.' In a footnote, Waddell explained that 'the Black Savages (Lalo or Laklo-Nagpo) are said to eat their prisoners of war, and at their marriage ceremonies kill and eat the mother of the bride if no other person is forthcoming.' The Scottish diplomat Reginald Johnston, who was tutor to the last Chinese emperor Pu Yi, published an account three years after Waddell in 1908 in which he corroborated this detail. 'The country between Assam and Tibet is unfortunately inhabited by tribes that are apparently hostile to all strangers. Their own domestic habits are of a somewhat repellent nature: it is said, for instance, that on the occasions of the celebration of marriages it is the genial custom of one of the tribes to serve up the bridegroom's mother-in-law at the nuptial banquet,' Johnston wrote.

Culinary doubts apart, there were also geographical ones, in particular about the great waterfall – suspected to be the highest in the world – that was rumoured to exist on the Tsangpo, as it made its way down from the Tibetan Plateau.

The most serious concern, though, was geopolitical. The Great Game had been sparked by British fears of growing Russian influence extending to the frontiers of India. In 1903-04, Colonel Francis Younghusband, with the support of the Viceroy Lord Curzon, mounted a little invasion of Tibet. The Viceroy feared that Tibet was slipping into the Russian sphere of influence. In 1912, the rule of the last Qing emperor of China, Pu Yi, ended. The centre could not hold; Tibet made its bid to shake off Chinese suzerainty.

The following year, Britain organized a conference in Shimla to discuss the status of Tibet. It was attended by the Dalai Lama's representative, Lonchen Shatre Paljor Dorje, on behalf of Tibet, 'Monsieur' Ivan Chen of Sun Yat Sen's newly formed Republic of China government and Sir Henry McMahon, foreign and political secretary of British India. Contemporaneous photographs show them all together in a row with Sir McMahon, in military uniform with a chest-full of medals, in the centre. The Chinese representatives, in natty suits and hats, flank him on one side. The Tibetans, in traditional outfits, are on the other. An accord emerged from this meeting in 1914, days before the outbreak of the First World War. The Chinese delegate had withdrawn by then, and only the Tibetan and British representatives signed the final document with its map demarcating the boundary between Tibet and India. The line between the two countries, drawn with a thick pen, was the work of McMahon. After that he moved on to the Middle East, where he began a correspondence with the Sharif of Mecca on future boundaries of Palestine and Syria. His mapmaking effort there, as in the case of Tibet, has not had happy consequences. India and China's war of 1962 was the result of a dispute over the line that bears McMahon's name. It is a dispute that continues to fester to this day, and periodically spirals into military standoffs between the two most populous countries on earth. China has never recognized the McMahon line that India considers the boundary between the two countries. In Chinese maps, roughly 83,000 square kilometres of the Brahmaputra river basin in Arunachal Pradesh and Assam is 'Southern Tibet'.

3

The Guide

THERE WAS NO DIRECT flight from Mumbai to Dibrugarh. When Akshay and I finally landed there after more than six-and-a-half hours of travelling, with a change of flights in Kolkata, it was obvious we had reached a town very different from forever abuzz Mumbai. An air of langour pervaded the place. Booking a taxi took a while as the people at the counter proceeded to do their work in the style called 'lahe lahe' or 'by and by' famous in Assam. Eventually we managed to get on our way, to the home of our kind hosts, my friends Millie and Masood. It had been many years since I last visited them, on which occasion we had taken a trip together into Myanmar, via the Pangsau Pass in the Patkai Hills, to the Lake of No Return. We did return, and were perhaps fortunate to do so. The old World War II Stilwell Road on which we were travelling was then motorable by four-wheel drive up to a point, some 12 km from India's border with Myanmar. From thereon, it was a trek. At the time, there were a lot of insurgents from various Naga militant groups and armed men of the Assam

Rifles paramilitary in the area. We crossed several military checkposts en route and were on the last leg of our hike when a few men in civilian clothes armed with AK-47s emerged from the jungle. We stopped in our tracks. Masood slowly began to step back into the jungle while I grinned foolishly and engaged the men in attempts at conversation. We had no common language and I did not understand them, nor they me. Fortunately, they were friendly and merely gave us some cardboard tokens that we were told to return on our way out. It was a version of border control, probably by soldiers of the Burmese military. We were not carrying passports or visas.

When we eventually got back to Masood and Millie's place, the first thing Masood did was pull a pistol out of a shoulder holster and place it on the centre table. He had thought the armed men with AKs to be militants and had backed up so he could draw his pistol. We would have died for sure if he had. He is of the nawabi mould; a man who likes to stroke his moustache while watching his minions, of whom there are several, scurry about.

Masood has spent most of his life in Dibrugarh. His family, the Khans, had lived there for four generations but traced their origins to Ghazipur in Uttar Pradesh. At an earlier time, they had been Hindu Rajputs in what is now Rajasthan, he said.

I had not heard of Ghazipur. Masood introduced it as a place in Varanasi district that was the site of the largest opium factory in the world. According to him, 'The monkeys of Ghazipur are all addicts. They drink the water from the factory effluent drain and get high. Then they go and piss on Lord Cornwallis's grave.'

Lord Cornwallis, who was Governor General of India in the late 1700s, died in Ghazipur in 1805 while on a journey around the country visiting military outposts. A good racist, like most people of his time, he had formulated something called the Cornwallis Code, which institutionalized racism in the British administration in India.

He had a poor opinion of Anglo-Indians as well, and wrote, ' ... as on account of their colour and extraction they are considered in this country as inferior to Europeans, I am of opinion that those of them who possess the best abilities could not command that authority and respect which is necessary in the due discharge of the duty of an officer.'[3]

Basically, only pure white men were of suitable 'colour and extraction' to be officers, according to Cornwallis. It seems a fitting tribute to him then that the opiated monkeys of Ghazipur tend to piss on his colonnaded tomb.

Masood's great-grandfather had come to Dibrugarh more than a century ago. The journey, a long and dangerous one in those times, was apparently triggered by a missing barber or oil-presser – family accounts differed on which. Every village in those days used to have a village barber, a village oil-presser for cooking oil and other such tradespeople. Travel was rough and took time. Each village or cluster of villages therefore needed to function autonomously, because it was pretty inconvenient to walk for days to buy oil or get a haircut.

The village oil-presser from Masood's ancestral village in Ghazipur, for some reason, ran away. Then one day, months or years later, word filtered back that the man had set up house in Assam – the first place in India where oil of another kind was struck in 1867. Masood's great-grandfather, on hearing that the precious oil-presser had been found, organized a search party. The men travelled down the Gangetic plains and up the Brahmaputra valley to Makum in Upper Assam, around 1,500 kilometres away. The mission was successful and the very important oil-presser was found.

It had been a long journey; the men of the search party decided to rest for a while in Assam. It seems that during this time, Masood's great-grandfather grew fond of its wild, open, fertile lands. When he returned to Ghazipur, he rallied his family, packed his bags and travelled all the way back to Makum. He had decided to move to Assam.

The family did well in Dibrugarh. As their business flourished, they slowly assimilated into the Assamese culture, eventually becoming Assamese. Masood was an influential student leader during the tumultuous All Assam Students' Union agitation of the early 1980s that saw student leaders Prafulla Mahanta and Bhrigu Phukan go straight from their university hostel rooms to ministerial bungalows.

Masood knew Assam well. The river, however, was not one of his specialities. Nonetheless, he assured us he was acquainted with just the right person to guide us.

This person happened to be a timber-smuggler. Since the smuggling business has traditionally thrived on the river, the gentleman knew its course and its people well. So on our first day in Dibrugarh, Masood, Akshay and I drove down to the riverside in his SUV in search of this man.

Our drive took us off the pucca road on to bumpy dirt tracks, and past a line of bamboo shacks out on to the riverbank. The sun was setting; in the near distance, we could see the river, and beyond it, sandbanks and water all the way to the horizon. Masood drove away from the water, back towards a hut on the riverbank. A genial-looking, middle-aged man with bloodshot eyes was sitting outside with an old laptop looking out at the river. He smiled a kindly smile and asked us to sit. It was Mr Smuggler. Pleasantries were exchanged, a flunkey summoned and drinks ordered.

Mr Smuggler came from a family of opium merchants. Opium was legal during the British Raj, and at one point, accounted for close to 20 per cent of India's revenues. In fact, India had been the largest exporter of opium in the world for centuries. The export of opium from British India, mainly to China, continued into the 1920s. It obviously took a lot of people to grow, process and trade all that opium and this man's ancestors were among those people. Then one day the British administration changed the laws, and the legal became criminal. A lot of people changed their line of work, but his forefathers did not. And that is how they became opium smugglers. This gent himself had diversified into a more popular and practical product: timber. Logging, too, was now mostly illegal, but when has a technicality ever stopped anything in India? Looking out from where we sat, we could see a few logs of wood stacked in the distance by the river. Big, thick logs – the trunk of an entire tree or two.

Masood asked the good smuggler for some tourist advice. What were the places we should visit? Dibru Saikhowa National Park was a must, he said. It was unique – a national park that was mostly water. Mr Smuggler remembered a story. Apparently, the Shah of Iran had visited Dibru Saikhowa some decades ago – he couldn't remember when – for hunting. 'The forest officer himself had acted as his guide for the hunt,' he said, admiringly.

'Hunting!' I said. 'But isn't that illegal?'

'It is illegal for other people,' he retorted.

We went back to talking about our travel plans. We would have to cross the river. There was no bridge. We would have to take a ferry. The friendly smuggler assured us that the ride would be free for us. 'I will send word you are my people. They wouldn't dare take money,' he said. I smiled awkwardly at his hospitable offer.

The conversation meandered into his troubles in life. He was having difficulties with the internet speed at this place on the bank of the Brahmaputra in Dibrugarh, with nothing around except an endless river in front and a few bamboo shanties at the back. He had spent his day downloading and watching *The Longest Day*, the epic World War II film about the Normandy landings. Now he was sitting there looking at the river, nursing his whiskey and waiting for *The Dirty Dozen* to finish downloading.

A tall, slim young man carrying a fancy DSLR camera and tripod walked in. He was Mr Smuggler's son, who was home on holiday from his college in Bengaluru. His daughter, Mr Smuggler said proudly, was studying abroad. Leaving Masood and him to chat, his son, Akshay and I walked down to the river that flowed before us, mighty and strong. The colours of a red sunset were reflected on its rippling surface. A few children played on the riverbank. A lone fisherman was still at work, knee-deep in the water, with a small net. Out in the near distance, a small wooden dugout canoe with a solitary boatman swept past silently and swiftly. It was our first glimpse of the river. I had only ever seen it in Guwahati before, where it is at its narrowest, and mostly from a safe distance. This looked different.

'It's very fast,' I said, looking towards the river. One of Mr Smuggler's assistants who was standing nearby replied, 'It has slowed down a lot since last week.' I looked at the torrent before us and made a mental note to stay away from the crumbling, sandy edge. I can't swim, and chances of survival looked negligible if I fell in. There was a sandbank across from where we were. I couldn't see the other bank, though. Maybe in better light ... but even then, some shape should have been visible on the other side. It wasn't dark yet. I had expected a big river but with a bank clearly visible on the other side, like in Guwahati. Why couldn't I see the other bank? 'It's very wide,' I said thoughtfully. 'This is not the main channel of the river,' the man replied. I was stumped. What I was looking at was a fast and powerful channel of water around a kilometre or more wide. And this was not the main channel of the river? 'So where's the actual Brahmaputra?' I asked. The man waved in the direction of the horizon, 'There.'

'How wide is it?'

'Oh, it varies ... maybe 20 km during rains.'

It sounded incredible.

4

Who Moved My River?

WE HAD NOT THOUGHT that the Brahmaputra would be hard to find. It's huge, it's a river, and it's right there. I had seen it many times in Guwahati, where it is a single channel of water flowing between two banks and the opposite bank is visible, and of course I had seen it neatly marked on maps. After our first day in Dibrugarh, I realized something was amiss. It was there all right, but it wasn't a neat, muscular channel of water flowing between two clear banks. It was this thing that had major and minor channels, all of shifting and varied names and identities. I figured that one of these, the most major of the major channels, was the 'actual Brahmaputra'. It would have to be tracked down. So, taking the advice of the friendly smuggler, we decided to go to Dibru Saikhowa to find the river.

Our drive took us to Guijan ghat near Tinsukia, where we found room onboard a large wooden houseboat. It was evening, and the sun was setting. The river raced past us, all whorls and eddies. We could hear it and see the odd tree branch or uprooted water hyacinth bobbing downriver at pace. Sometimes there would be a little splash in the near distance as a chunk of earth fell into the river. It was a sound that would become familiar. It was the sound of the water eating away the land.

I wondered whether we had found the 'real' Brahmaputra. 'Is this the main channel of the Brahmaputra?' I asked Madhab, the Ahom boy who was our porter, guide and general handyman on the boat. I got the response I was getting used to. 'No, this is the Dibru. The Brahmaputra is … ' – and he waved his hand in front to point to the expanse in front of us – 'there'.

'There' across the Dibru river was a large sandbank that turned out to be a river island.

Night fell. It was a night of deep darkness, darkness of a kind that you can never see in cities. The silence was broken by the sound of distant folk music from somewhere across the water. We had seen no land around us apart from the river island. There was no light visible. However, it was clearly inhabited … and the inhabitants in this distant outpost in Upper Assam seemed to be Bengali. The song was in an eastern dialect of Bangla.

The sky was more lit up than the earth, the pinpoints of countless stars sparkling above us. It was nothing like the sky that's visible in the city; we might as well have been on another planet. Here on the river, I turned my gaze up and sat looking, transfixed. A band of light was clearly visible. 'The Milky Way,' I said to Akshay. I had never seen it before.

'Hathi Pathi,' said Madhab.

Hathi Pathi: the Elephant Path in the sky.

There's a quote, attributed to various people from the Buddha to Anaïs Nin, that goes something like: 'We do not see things as they are, we see them as we are'. The ancient Greeks and Romans had seen the band of stars in the night sky and thought of a trail of milk.

The ancient Hindus had seen it as Akash Ganga, the holy Ganges in the sky. Some Assamese had seen the same band of stars and thought of an elephant trail drawn in stars.

Almost everybody around the world, including Assam, now sees that band as the Milky Way. Hardly anyone sees it as the Elephant Path.

Down on the horizon, upriver, looking past the bow of the firmly anchored boat, we could see only one other band of light. It was an orange glow in the distance: the light of a massive fire – a flare from an oil well.

It was the kind of scene where one could conceive, a hundred years ago when the forests around were thick with wild animals, a person might easily have been awed by the river, the jungle and the dark. The song wafting in from the distance may have added to the sense of wonder and dread if one did not know the language. The milieu might have evoked a sense of a journey into the heart of darkness.

We sat on the deck of the boat stargazing. Time had slowed down. In the silence and the dark it felt like late night; it was quieter and darker than it ever gets in Mumbai at any time. I knew it couldn't be very late but found it hard to reckon how long we had been up there. An hour? Two hours? We tried guessing the time. It felt like 10 p.m. at least. It turned out to be 6.30. By 7.30 we were done with dinner and ready to sleep.

The night passed with little incident and in reasonable comfort, except for a brief period around three in the morning when the power failed. The fan stopped whirring. It was sweltering hot. I threw off the covers and was immediately set upon by hordes of mosquitoes. The only other sound was that of water lapping against the hull of the boat. There was nothing to see; it was pitch dark. Someone was walking about in the narrow passageway outside my cabin. The power came back after a while. I went back to sleep.

We were up at first light around 5 a.m. without any alarm or wake-up call. The time zone in Northeast India is certainly different. Morning started early with cups of chai and biscuits and the only perennial activity here: river gazing. Then a man in combat fatigues carrying an AK-47 walked in. The boat staff seemed to barely notice his presence. I looked around, to see if there were more. Soon enough, there were four men in fatigues with AKs on the boat. They walked around, avoided conversation and soon left. They were soldiers from the Indian Army's Kumaon Regiment out on patrol. No one on the boat seemed to have anything to say about their little visit.

We started on our water journey into the Dibru Saikhowa National Park soon after. Our transport for this leg of the journey was a small wooden country-boat fitted with a very loud motor. These are locally known as 'bhut-bhuti' for the sound they make. The crew included a small, wiry boatman and his underage apprentice, a boy of thirteen, whose job it was to constantly bail water out of the leaky boat with a plastic bucket improvised from a used cooking oil can.

Boatman Radhabinod Pal was from Sivasagar, also in Upper Assam. He had moved to Guijan ghat in 2005. Dibru Saikhowa had been declared a national park in 1999, and the first tourist lodge in the area, run by a reformed poacher named Joynal Abedin, had come up. The United Liberation Front of Asom's insurgency, which had severely affected these areas, was winding down. Tourism was starting, and there was work for him.

The river we were on, the Dibru, had been a smaller river then, Pal said. It started growing. More water coursed through it. Year on year, it kept becoming more powerful.

The river's swift current swept us downstream, out of sight of the ghat and the houseboat. We passed the tip of the river island with its emptiness of white sand and turned into a channel that Pal said would eventually connect with the Brahmaputra. Our boat was now travelling upriver; we had changed direction. The forest thickened gradually on both sides. From tall kaash grass with their tufts of white it turned to thick undergrowth and tall trees. The only inhabitants we saw were birds on the sparkling white-sand river beaches. Terns, herons, storks and kingfishers observed our noisy passing.

That other humans passed this way, however, was evident from little signs. Somewhere in the mud, a few incense sticks. What were those incense sticks doing there? Who was the God being worshipped here in what looked like the middle of nowhere? Why, Ganesha of course, said Pal ... but it could also be Shiva ... who is Ganesha's father.

The channel we were on, which varied between 70 m to 100 m wide, flowed strong. Stumps of big trees stood almost concealed in the water at intervals; they had succumbed to its flow. Boatman Pal stood at the prow of the boat, peering ahead for signs of submerged danger. His apprentice Amit steered following his hand signals. The speed with which he waved his hands seemed to be an indication of the urgency with which the boat needed to be turned. On one or two occasions he also turned and glared at Amit. We probably had a few close shaves.

The heat increased. The hours wore on. We stopped taking photos. Conversation ceased. We began wiping sweat and drinking water in silence. Three hours later, we had still not reached the 'real' Brahmaputra. The river we were on had widened. The forest had thinned; now it was sandbars on one side and grassland on the other. We were getting close, Pal said.

We came upon it quite suddenly.

It was like nothing I had ever seen or imagined. In every direction before us, as far as the eye could see, there were only channels of water separated by sandbars and river islands. It was a waterworld. This vast entirety of sand and water was the great Brahmaputra.

Here, at the edge of the Dibru Saikhowa National Park, is close to where it is, in truth, born. This is where the rivers Siang, Lohit and Dibang merge in the area around the massive river island, roughly 35 km long and 10 km wide, on which the park is located. The untidy tassels of water they together form is the Brahmaputra.

To think only the main channel is the river is folly; in fact, the whole combination of channels and sandbanks constitutes the river. The Dibru, too, is a part of it. So is the river channel we had seen on our first day out in Dibrugarh.

The river is the sum of its parts, and much more.

It has come to be that the Siang, which is the longest and strongest of its three formative tributaries, is seen as the Brahmaputra; but the part is not the whole. In terms of water volume, the Siang is at best about a third the size of the Brahmaputra. The Lohit, which meets the Siang on the northern shore of Dibru Saikhowa, is no minnow. And the Dibang in monsoon carries a surprisingly large volume of water, more than the Lohit. It is almost as big as the Siang in the rainy season. Many other tributaries that are great, powerful rivers in themselves, such as the Subansiri, Manas, Teesta and Kopili flow into the Brahmaputra, making it the phenomenon of nature that it is.

Hydrologists call it a 'braided river'. The term starts to make sense when you see the Brahmaputra, not from a bank, but from somewhere in the middle. Braids of water run into one another. Sometimes a channel seems to flow in a direction opposite to the channel next to it. The dance of creation and destruction is visible in the play between sand and water. The fine, silvery white river sand accumulates over time to form sandbars, which turn into little islands. Then some subtle balance in the forces at work may shift from one side to another. The water may start to nibble away at the island.

It is possible that the island may disappear. Or it may not.

Perhaps a bit of grass will start to grow on one of the countless sandy islands. Perhaps the tall kaash grass will take root. Sand may slowly start to turn into soil. A seed may float in from somewhere, and grow into a tree. One tree may turn into many trees. Animals and humans may come to settle. Then, one monsoon day, the river may rise, and lay waste to it all. It may start eating away the island, until no more than a sliver of a sandbar remains. And the cycle of creation and destruction starts again.

5

Quicksand

AKSHAY AND I STARED awestruck at this waterworld. It seemed impossible to tell direction in this place without a GPS, or even with one ... because a navigable river channel that exists today may become too shallow for boats next month. Or even run dry. Which channel does one point the boat into?

Boatman Pal seemed to know from memory and instinct. He navigated with ease past a big channel into another narrow channel. We were once more riding upriver. There was only an endless wasteland of sandbars dancing in the heat on one side. In the far distance, we could see a thin line of land ... or maybe it was the horizon. On the other side, land was close to us, a few feet higher than the channel. It formed a sharp edge with a drop of some seven or eight feet. The shallow channel dispersed into smaller braids that were running dry. By now it was past midday. The heat was oppressive. No one was talking; it was an effort to speak.

We went up one of those braids that ran dry ahead of us. The boat halted. Wordlessly, Pal got out and climbed up the verge. Madhab, the boy from the houseboat who had accompanied us, climbed up after him. They motioned for us to follow.

I thought we had taken a wrong fork in the river and were going to back up. Instead, Pal and Madhab set off in opposite directions, with Pal motioning for us to follow him. We were now on sandy earth that soon turned to grassland dotted with brush and a few stunted trees. Pal walked into the grassland. We followed. The sweat poured off us in buckets. Akshay said, sourly, 'I wasn't expecting this. This is a green desert.'

'Where are we going?' I asked Pal.

'To see the wild horses,' he replied.

Dibru Saikhowa is famous for its feral horses, which inhabit the grasslands. The more thickly forested areas have wilder animals, including elephants and tigers.

We walked fast and in silence through a thin track in the grassland until we came to a place where a riverbed had recently run dry. We could see pools of water in the sand. Across, on the other side of this riverbed, was more grassland.

Pal shaded his eyes with his hands and looked out across the riverbed. I was carrying a small monocular, what old seafarers used to call an eyeglass. I peered through it in the same direction and saw sand, driftwood and grass. Pal asked if he could take a look, and announced, 'They are there.' Saying this, he set off to cross the riverbed.

'Run across, and don't stop,' he said, as we were about to put our feet onto the soft sand. 'This is quicksand.'

Akshay and I looked at one another.

Pal had nimbly made his way to the other side. 'Heavy people are more prone to sinking,' he shouted helpfully from the other side.

Akshay, almost six feet tall and bigger than Pal or me, weighed over 80 kg then. With some trepidation, I waited for him to go next. He charged off, leaving footsteps at least six inches deep in the sand, which vanished soon after. His pace slackened with each step; pulling out the leg after a step clearly took effort, and the heat had sapped our energies. But he kept going, and I was very glad to see him finally stagger across to the other side.

I made a dash for it next, feeling my legs go in, and forcing myself to run on as if my life depended on it ... which it did. If one of us had started to sink in there, it may have been difficult for the others to effect a rescue. We were not carrying anything apart from my pocket umbrella and a one-litre bottle of drinking water, shared between the three of us. There was no gear, no mobile signal and no human habitation for many miles.

The crossing was made without incident. Reaching the other side, we made a rest stop, washed our sweaty, flushed faces in the remaining water of that channel and drank a little of the water we had in careful sips. Then we walked on into the grassland in front of us. A little path ran on the edge of the river channel, at a height of some six or seven feet above the water to our left. To our right was grassland and brush. We were walking single file at a strong, steady pace, in silence, with Pal in front, Akshay next, and me bringing up the rear, when I heard some rustling in the undergrowth. Then, snorts. It sounded like some large animal. A horse? Or ... could it be a leopard?

I looked towards Pal. He had disappeared around a bend in the path. Akshay was busy wiping sweat and walking on unhappily, totally oblivious to the sounds. I quickened my pace to catch up with Pal, and spotted him up ahead. Suddenly, there was a clatter of hooves. Pal ducked and froze. I copied his movements. Akshay, after a few moments of masterly inactivity, did the same.

It was a herd of wild water buffaloes, a rare and endangered species. There are only around 3,400 of them left in the world.

The wild buffalo is one of the most dangerous animals in the jungle. The Cape buffalo was considered one of the 'big five' by hunters in Africa, the other four being the lion, elephant, rhino and leopard. In India, the tiger substituted the lion in most places in the big five rankings. The water buffalo, which weighs around a ton, replaced its smaller African cousin, the Cape buffalo.

Ahead of me, I saw Akshay straightening up. He seemed unimpressed by the herd of snorting, cantering buffaloes with their sweeping, wicked horns, visible hardly 20 m away in the brush. The skittish buffaloes seemed undecided about whether to charge towards us or away. The former would be fatal, of course. I had made up my mind to jump into the river if they came at us, even though I can't swim and buffaloes can.

The buffaloes snorted, pawed the ground and eventually cantered off into the brush after a brief while. I heaved a sigh of relief. We resumed our march in silence.

We came to more open grassland. There, in front of us, a few beautiful horses and a little foal stood grazing. Pal went around behind them. We took up position behind a little tree. The horses broke into a run and went galloping past us.

That was it. Show over. It had lasted barely a couple of minutes. We had to embark on our long trek back.

'Did you get any pictures?' I asked Akshay.

He had some great ones of the horses galloping past.

'What about the buffaloes?'

'Buffaloes?' Akshay snorted. 'They looked just like regular buffaloes.'

'So did the horses,' I replied.

He wasn't convinced.

'The circus lions also look just like the wild lions,' I pointed out. 'Same with elephants too.'

The logic was impeccable. Akshay stomped off.

We retraced our path. The run across quicksand was harder this time since we were more tired, but in a way easier because we knew what we had to do. The march in the heat seemed interminable. Our drinking water ran out. I had also brought along a fancy water bottle with a built-in filter, but there was no water on our route. The nearest place for water was the channel where our boat was parked.

We finally reached the boat, hot and tired and irritable from the discomfort. Then I had one of my good ideas. We stripped down to our underwear, and jumped into the river.

The water was icy cold. Even there, hardly a foot from the bank, it was around three-feet deep with a steady current. It looked green, probably from some effect of the soil it was cutting through. The mud under our feet was soft. We cooled off for a bit, wallowing like our friends the buffaloes, before returning to the boat for a wonderful packed lunch of Assamese food – rice and wild chicken curry – that Madhab had brought. I rounded off the meal with a sip of Brahmaputra river water, filtered through my water bottle. It was a moment of some satisfaction. We had finally seen the elusive son of Brahma, taken a dip and sipped its waters. We were now ready to deepen our acquaintance with the great river.

SECTION I

Tributaries

PART 1
Lohit

6

Red River

AMONG THE TRIBUTARIES OF the Brahmaputra, it is the Lohit
that has traditionally had pride of place in Indian myth and
song. The Brahmaputra is synonymous with the Lohit – and not
with the Siang or Tsangpo – in the popular Assamese ballad by
Bhupen Hazarika, 'Bistirno Parore'. The ancient mythologies of
Brahma Kund and Parshuram Kund relate to the Lohit. The earliest
colonial accounts, such as one by Lt R.Wilcox dating to 1825-28,
simply describe the Lohit as the Brahmaputra. Even authoritative
British colonial accounts as late as 1888 referred to the two rivers as
one; the account of J.F. Needham, published that year, was called
*Journey Along the Lohit Brahmaputra between Sadiya in Upper Assam
and Rima in South Eastern Tibet.* Needham, an officer of the Bengal
Police who had been appointed political officer in Sadiya, made the
journey to determine whether or not the Tsangpo did indeed flow
into the Brahmaputra rather than the Irrawaddy and was satisfied
that it did.

The Lohit valley was the route by which colonial explorers continued to make their way into Tibet until decades later. Ronald Kaulback, the surveyor and cartographer who accompanied the celebrated botanist Frank Kingdon Ward on his journey from Sadiya to Rima in 1933, explained the reason behind this choice of route in a paper read at the Royal Geographical Society in London in January 1934:

> From Sadiya there are three possible routes through the mountains into Tibet. The first of these is the valley of the Dihang, or Tsangpo, the main stream of the Brahmaputra. This was closed to us on account of the hostile attitude of the Abors, and we should never have got through that way, even if the Indian government had given us permission to try. The second, the Dibang Valley, besides being comparatively short, and with a pass at its head, is almost uninhabited, and we should have had great difficulty in procuring coolies. The third and only practicable route is the Lohit Valley, which leads up into Zayul, the most south-easterly province of Tibet.[4]

One man who came to grief due to the 'hostile attitude of the Abors' had earlier made a journey along the Lohit. Noel Williamson's account, *The Lohit-Brahmaputra Between Assam and South-Eastern Tibet, November, 1907, to January, 1908*, begins as: 'The river shown on the maps as the Brahmaputra enters the north-eastern corner of Assam through the Mishmi hills. To the Assamese it is known as the Lohit; Tibetans call it the Zayul Chu and the Mishmi name is Tellu.'

Today the Brahmaputra is identified with the Tsangpo, and maps everywhere show the Tsangpo as the Brahmaputra. The identification of the two rivers as one feeds into fears in India about Chinese projects to divert or dam the river. It is a gross exaggeration to call the Tsangpo the Brahmaputra; the part is not the whole. Indeed, even the Siang is a far more considerable river than the Tsangpo; numerous rain-fed tributaries join it in Arunachal, and the river in monsoon is a very different beast from the beautiful stream that it becomes in winter.

The Lohit starts life in eastern Tibet as the Zayu or Zayul Chu. It enters India close to the trijunction of the country with China and Myanmar, near a place called Kibithoo. At that point, it is a cascading mountain stream flowing through a gorge with forested hills on both sides. There is a small village called Kaho inhabited by a Buddhist tribe of Tibetan origin, the Meyor or Zakhring. These people, according to a research paper by Mridul Kumar Chakravorty, crossed over from Tibet in 1906-07 and settled in the Dri Valley (further west) where they came into conflict with the local Mishmi tribe. He puts the total population of the Meyor tribe at around 1,000, which is substantially higher than earlier estimates that put the population at around 300.

The river flows through these sparsely populated, mountainous lands down to Dong, the easternmost inhabited village in India. From there it flows towards the relatively open valley of Walong where, in the surrounding hills, in November 1962 a fierce battle was fought between the Chinese and Indian armies. The Chinese Army had by then overrun nearby Kibithu. The saga was repeated in Walong, where despite heroic resistance from the fighting men of 4 Sikh, 3 Gorkha, 6 Kumaon and 4 Dogra regiments, mismanagement led to defeat. The survivors were forced to withdraw further downriver along the Lohit to Hayuliang. The Chinese halted their advance at the outskirts of this village.

Hayuliang is located at the confluence of a river called Dalai with the Lohit. The name in the language of the Mishmi tribals who inhabit the area means 'place of my liquor'.

Mishmi liquor, though an interesting prospect, was not the liquid I wanted most in this part of the world. I was after something both more precious and mundane: H_2O.

What I wanted was to *taste* the water of the Lohit. And the Siang, and Dibang and Brahmaputra.

There is a pull, very ancient, among people from cultures around the world to take a dip in certain waters and to sprinkle the sacred water or touch it to the lips. This practice is common in one form or the other among the Hindus, Christians, Muslims, Sikhs, Jews, and Buddhists. Christians have their holy waters in Israel, where the River Jordan flows. Muslims consider the waters of the well of Zamzam in Mecca holy. The Ganga, polluted beyond belief, is considered pure and holy by devout Hindus; sprinkling its water on places and people is a Brahminical ritual of purification. The Brahmaputra, perhaps fortunately for it, has little such holiness attached to its waters, and is spared some of the tortures that the holy Ganga must daily go through. There are, however, certain spots along the river that acquire special sacredness on certain days. It so happens that the most sacred of these spots, the places known as Brahma Kund and Parshuram Kund, are in the upper reaches of the Lohit in Arunachal Pradesh.

I am an irreligious Hindu. Yet once I embarked on the journey to follow the Brahmaputra, I fell sway to this same pull and found that I wanted to drink the water of its tributaries, and of the river itself, and to take a dip in its waters. Perhaps the thought had been there all along, when I bought the water bottle with the inbuilt filter from a shop in Matunga in Mumbai. It was there when I immersed myself, after our first real glimpse of the river around Dibru Saikhowa, in its waters. It was a gesture that made me feel close to it. It was a way of feeling that the waters were a part of me. True immersion in the task seemed somehow incomplete without immersion of the physical self. Where immersion might prove difficult, I wanted to risk ingestion; at least the common Hindi boast of '*Ghat ghat ka pani piya hai* (I have drunk the water of many ghats)' would have some basis.

The appropriate ghat to drink and take a dip in the Lohit is undoubtedly the Parshuram Kund. The word Kund in this usage means pool, but it's a natural pool in a flowing river. Getting to Parshuram Kund by boat is impossible. The only approach is by road. But even before hitting the road, there is a hurdle that needs to be overcome. Entry into Arunachal is restricted even for Indian citizens, and a special pass, the Inner Line Permit, must be obtained first. As with any task involving the great Indian bureaucracy, this can be a mini adventure in itself.

7

Battle of Inner Line Permit

'AKSHAY,' I SAID, 'LET'S stop and get the Inner Line Permit. The office is right here.'

We had just disembarked at Dibrugarh's Mohanbari airport, and eventually, after an experience of lahe lahe had managed to procure a taxi for Masood and Millie's place.

We had driven just a short distance from the airport when I spotted a sign for the office that issued the Inner Line Permits for Arunachal Pradesh. This is a permit required to enter some states in Northeast India by Indian citizens from other parts of the country. Foreigners who want to visit these areas need another permit called the Restricted Area Permit, although a temporary exemption for tourists of countries other than China, Pakistan and Afghanistan has been declared by the Union government.

The Inner Line Permit has a long and curious history. It was introduced by the British when they were extending their Raj into the hills of what is now Northeast India, back in 1873. It was the first Indian law passed for Assam. The sarkari name of the law is Regulation 5 of the Bengal Eastern Frontier Regulations dated 27 August 1873, and it is subtitled as, 'A Regulation for the peace and government of certain districts on the Eastern Frontier of Bengal'. The districts that fell under the regulation included Kamrup, Darrang, Nowgong, Sivasagar, and Lakhimpur, in Assam, the Khasi, Jaintia and Garo Hills that now constitute Meghalaya, the Naga Hills of what is now Nagaland, and the hills of Cachar, in the Barak Valley of Assam. It was later extended to the Sadiya Frontier Tract, Balipara Frontier Tract, and Lakhimpur Frontier Tract, and the Lushai Hills which are now Mizoram.

Barring the Naga Hills, the original areas covered by the ILP – the districts such as Kamrup and the Khasi Hills mentioned in the 1873 regulation – are now in Assam and Meghalaya and no longer require the Inner Line Permit, though there is on ongoing demand in Meghalaya for its restoration. The Frontier Tracts of Sadiya, Balipara and Lakhimpur, which were administratively carved out of the Darrang and Lakhimpur districts in 1914 as parts of the North East Frontier Tracts, subsequently became parts of the North East Frontier Agency, known by the acronym NEFA. This is now the state of Arunachal Pradesh, and visiting it still requires the ILP.

The ILP office was in an old, classic Assam-type[5] bungalow, with sloping corrugated metal sheet roofs and wooden wall frames holding panels of bamboo and Ikra reed covered with mud plaster. These houses were designed by the British in the colonial period from local building materials and were beautifully adapted to the environment. They speak of an elegance that is now lost.

Other than a group of men and women who stood idly by, there were no visitors. We were pointed to a door and went in. A woman, clad in a saree and with sindoor on her forehead, sat at a desk, looking unhelpful. We had already checked on the Arunachal government website, but just to make sure, I asked her what documents we would need. 'Driving licence or passport or election ID card,' she said robotically. 'And passport photos and photocopies of documents.'

We stepped out. The man who had pointed us to the right door was helpful, suggesting that we go get the photocopies and return immediately to save ourselves a trip. But it was already past 3 p.m. and Millie and Masood were waiting to have lunch with us. Nothing ever gets done in a jiffy in any government office anywhere in India. Here in Assam, it was even more unlikely to be speedy. We decided to return on full stomachs, furnished with the required documents and plenty of time, the following morning.

If you've ever been to an Indian government office, you can probably guess what happened next.

We hit a roadblock.

As soon as we handed in our filled application form with photocopies of passports and photos the next day, the woman asked, 'Originals?' I had mine, but Akshay's mother had thoughtfully taken his passport out of his bag out of concern that it might get lost. 'We have PAN card originals,' I said, but the three women in the room replied in chorus, 'PAN card won't do.' The game was on. They were the goalkeepers, and we were there to score an ILP goal. I noticed that the form allowed for an applicant to apply on behalf of another person. Could I apply for Akshay? Yes, I could.

I filled a fresh form, and entered the room again while Akshay stood outside in the humid heat, smoking a cigarette and sweating profusely. 'Room number 3,' the robot-like woman said without bothering to look up at me. Of course none of the rooms were numbered. After asking around, I finally found my way to room number three. Inside, a very small man sat behind a very big desk. The desk was empty save for a piece of paper in front of him.

I have learnt from experience that the size of the desk and the number of people sharing a room are excellent indicators of status in offices, especially government offices. This was clearly an important man in the Inner Line Permit scheme of things in Mohanbari on the outskirts of Dibrugarh, where not much happens.

I handed him my papers.

He peered at them perfunctorily.

'Originals?' he asked.

I fished in my wallet and pulled out my driving licence.

'And this one?'

I told him we had an original PAN card for that one.

He waved his hand. Dismissed.

I deliberately sat down unasked and started reading from the Arunachal Pradesh government website on my phone, where it said that the PAN card was one of the documents on the basis of which an Inner Line Permit could be issued. I pushed the phone across the massive desk in his direction.

He did not touch it. He frowned.

Now he sounded a little unsure of himself. 'We got a notice. This is old,' he said. The Arunachal government's tardiness in updating its website was really not Akshay's fault, or mine. It wasn't this guy's fault either; we were stuck. If he stood his ground, we were sunk. Our big trip was going to flounder on the rock of Inner Line Permit.

There was a pause as we regarded each other across the table.

'Will an attested copy work?' I finally asked him.

'Yes,' he said, seemingly relieved that our standoff had ended.

Outside, Akshay and I had a quick conference. The executive decision was that he would try and find someone who knew someone to certify a copy of his passport on trust, without insisting on seeing the original. This was a possibility since he had a picture of the passport somewhere online.

His wife Mrigayanka's grandmother had passed away just the day before. She had died where she had spent her last years, on a tea estate near Dibrugarh. Mrig's mother, a lawyer, would be flying in from Goa for the funeral, and was expected to reach in an hour or so. It was not the occasion to be looking for people to attest documents, but it would have to be done.

I handed Akshay the documents and my driving licence, dropped him off at the nearby airport to wait for his mother-in-law, and left to return to Dibrugarh town.

I did not witness the final act of the battle, which Akshay heroically fought on his own the following day. The attestation idea did not work. A mix of desperation and frustration drove Akshay to reach the office unarmed with the document and march into the cabin of the topmost officer in charge of that Inner Line Permit office. He somehow managed to convince the lady there that we were really who we claimed to be and not illegal Bangladeshi migrants trying to sneak into Arunachal Pradesh, and emerged triumphant with two ILPs in hand. With this great victory in the battle for the permits, our journey to Parshuram Kund finally began.

8

Oil, Opium, Apong

THE ROAD TOWARDS ARUNACHAL Pradesh cuts through Upper Assam. We spent the first night of our journey in a highway lodge on the road between Margherita and Digboi. The histories of the two neighbouring towns are entwined; Digboi owes its existence to Margherita and lady luck. According to local lore, in 1867 a crew under an Italian engineer, Roberto Paganini, while cutting a path through the jungle for a rail line via Margherita, noticed oil stains on the feet of the elephants being used to haul logs. The English sahib on the spot, a Mr W.L. Lake, is said to have responded by crying out 'Dig boy, dig!' And so oil was found, and the town got its name. 'Dig, boy' became 'Digboi'.

It's still very much an oil town. The boys are still digging. The refinery that started in 1901 is still in operation. The whole air smells of oil in places. You can see the flares burning like giant torches in the night.

We drove past the town to a spot near Ledo for dinner.

Ledo is the starting point of the Stilwell Road, a road that was built under the directions of the American General Joseph Stilwell during World War II. It was a route from India to China via Burma, and it was meant to help the Allies prop up the Chinese in their fight against the Japanese during the war. Stilwell himself commanded a Chinese army, and was reputedly the first foreigner since Marco Polo to do so. He was chief of staff to Generalissimo Chiang Kai Shek, the nationalist rival of communist leader Mao Tse Tung. Eventually Mao would win the Chinese civil war that followed World War II and Chiang would found the country of Taiwan, but that is another story.

The official British account of the Allied campaign in Burma recounts the building of this legendary road. Burma had fallen to the Japanese. Stilwell himself had trekked out of the country at the head of a band of retreating soldiers armed with a stick. A tough man of few, often acerbic, words, he carried the sobriquet 'Vinegar Joe'. He was firm in his belief that this road could now be built in the face of Japanese opposition, through densely forested hills where the rain came down in torrents and diseases brought down soldiers even before enemy bullets could.

The account says a crew of 'Chinese, Chin, Kachin, Indians, Nepalis, Nagas, Garos, slashed, hauled and piled. In one camp 2,000 labourers spoke over 200 different dialects. Negroes drove machines. Black, brown, yellow, white men toiled shoulder-deep in the streams, belt-deep in the red mud. Bulldozers were lost when rain-soaked shelves collapsed and slid into streams 1,000 feet below. After a cloudburst, in some places the road would literally be lost.'[6]

After tremendous effort, the road was completed.

One day during the monsoon when Mountbatten was flying over the Hukawng Valley in Burma on a visit to see Stilwell, he enquired about the name of the river that lay beneath. 'That's not a river,' said an American officer, 'it's the Ledo Road.'

After the war, India and Burma became independent. Borders came up. The road fell into disuse and became a ghost road, remembered and used only by those who walked dangerous paths – smugglers, drug and arms traffickers and insurgents.

In the past couple of decades it has gradually returned to more mundane use, at least in some stretches. I had travelled a short distance on it with Millie and Masood years ago, when we went to The Lake of No Return. Our chosen halt on this trip was less exciting and more appetizing … a restaurant called Singpho Hut. It is, as the name suggests, a hut built in the Singpho style that serves the eponymous tribe's ethnic cuisine. There is a Singpho population in this area; the same people are known as Kachin in Myanmar and Jingpo in China. They are scattered across the three countries.[7]

It was a good thing we had called in earlier to say we would be arriving for dinner. We were the only guests. The food was fresh and delightful, cooked especially for us. There was fried pork on a bamboo skewer and pork curry with diced potatoes. The curry had a strong, pleasant flavour, probably from the raw turmeric. I could not detect any spices apart from turmeric and green chilli. The accompaniments included a bowl of chilli paste, a bowl of dal, and a lightly fermented fish chutney. The rice was steamed and served in banana leaves.

Akshay and I agreed that it was a wonderful meal. We retired happy from our dinner excursion, and slept the contented, comatose sleep of those who have eaten small mountains of rice.

Early next morning we drove out for Bordumsa, the main settlement of the Singpho tribe in India, via a road that runs through an elephant reserve. A wall of tall, leafy trees stood on both sides of the potholed road on which, once in a long while, a car came along. Otherwise, there was no traffic other than the occasional motorcycle.

Hoolock gibbons inhabit the trees some of which run, by my reckoning, to over 100 feet tall. We heard their loud, squeaky cries and stopped. The gibbons fell silent as soon as we stepped out to try and see them.

In some places, the forest gives way to fields on one side of the road. We crossed an occasional village with thatched bamboo houses, paddy in the fields, banana plants and coconut trees, chickens, goats and cattle. The people there are not rich, but they seem to have enough of what they need – food and shelter, clean air, good water. Small dish antennas on the roofs of some huts indicated that they also have entertainment, but that's where trouble starts: they might not remain contented with their simple life for long. The advertisements with their siren songs and TV news with its frequent messages of hate must have, along with all the wonders that flow into mobile phones, started working on their minds.

An Arunachal state government check gate stands on the edge of Bordumsa, which is in the Changlang district of Arunachal Pradesh. We had reached the border between Assam and Arunachal. Inner Line Permit country lay ahead of us. As our car pulled up, we rummaged through our wallets to find the precious Inner Line Permits that we had obtained with so much effort on arrival in Dibrugarh.

The driver calmly told us to remain seated in the car. He stopped, walked over, and was back in a minute. We drove across without any permit being checked. After all the trouble we had gone to for the pass, it was a bit of an anticlimax.

A little further down the road there's a Singpho cultural centre in Bordumsa where the tribe's annual festival is held. We walked in after seeing a large, colourful structure that seemed to depict a giant hornbill with what looked like a gate on its back. Inside, a concrete building on stilts with sloping roofs had been decorated with sketches of birds, buffalo heads and women's breasts. We looked around but could not find anyone to explain these symbols of Singpho culture to us. An attractive young woman who was running a canteen at the place asked us where we were from and told us, in crisp English, that the key people were all away to attend a Bharatiya Janata Party meeting.

The apparent popularity of the conservative Hindu nationalist party in Changlang came as a bit of a surprise. The Singphos in India are mainly Buddhists, while their cousins in Myanmar and China are predominantly Christians. Nor was this place known for its Indian nationalism. Naga separatist militant groups fighting for independence from India had a presence in the area, and in neighbouring Tirap district. The place was also historically an opium-growing region, and use of the drug was widespread; even now, local police still carry out special drives against opium poppy cultivation.[8]

The habit of opium consumption among residents of the area was already well established when the first British colonial administrators got to these parts. Historian Edward Gait noted in *History of Assam*, 'Their pacific attitude in recent times is attributed by some to their now universal habit of eating excessive quantities of opium, which, it is said, has sapped their energy and robbed them of the old warlike proclivities.'[9]

His account was published in 1906.

Opium is believed to have come to Assam with the Rajput army that fought on behalf of the Mughals during their invasion of Assam in the seventeenth century.[10] From there, its use spread further with trade.

In recent years, from roughly around 2007 or so, a drive against opium has penetrated to the interiors of this district. There is also a Singpho cultural revival, of which the cultural centre in Bordumsa – opened in 2009 – is both an example and evidence.

Other neighbouring tribes are also rediscovering their cultural roots and establishing links with long-lost cousins in neighbouring countries.

A few kilometres down the road, at a place called Tengapani, we came to a spanking new golden pagoda set atop a hill. The green plains lie at its feet. A river meanders through, a glistening silver line in the distance. The way up is a long climb of many steps. At the bottom of the steps, two Indian Army soldiers in full battle gear stood guard. Halfway up the steps, we met a couple of more army men, looking out over the peaceful scenery, their assault rifles in their hands and old Bollywood numbers playing softly from a mobile phone.

The pagoda at the top is of recent vintage, and looks like something one might see in Burma. There is a golden-coloured pillar near it, reminiscent of the Ashokan pillars named after the Mauryan Emperor Ashoka who had them erected in the Third Century BC. A large prayer hall with a statue of the Buddha beautifully made from woven cane sits near the pillar. The entire complex is set amid well-tended lawns and manicured gardens. It is both pretty and serene. There was not a soul in sight that day. No sound disturbed the silence. We automatically began to communicate in gestures and whispers, as though our voices might disturb the Buddha statues, or the other gentleman whose statue sits under an umbrella outside the small library that bears his name – Chow Chali Mein.

Chow Chali Mein, born in 1886, was a leader of the Tai Khampti community that inhabits the area around Namsang. He made a small fortune supplying timber from Arunachal to the British, who awarded him a contract to supply wood for the Assam Match Factory in Dhubri. The logs used to be tied onto rafts and floated down the Brahmaputra from Sunpura, a village by the Lohit, which flows about 5 km from the golden pagoda. At the back of the pagoda, on the side facing away from the highway and the river, is the Namdapha National Park – a vast forest of 1,985 sq. km, home to many rare animals and a tribe called the Lisu, famed for their hunting skills.

Building on their success in the timber trade, subsequent generations of the Chow Mein family have done very well for themselves in Arunachal. Chowna Mein, one of his descendants, became the Deputy Chief Minister of Arunachal Pradesh in 2016.

We paid our obeisance to the Buddha, and drove on.

Our road led past a weekly bazaar beside a village some kilometres away. It was bustling. Traders had spread their goods on the ground in front of them. Cheap clothes, cheap electronics, various kinds of food. At the edge of the bazaar on the roadside, a tight knot of men stood or squatted around a game of dice. Bets were being briskly made. Near the gamblers was a local food and drinks shack. Rough wooden tables and benches, a wooden floor, plastic jugs for water and beer bottles with a white liquid inside that I recognized as the local brew, apong, lay on the counter.

Naturally, we sat down to try some. The apong cost Rs 30 a bottle and was delicious.

We had barely had a swig or two when I noticed three men sitting at a table at the end of the bar looking at us, the obvious strangers, with interest. One of them called out and waved. Picking up our glasses, we walked over to join them.

Two of the men were from the local Khampti tribe. The third was from an Arunachali tribe from further away.

A meeting with strangers in a rough country bar can turn into a serendipitous encounter or a murky one. Fortunately, the locals were merely curious. They soon became very hospitable. They were drinking Super Strong He-Man beer and cheap whisky, which were clearly considered the posh drinks in those parts. They offered us some. We declined after expressing admiration for the apong, at which they laughed. They were having spicy meat nuggets and ordered some for us. I have no idea what meat it was. Sometimes, ignorance is indeed bliss. It was delicious, and I left it at that.

Our cheery halt had to end all too soon as we had a long way to drive. We finished our apong and restarted the journey with a happy buzz about us.

An hour or so later, we were driving on a perfectly smooth road through lush green country when we came to a bridge over a mountain stream, one of the many that eventually find their way into the Brahmaputra. In the near distance, some young men, most of them fit, lean and bare-bodied, were sitting on rocks near the water. It looked like a picnic.

In our apong-fuelled haze, we stopped and climbed down to the water. The stream was crystal clear. The smooth stones at the bottom of the stream shone in the soft golden sunshine. I touched the water. It was icy cold.

The men on the rocks had spotted us. They beckoned to us to join them. We went across, picking a path through the brush and undergrowth. They were locals, young police recruits out for a bit of fun.

The customary questions followed. Once satisfied that we were all right, they immediately became hospitable like the men at the bar. Food and drinks were offered. They too were drinking cheap whisky.

We sat down to chat. By and by, some of the men clambered down to swim. After a while, plucking up my courage, I decided to risk the swirling, freezing water. It was a terrible idea. Less than a minute later, I had leapt out, shivering. My lovely apong high was gone. New jungle saying: Pretty mountain stream makes for nice scenery, not nice swim.

9

Parshuram's Bath

SHORTLY WE GOT ON our way again. This time we didn't stop until we had reached our destination, Parshuram Kund, the site of a centuries-old and legendary pilgrimage.

The story of Sage Parshuram, who washed away his sin of matricide at the Kund and flung his battle axe into the mountains, releasing the Lohit river – red from the blood of his axe – has drawn Hindu pilgrims to this site ever since it was 'identified' by an itinerant sadhu sometime in the seventeenth century as the spot of Parshuram's famous bath. The story itself is recorded in the tenth-century Kalik Purana, which describes the tirthas or pilgrimage spots of Kamrupa, an ancient kingdom whose shifting map at different times spanned parts of what is now Bangladesh, Assam, West Bengal, Arunachal Pradesh and possibly Meghalaya.

Getting to Parshuram Kund is considerably hard even now, in the age of aircraft and motorable roads. It must have been a forbidding trek before these advancements reached what is now Northeast India.

And yet for at least three centuries, and possibly for much longer, people have been making this pilgrimage for a holy dip in the raging, cold waters of the Lohit in large numbers at least once a year, during the festival of Makar Sankranti – a rare Hindu festival based on the solar rather than lunar calendar – in mid-January, which marks the beginning of the end of winter.

We had arrived during 'off season'. The only place to stay was a Hindu ashram dedicated to Parshuram, and save for a few sadhus and goats and dogs, it was empty. Our driver went and asked if we could take one of the rooms. The sadhus agreed. After some time, a man carrying a bunch of keys emerged from the only inhabited part of the ashram and wordlessly set off up the hill. We followed. A fair way up was a small Shiva and Durga temple. The jungle was close behind. There were a couple of make-do rooms with tin roofs next to the temple. This was to be our accommodation for the night.

The place had not been opened since the previous pilgrimage season in January. It was now September. There were giant black spiders, the biggest I had ever seen, in huge cobwebs in various nooks. One of them had built a cobweb that was blocking off access to the Indian-style squat toilet. The beds had mattresses with rat droppings and vague patches of discoloration. Mould was everywhere.

I wondered whether sleeping in the temple verandah might be a better idea. However, we didn't know whether there were snakes and other creatures about. We took the room.

By 6.30 p.m. it was pitch dark all around. The roaring river in the distance was the only sound. Sometimes a leaf would rustle or an insect or animal would call out. The lights, weakly battling the surrounding dark, had succumbed to power failure. The only bright spots visible anywhere were the stars.

Time stretches in places like this. We sat and listened to some old Bollywood and Baul music on my phone. After that, conversation dried up. There was only silence and darkness. Sleep seemed the sensible option.

But sleeping was easier said than done. The dirty, musty room had no fan. We had cleaned up and spread our sleeping bags, but it was still too hot inside without a fan. The best option was to sleep with the door open and allow the cool breeze – and anything else that chose to enter – in.

We spread out our sleeping bags and prepeared to turn in for the night. We were sitting on our beds having a last smoke with the beam of the torch light pointing at the wall in front of us, when Akshay suddenly said, 'That installation is alive!'

I followed his gaze. There on the wall near the foot of the beds, where we had seen a number of black blotches that we took to be some sort of damp marks, one blotch seemed to be moving. We looked more carefully. It was a colony of giant slugs.

I gingerly lay down, wondering if the slugs would make their sluggish ways towards where we were sleeping, if the giant black spiders might be so inclined, and if there were other, larger or more poisonous creatures about. Akshay was soon emitting gentle snores, for which I greatly envied him. I had only managed to fall into a kind of half sleep, in which I dreamt of – or imagined – a variety of animals, such as leopards and snakes, invading the room, when a shout woke me. I opened my eyes to find myself blinded by a torchlight. Gripping the hilt of my hunting knife that I had kept next to me, I sat up.

It was a guard.

'Babaji has sent me to call you for dinner,' he said.

I propped myself up on an elbow and checked the time on my phone. It felt like the middle of a very long night, but it was only 9 p.m.

Akshay absolutely refused to go anywhere. I dragged myself out of bed reluctantly and trudged down the small hillock to Babaji's house. The watchman asked me to sit on a mat in the verandah and vanished. The door was shut. Sometimes someone would walk in or out, revealing a log fire burning in a pit inside the room. A big bunch of fresh marijuana leaves lay near the door.

After some time, a tall, slim, bearded man with long flowing hair came and sat on the mat next to mine. I greeted him with a namaste; he returned the gesture. He did not look like a regular sadhu, so I asked him where he was from. He had come from Punjab, he said, and he had been there five days. He was running away from pollution. 'Pollution is in everything in cities,' he said. 'You can get high on fumes by simply breathing.' In these pristine environs, one presumably had to get high through other herbal, organic ways.

The food we ate from city marketplaces had too many chemicals for his taste. 'Too much urea is thrown into the ground,' he went on. He spoke at length of sugarcane and the varieties of sugarcane that grow in different states of India and the ways in which they are grown. None except the Arunachal variety met with his approval.

He asked me where I was from. I explained that I was from Shillong, but working in Mumbai. He had nothing to say about Mumbai. 'I have been to Shillong,' he said. 'I did not like it.' There was a small pause. 'The areas outside the town are very nice.'

The food arrived. It was a thick stack of giant rotis and a small hillock of sabzi. I said I could eat only one of those rotis, each of which was as big and thick as a naan. My neighbour kept his bundle of six. We ate in silence. I finished before him since I had a sixth of the food, and sat back, feeling full. He looked at my plate, on which a little of the sabji was left over. In his soft but steely tone, he said, 'You can feed that to the cows. I don't like food being wasted.'

As it happened, a few cows were conveniently standing at the gate of the verandah. I went to feed them the leftovers, but the five dogs got to it first. Clearly, they had no issues with pure vegetarian fare.

I asked Babaji, who had by now appeared on the verandah, what I should do with the plate. The tall man whose name I did not know answered on his behalf in perfect BBC English. 'There's a tap outside. You can wash it and keep it on the verandah wall.'

Just as I was leaving after keeping my washed plate atop the low wall, he called me back.

'You forgot the glass.'

I went to pick up the glass.

'Rules,' he said.

I washed my glass, kept it to dry, thanked Babaji for the meal and bade the refugee from polluted city life goodnight.

The rest of the night passed without incident. We awoke next morning to the steady roar of the river and went to take a look. It turned out to be a bit of a trek, uphill then downhill. That roar was coming from a kilometre or so away.

At the bottom of the hill, suddenly the narrow cement path slippery with moss ended before a torrent. Conversation was difficult. We had to shout to be heard over the river's thundering roar. Words seemed superfluous. This was a space beyond words. It was a zone of primal natural energy.

The Lohit storms down into the plains here at this point. There was a 'kund' or lake here known as Parshuram Kund or Brahma Kund – and it was believed, in past centuries, to be the birthplace of the Brahmaputra. The kund was around until a great earthquake in 1950 broke the barriers that enclosed the lake. Now, the lake had disappeared and there before us was the river, an icy, raging torrent. It rushed over boulders and smashed into the rocky cliff. Over time, it would wear these boulders down, and perhaps even the cliff – if allowed to flow freely.

There is, like everywhere else in Arunachal, a plan to dam the river. The 1,750 MW Lower Demwe project, a controversial hydroelectric project located near the Kamlang Wildlife Sanctuary and just a short distance upriver from Parshuram Kund, was finally cleared by the National Board for Wildlife in late 2018. The project had been on pause since 2014 following orders of the National Green Tribunal.[11] The impact of this project on wildlife and riverine life is likely to be harmful, a fact acknowledged in the report of the Wildlife Institute of India, on the basis of which the clearance was given. The report noted the presence of eight endangered species of animals, birds, turtles and dolphins in the vicinity, two of which are critically endangered. It warned that the dam would lead to 'possible loss of critical habitats' and 'daily flooding' as well as 'strong currents on daily basis' that would 'affect the movement and survival of endangered turtle species'. The changes in the 'hydro-morphology of the river due to daily flooding will also affect movement and survival of river dolphins and their major food species,' it noted.[12] But there's a lot of money at stake – at least Rs 5,500 million (550 crore), which is the amount owed by the company building the project to banks in 2018. The company, Athena Demwe Power Ltd, has been facing legal proceedings for insolvency.[13]

The Demwe dam is not the only one envisaged for the Lohit. In fact, it is one of a cascade of seven large hydroelectric that some bright sparks dreamt up. If implemented, these dam projects would effectively cut up the Lohit into several pieces. They would also undoubtedly enrich several contractors, bureaucrats and politicians.

I walked down to a boulder in the river and filled my water bottle with the cold, clear water. Dipping more than a finger or toe was out of the question. No one who got into this water was likely to get out alive. It's said that everyone wants to go to heaven but no one wants to die, and that is absolutely true – and quite sensible. After all, the existence of heaven is a matter of considerable doubt, whereas the existence of death is not.

I gulped a bit of the icy water and – satisfied that I had drunk the water of the Lohit – busied myself looking around.

The untamed, undammed river might wear down most of the rocks around but there was one rock it would have a hard time eroding. This was a giant rock that stood defiantly in the middle of the river, a thin wedge with a sharp top; a shape that might bring to mind an axe-head. Perhaps an axe wielded by a giant. The axe of Parshuram!

The drive back took us via Tezu on the north bank of the Brahmaputra. After a small climb into the Arunachal hills from Parshuram Kund we found ourselves on a beautiful, deserted single-lane road, from where, far in the distance and a long, long way below, lay the Assam plains. It was a grand spectacle. The Brahmaputra shimmered silver in all its braided glory. The earth around it was green and gold. A mist enveloped the scene.

Our road wound down the hill towards this place.

PART 2
Dibang

10

The River Damned

THE SIANG HAS THE advantage of length. The Lohit has myth and lore on its side. Of the three tributaries that come together in a profusion of watery braids to create the mighty Brahmaputra, the Dibang is the one that gets the shortest shrift. Perhaps it is natural that this should be so; the Dibang, after all, is the shortest and most seasonal of these rivers. Its length is only 195 km. During the dry season, its bed is all rocks and sand, on which for vast stretches the tall kaash grass grows. Come rains, and the myriad channels that flow into it swell the river to a torrent. Sometimes there are floods, and during those days the river and the tracks, euphemistically called roads, become impassable, except to elephants that are then pressed into service on rescue missions.

How much water flows in the river during the rainy season or the dry season – these matters are, for reasons not quite clear to me, national secrets in India. Nonetheless, it is clear even at a glance that the size of the Dibang varies greatly from winter to monsoon. Old records of the volumes of water flow also exist. The British explorers who mapped these areas in the latter part of the nineteenth century were meticulous about their measurements, and have left accounts. In the *Journal of the Asiatic Society* in 1879, a researcher can find a study by H.J. Harman on the 'Discharge of large rivers in Assam'. From his detailed experiments, Mr Harman found that the discharges of the rivers increased fivefold or more in the monsoon season from the dry season minimums. He identified the Brahmaputra with the Lohit, as was the convention then, but reckoned that its discharge was less than that of the Dibang and the Siang, the latter of which he called by its alternative name, the Dihang.

A journey up the Dibang valley by British explorers in those times has had a role in the shaping of India's current boundaries. It was from a village called Mipi far upriver in the Dibang valley that Captain F.M. Bailey of military intelligence and Captain Henry Morshead of the Survey of India launched their celebrated expedition to explore the Tsangpo gorge. 'During the winter of 1912-13 an expedition was despatched by the Government of India to survey the basin of the Dibang river, in one of the upper valleys of which was found the small village of Mipi, inhabited by Tibetans who had settled there a few years previously, after driving out the Mishmis who were the former owners of the land,' Bailey wrote in his account of the expedition published in *The Geographical Journal* in October 1914.

Mipi is still a small village beyond the last town in the upper reaches of the Dibang on the Indian side of the McMahon Line, a place called Anini. The epic journey that Bailey and Morshead undertook from there has had a lasting impact. It was their expedition surveying the watershed of the eastern Himalayas that contributed to the drawing of the McMahon Line as the boundary – still disputed to this day – between India and Tibet. Their work built on that of the great Indian explorer-spies known as 'pundits'.

The line was drawn, with one notable exception in the Tawang tract, along the crests of the ridges of mountains where the waters separate. Where the waters flow south, is Arunachal Pradesh. Where the waters flow north is the Tibetan Autonomous Region of China. The Chinese claim line, however, places the boundary where the hills end in the plains of the Brahmaputra Valley far below.

The Dibang originates in the southern slopes of the Himalayas at the edge of Tibet. It merges into the Lohit 195 km downstream near Sadiya.

Like the Lohit river valley, the Dibang river valley has its own claims to ancient mythical fame. Sadiya is believed to be the location referred to in the Mahabharata as Kundil Nagar. There is a locality by that name in the present town. Rukmini, the wife of Lord Krishna, is said to have hailed from there. Another place not very far away is named Bhismaknagar after King Bhismak, the legendary ruler of the Vidarbha kingdom who was said to be Rukmini's father. In Hindu culture, the same stories and names often pop up at multiple places and thus there is a part of Maharashtra in western India that is still known as Vidarbha, which is also associated, more plausibly given its relative proximity to Sri Krishna's Dwarka, with Rukmini and King Bhismak.

The ruins of an old fortress survive in Bhismaknagar in Arunachal, about 40 km away from Sadiya in a straight line. This fortress dates back to the twelfth century AD and was the stronghold of a kingdom called the Chutiya kingdom. The name is now usually spelt as Sutiya, because the word 'chutiya' is unfortunately a popular cuss word in Hindi – a language unknown in these parts in previous centuries, but now the lingua franca of Arunachal Pradesh.

A smooth new road now winds between the fields and over numerous riverbeds on brand-new bridges from Roing in Arunachal past the near-forgotten, nondescript village of Bhismaknagar. The biggest of these bridges bears a sign announcing that it was inaugurated by Kiren Rijiju, the Union Minister of State for Home Affairs, who is from West Kameng in Arunachal Pradesh, in July 2017. The riverbed was dry.

On one side of the road, the river valley gave way to tall, craggy green hills a short distance away. Behind them the white peaks of snow-capped mountains were visible. On the other side, the plains stretched into the distance interminably. The area was thinly populated by a mix of Mishmi tribals and Nepali settlers.

We drove past Bhismaknagar without quite noticing it was there. Along with roads, mobile connectivity has also come to these lands, but the data signal was intermittent and the navigation didn't work. We fell back on the old method of simply asking our way around. The first person we met was a lone old man with a weather-beaten face, walking the emptiness of the highway, who told us to go back the way we had come, to a basti or settlement. We drove back to a few huts and some decrepit Assam-type cottages. There was not a soul about. A little shop in a bamboo and thatch hut was 'open' but there was no one inside. I called out but no response came. Nazir, our driver, went up to the gate of a nearby hut and shouted at the top of his voice. A man emerged from inside the hut. 'Where is the old fort?' Nazir asked in Hindi without further ado. The man, from the door of his hut, pointed to a place somewhere behind us. 'It is nearby,' he said cryptically.

We explored further. There was a dirt track branching off from the highway. A couple of hundred metres in, a concrete wall enclosed a structure of some sort that was guarded by a rusty iron gate. Somewhat surprisingly, we were not the only visitors to this remote spot; an SUV and a motorcycle stood outside. We were about to enter when a Husky came bounding up, followed by a little girl of ten or eleven who clung to the dog's leash as we made our way in. The family inside were Arunachali folk from Pasighat, making a pit-stop on their journey back from Tezu to see for themselves this famed place of which there were legends.

Now, only the legends remain. The roofs and walls of what must have been a small fort or palace are gone. Only the raised plinth still stands in its place. It is made of small, flat bricks. All around, there are only the fields and the trees and the loud squeaky whoops of Hoolock gibbons. They seemed to be berating us for invading the privacy of the forgotten fort.

On the way to Roing, the beautiful new highway briefly paused in its progress. A bridge was still not quite complete. There was a diversion, a dirt track that led down between the kaash grass towards the dry riverbed. We drove at a crawl over the riverbed and across an unreliable wooden bridge that was just some rough beams of wood tossed over the water. It was a sample of what much of the road had looked like until very recently.

Roing has little to commend it. Life here is concentrated along the road that passes through it. It is a way stop for tourists on the way to Mayudia, in the mountains ahead. Assam has discovered Mayudia; it is the nearest place the state's residents can see snow. The new Dhola-Sadiya Bridge means the Brahmaputra is now no barrier. Roing is a busy place on weekends.

The Dibang flows a few kilometres out of Roing on the road to Dambuk. A brand new road was near completion here as well when we made our journey. A bridge on the river was under construction.

The riverbed was mostly dry. A couple of little streams of clear water flowed here and there. Most of it was now white river sand on which endless fields of kaash grass grew. The riverside below the bridge, pretty as a picture, had become a picnic spot. There were two groups about. One was a carload of young men and women from Assam doing the usual picnic things … eating, drinking beer, taking selfies, splashing the cold water on one another. They were

stereotypes of the new 'middle class' Indians, part of the globalized
world. At a distance of about 100 m downstream from them was a
busload of people who appeared to be tea garden labourers. Their
clothes were scruffier, but it was not this that gave them away; they
sat with their backs to the river, huddled quiet in small groups. Near
them, a man had set up a gas stove and was cooking in the open.
They sat facing him, waiting for him to finish. A few minutes later,
they were all sitting in rows on the ground, for the lunch that was to
be served. They had no interest in the scenery.

There was a path below the bridge – the old road. It was a dirt
track along the riverside running between tall kaash grass and trees
just wide enough for one car. A short distance along this track was
a shallow channel of water that connected to the Dibang. The drive
was through the water. Even as we were assessing our situation, a
middle-aged couple on a beat-up old 100cc motorcycle rode calmly
through the water and crossed to the other side. The 'ghat' itself was
further down the track. Called Nizamghat, an Indianized version of
Needham-ghat, named after the British colonial explorer Needham
who was in these lands in the late nineteenth century, it is simply
a place on the riverbank where two wooden canoes nailed together
with wooden planks ferry the scant vehicles and passengers across.

During the rainy season, the river grows into a powerful
torrent. Numerous smaller rivers and mountain streams from the
hills and mountains of Arunachal feed into it. Sometimes there
are monsoon floods, which make the old roads impassable for all
modes of transport except the oldest. Then elephants are called out
for duty, to move people and essential supplies to the villages in the
Dibang valley.

The river's days are numbered. Just a short distance upstream
from Nizamghat, where the river breaks out of the mountains into
the valley, its nemesis is being built.

At 278 m, the Dibang multipurpose dam is envisaged to be India's biggest and the world's tallest concrete gravity dam when completed. It was rejected twice by expert groups due to environmental concerns.[14] But money is a great remover of obstacles, and we are talking at least Rs 29,839 crore – the latest estimated project cost according to NHPC Limited, which is building it; a sum almost double the 2007 estimate of Rs 15,886 crore.[15] That is a massive sum. The dam eventually found approval without any study on downstream impacts. Protests from locals have been of no avail.[16]

The Environmental Impact Assessment (EIA) report of the dam states that it will have the installed capacity to generate 3,000 MW of power. According to it:

> Most of the submergence area falls in the gorge area, therefore, it is restricted longitudinally, and no major submergence is observed laterally. In such conditions, impacts do not spill over to a large area. Thus, beyond the designated study area, the impacts likely to accrue as a result of project construction and operation are not expected to be significant.

However, it goes on to say that the area is prone to landslides and earthquakes, that two of the most powerful earthquakes in world history have occurred in Northeast India, and that 'The proposed Dibang Multipurpose project falls within Zone V of the Earthquake Zoning Map of India', which constitutes the zone of highest risk.

The EIA report continues to say that:

> The Lower Dibang Valley and Dibang Valley districts of Arunachal Pradesh are true representatives of East Himalayan Biodiversity ... Many herbs and shrubs including trees and climbers have been used traditionally

by the local people as medicinal plants for the treatment of different ailments. Some of these plants have been smuggled through international borders by the active participation of the local people for money. Due to this reason and other ecological factors many of these plants are on the verge of extinction. The whole Arunachal Reserve Forests can be termed as reservoir of ornamental plants mostly orchids and other flowering plants.

There are thirteen endangered species of flora listed. The list for fauna and fish are, by the EIA's own admission, incomplete because the short span of the study did not permit a detailed survey. However, the EIA notes that the area is thickly forested and notes the presence of forty-three mammal species, seventy-one fish species and various other types of fauna found in the area.

The proposal was rejected twice by the Forest Advisory Committee. Independent experts ridiculed the latest EIA for its lapses and errors, pointing out that, for instance, it spoke of 'different tiger species' being sighted whereas only one tiger species is known to exist in the world. The presence of tigers at high altitudes in the Dibang Valley, earlier considered doubtful, has been confirmed.

Even the shoddy EIA exercise could not adequately hide the fact that the 5056.50 hectares of forest land required for the project is rich in wildlife. Around 350,000 trees in this ecologically diverse area would have to be cut for the project ... a whole forest.

Moreover, the dam-building exercise is likely to turn the water, which is used by animals and humans alike, turbid. There will be sewage from the labour camps, because thousands of workers will be required, and effluent from the crushers, the EIA notes. Fish species, especially migratory fish such as the mahseer, will be severely affected.

Local villagers, mainly of the Idu Mishmi tribe, some of whose villages are in the area that will be submerged, have been protesting the proposed dam right from the start. In an article for the South Asia Network on 'Dams, Rivers and People', academic Parag Jyoti Saikia wrote:

It is important to note that the public hearing for the project faced vehement opposition of the local people. The public hearing of the project has been halted several times. The local people expressed serious concern regarding Dibang multipurpose project and feared that influx of outsiders for dam building will lead to a demographic imbalance in the Dibang valley. This is a serious issue since the primary inhabitants of Dibang valley are Mishmi (Idu) which is a very small community with a population of 11,023 according to 2001 census. According to NHPC estimation a workforce of 5800 people (labour and technical staff) would be needed for the Dibang multipurpose project. But All Idu Mishmi Students Union (AIMSU) has contested this figure and opined that a single project would bring about 15,000 people into the region. It is also reported that NHPC claim that the project will cause 'negligible human displacement' grossly undermines its harmful impacts on smaller ethnic community such as Idu Mishmis.[17]

Saikia also pointed out that there were other, smaller projects in the area, and no cumulative impact assessment of the various hydel projects in the Dibang valley region had ever been conducted. Moreover, there was no proper assessment of the downstream impact of the dam in Assam, and no public hearings had been held there.

Saikia further wrote:

Mining of boulder, sand and other construction material for the Dibang multipurpose project will have very severe impacts on the river as well as on the local environment. The amount of boulder required for the construction of this project is 193 lakh cubic meters as stated in the project document. This is a really astonishing figure and impact of such mining on the river bed and nearby areas will be catastrophic. The fragility of the Himalayan mountain range is not unknown to anyone and mining in such a sensitive hilly area will only increase the risk of landslide and disaster. The catastrophe of Uttarakhand floods is a clear example of this.

The EIA prepared by National Productivity Council, Guwahati, suggests compensatory afforestation, hatcheries and similar mitigation measures and ends by presenting a bill of Rs 3,686 lakh for the cost of 'environment management plans' – meaning more money, and a pretence that something is being done for the environment – because the damage done by the dam cannot be so easily undone.

The insensitivity is appalling. What is the price of the priceless Brahmaputra river and its ecosystem, of which the Dibang is a vital part? Who is this project for, if the local people hate it and want no part of it? Claims that big dams stop floods have been proved to be a lie. The largest concrete gravity dam in existence is the Three Gorges Dam on the Yangtze river in China. It failed to prevent the worst recorded flooding in the Yangtze basin in central China in 2020, and there were serious concerns that it might crack. What mitigation measures would mitigate the possible effects of a powerful earthquake, in the highest risk seismic zone in India, that might crack open the world's tallest concrete gravity dam?

11

Temple of the Dread Goddess

NEXT MORNING, TURNING OUR backs towards the mountains and the dam, we drove towards Sadiya. There is a small temple complex there, a few kilometres off the highway, at the end of a bumpy, single-lane road. The surrounding countryside is ridiculously pastoral. The green of paddy fields alternates with the golden yellow of mustard. Little streams flow through the land against a backdrop of hills with snow-capped mountains standing behind. The surrounding population includes a mix of Adi and Mishing tribals, the Sutiyas who once ruled the land, Nepali settlers and a smattering of others. We managed to find our way to the temple by asking villagers; it is a temple with a fearsome past whose memory is alive, at least among the Sutiyas. It is called Bura Buri Than. Majestic old trees stand around three small, conical concrete structures shaped like rather squat pencils. The one in the centre is taller than the other two, and is obviously the main shrine. These were the Bura Buri temples … and they were closed on the day we visited; there was no one inside the temple compound.

I pushed open the creaking, rusted gate and walked in. A small man with a scraggly beard soon appeared and fell in step with me. He had been hanging around outside. He was from the adjacent village; his name was Satya Gogoi and he was the secretary of the local village committee. The temple opened only thrice a year, he told me. On those days, people of various Hindu communities of the area – Sutiyas, Ahoms such as him, Nepalis – gathered here. The place was abuzz. There were duck and goat sacrifices in the open hall in front of the temple. Once every three years, a big festival was held. The big festival required big sacrifices, and for that purpose a large hook had been set in concrete in the ground of the courtyard outside the temple. It was used to tether the buffalos that were slaughtered on the occasion.

'How old is this temple?' I asked him. It was only a couple of decades old in its present form, he said, but it was an ancient place of worship. There were a few scattered remains of an ancient temple behind the present one; he did not know how old those were. Some hundreds of years old … or maybe a thousand or a thousand five hundred. We walked to the back of the temple where, amid bushes and bits of plastic, there lay the shattered stone remains of what must once have been the columns of a temple. There were figures carved in the stone, but they had been worn down to blurs by the passage of time. From their appearance it was evident they were many centuries old.

We were walking back towards the sacrifice hall when a gnarled hunchbacked man, evidently drunk at ten in the morning, accosted me. He wanted twenty rupees. He was very clear about this amount, and insistent. He did not beg; he impatiently demanded. I gave him ten rupees but he was not satisfied. He began to claw at my arms.

Gogoi shooed him away, first gently and then with some anger, after which the man fell behind to a distance of about five or six feet away, but he did not leave.

I stopped to admire a giant tree, more than 100 m tall and, by its appearance, of great age. It had strange growths on it that I did not recognize; it was not all one foliage. There were orchids and ferns and creepers. Its roots seemed to hang in the air, spreading out, before touching the earth.

The hunchback stood muttering and glaring at me, probably unhappy that he was still ten rupees short for his next drink. We walked out of the temple compound to the road outside in a small group. Two men were standing outside the gate. One wore a white dhoti and kurta and had on his head a white turban tied in an unusual manner. His features were a curious combination of the East Asian and Indian. The other, a burly, swarthy fellow of somewhat similar appearance, with bloodshot eyes, stood next to him surveying me curiously.

'This is the Deori,' Gogoi explained. We went up to him. He was the temple priest.

The temple, the Deori explained, was one dedicated to Bura, meaning old man, and Buri, meaning old woman. The old man, he explained, was Shiva. The old woman was Parvati. There were idols of the duo inside the locked temple sanctum.

'And what are the smaller temples on the side?' I asked him.

'Oh, that's for their children … the boys on the right, and the daughter on the left,' he said.

'Children?'

'Yes.'

He did not explain further.

'Who are the children?'

He seemed a little surprised at my ignorance.

'Karthik and Ganesh, and Kechai Khaiti.'

Karthik and Ganesh, I knew. Karthik was the god of war in the Hindu pantheon. Ganesha was the popular elephant-headed god of beginnings, the remover of obstacles. But who was Kechai Khaiti?

I asked the hereditary priest, descendant of a long line of Deoris. She was Kali. She was Durga.

She was, I realized, the 'dread goddess' of early colonial accounts who had to be propitiated with human sacrifices.

The ritual was still alive when the British began to rule the area, and finds mention in records. Author and historian Colonel Leslie Waterfield Shakespear says there was a shrine in this area connected to Cooch Behar, in what is now north Bengal, by a raised road. He wrote in his *History of Upper Assam, Upper Burmah and North Eastern Frontier*, published in 1914:

> Several generations have passed away since the votaries of these temples were numerous enough to keep the roads leading to them open. The Tamasari Mai was dedicated to Kamakhya and the Yoni; but Shiva and the Lingam were also worshipped with all barbarous rites including human sacrifices, which latter obtained it is known in the early part of the nineteenth century. In 1850 Hannay knew of certain families living near Sadiya who for generations past had been specially set aside to provide the doubtful honour of becoming victims to the dread Goddess.

He further wrote:

> Colonel Dalton has given an account of these sacrifices, which obtained almost up to the British occupation of Assam, by certain Deori Chutiya priests of the Tamasari Mai. These described how the victim was detained some

time at the temple, being fed until deemed sufficiently fat to please the flesh-eating Goddess. On the appointed day he was led forth in magnificent clothes to be shown to the crowds assembled for the hideous ceremony. He was then led by a private path trodden only by the priests to a deep pit at the back of the temple. Here his gay raiment was stripped off and he was decapitated, the body flung into the pit, the head being added to the heap of ghastly skulls piled in front of the shrine.

The temple had long outlasted the rulers who were its original patrons. The Sutiya kingdom fell in 1522 when the last Sutiya king, Nitya Pal, was defeated and killed by the Ahoms in Sadiya after more than two centuries of skirmishes between the two sides.

There is a second temple called Kechai-Khaiti near the Brahmaputra here. A dirt track descending from the highway led through paddy and mustard fields to a bamboo bridge over a stream. Nothing bigger than a motorcycle could possibly pass. I walked out alone over the bridge, in the silence of the still morning on a track beaten by feet on the earth.

The temple itself was again a fairly new concrete structure with nothing much worth looking at. Was this, perhaps, built over the remains of the temple of Dalton's account? There is an earthen embankment that runs around the place. It was impossible for me to tell how old this was, or who built it. At the Bura Buri temple, the Deori had pointed to the tall trees. 'These form a circular avenue around the shrine,' he had explained. I wasn't able to discern any avenue.

It is possible that the past exists around us, barely visible, all along the Brahamaputra Valley. The few architectural remnants hint at an ancient past vastly different from the present conceptions of indigeneity and migration. About 100 km downriver, at the foothills where the present border of Assam and Arunachal lies, there is a place called Likabali where the ruins of an ancient temple called Malinithan have been found. According to myth, it is the location of the marriage of Lord Krishna with Rukmini, the princess of Vidarbha. Multiple stories being the norm in India, the same site is also believed to be the easternmost of the nine 'Shakti peeths' of Hinduism. The ancient idol of the goddess worshipped here is of Durga astride a lion, slaying Mahishasura – an image familiar to anyone who has seen a contemporary Durga Puja at a Puja pandal. In a book on the temple's iconography, archaeologist J.C. Dutta concluded that it was built by the Pala dynasty of Kamrupa sometime in the eleventh or twelfth century. A similarly intriguing architectural site exists on the other side of the Brahmaputra, near Numaligarh in Upper Assam. It is called Deopahar. Here there are ruins of an ancient temple estimated to date to the tenth or eleventh century. The structure was built before the arrival of the Ahoms to Assam. Who were the people who built those ancient temples, and what became of them?

PART 3

Siang

12

By Magic, Ferry, Winger and Tempo

THE SIANG, ALSO CALLED Dihang, is the Indian avatar of the Tsangpo, the longest of the Brahmaputra's formative tributaries, and the one nowadays associated most closely with the river. After a 1,625 km journey east from its birthplace in the Angsi Glacier near Mount Kailash, past the cold high-altitude desert of Tibet, it turns its direction of flow westwards at what is called the 'Great Bend' and, curving around the 25,531 feet tall Namcha Barwa peak at the eastern end of the Himalaya, flows through a gorge, about thrice as deep as the Grand Canyon in the USA, to enter Arunachal. From thereon, gathering more streams into itself, it flows as the Siang.

Pasighat in Arunachal is where it enters the plains after its long journey.

Our own journey to visit it began early one morning from Millie and Masood's house in Dibrugarh in a hugely overcrowded minivan, a Tata Magic, which folks in these parts use for public transport.

This vehicle would take us to Bogibeel Ghat, the makeshift river port from where the ferry would take us across the Brahmaputra to the north bank. A massive bridge across the river was then nearing completion. It had been two decades in the making. When finished, it would be 4.94 km in length, making it the longest rail-cum-road bridge in India.

There are no tickets on these Magic vans, no timings and no concept of seating capacity – the real magic is in the astonishing numbers of people that fit into them. Despite the overcrowding, the van operators are often keen on a quick extra buck. We watched our fellow passengers, packed in with us so everyone was practically sitting on their neighbour's lap, fish out Rs 50 each at the destination, but the teenager who was the driver's assistant demanded Rs 100 each from me and Akshay – a 'tourist surcharge', presumably. We refused to pay this amount, at which he began to get aggressive. Things might have turned ugly if the driver, older and more sensible than his young apprentice, had not told him to back off. I suspect his good sense was born out of the realization that we had been dropped off by local people from the fuel station outside which he parked his vehicle. Without the fear of getting caught, it is possible, even likely, that they would have chosen to pick a physical fight over the fraudulent ticket price.

After this unpleasant start, the ferry ride was great. It was an overcast day with a wind blowing and the river looked choppy and grey. There were wavelets on the water. It started to rain soon after the ferry had left port, and the rain came slanting into the old wooden craft loaded with cars, motorcycles, bicycles and people. We had found ourselves seats near the engine, below the deck. The man sitting next to me, unfazed by the conditions, did not look like a local. He turned out to be a colonel in the Indian Army who, after a stint as instructor at the army's High Altitude Warfare School, was now posted somewhere in Dhemaji district on the Brahmaputra's north bank. The army had work to do in these parts, because of the presence of armed insurgent groups. There was also, always, the dragon to the north – mainland China, which is less than 170 km from Dhemaji town as the crow flies.

It was still raining when the ferry reached the other side, about forty-five minutes later. Picking our backpacks, we made a dash for a ramshackle bamboo tea shop. We would have to take shelter from the rain, and a cup of hot chai would make the waiting more pleasant.

A group of bikers on big motorcycles, togged out in fancy biking gear, had also been on the ferry with us. Now they entered the same tea shop. They were from Pune and Bengaluru, and were heading into Arunachal for some hard riding.

We had to find our own wheels to get out of the ghat. A tempo agreed to take us to Silapathar, the nearest town. We had booked the vehicle for ourselves but of course that meant nothing. We had gone hardly 100 m on the very bumpy mud track when a man flagged the tempo down. The driver stopped and asked the man to sit in front, next to him. The mud track curved up towards a metalled road built on an embankment. A woman and her three daughters waved at the vehicle. The driver stopped for them. They trooped in next to us. Now we were seriously overloaded, eight people and luggage in that precarious tempo. In other words, the tempo was full enough to satisfy the driver.

The road seemed designed for dirt biking, and would doubtless challenge the bikers we had met at the ghat. It had good stretches, but these were interrupted frequently by the presence of potholes. It was one lane, with traffic moving in both directions, and with all drivers swerving constantly to avoid potholes, it was a bit like being in a car racing video game with cars going both ways, only real. To make it more interesting, the road was built on an embankment at a good height over the surrounding lush green paddy fields, and of course, it was wet from the rain. Fortunately, there were not many vehicles and visibility was good.

Eventually we reached Silapathar and disembarked to take the next, slightly larger vehicle, a minivan called Winger that would take us to a place called Jonai on Assam's border with Arunachal. A little scrum of young ruffians who work as drivers and conductors on these vehicles surrounded us and exhorted us to load our bags and board one of the Wingers. As soon as we did this, they changed their minds and asked us to board another. Then they packed us in, in the fashion that foreigners call 'sardines in a can' and Mumbaikars call 'local train at rush hour'. After this, we waited. The vehicle, in the considered judgement of the driver and conductor, was not adequately full.

I remember reading many years ago, the journalist and writer Ryszard Kapuszinski describing taking a bus somewhere in Africa. He asks his fellow passengers what time the bus will leave. Everyone looks at him like he is stupid. Then someone explains, 'The bus will go when it is full.'

This is a principle followed for all modes of privately operated public transport in Northeast India as well. The vehicle will go when it is 'full', full being a matter of perception. It is full only when the driver feels it is full.

An hour later, after all possible spaces had been filled and the spaces between the spaces had been filled, the driver picked up one for the road – an extra passenger, as is customary here. We were finally ready to move.

The road, after the previous patchwork of potholes joined by little bits of tarmac, was excellent. It was a road built and maintained by the Border Roads Organisation, which works in the most difficult terrains and frontiers.

We drove through that straight line of blacktop cutting through the fields of brilliant green, with the Arunachal hills in the distance. The driver told me the population here is mostly from the Mishing tribe; he himself was a Mishing too. There is a Mishing Autonomous Council in these parts. We passed bamboo huts with women,

Mishing by appearance, with their distinctive East Asian looks, weaving at looms outside. Most lampposts had been plastered with bright red posters and the word 'Ganashakti', meaning 'people's power', emblazoned on them. These were posters put up by the supporters of Bhubon Pegu, a Mishing leader who was member of the legislative assembly from the area.

There were also pockets dominated by the Bodo tribe, the largest and most powerful plains tribal group in Assam, who have after long years of fighting for a separate Bodoland state – by means including armed insurgency – finally settled for a 'Bodoland Territorial Region', which is something like a state within a state. Simen Chapori, which we drove through, was a Bodo area. The place was full of banners and posters announcing the arrival the following day of Hagrama Mohilary, a former insurgent leader who used to head the Bodoland Liberation Tigers, a dreaded group of armed militants, before he surrendered arms and became a politician and chief executive of the Bodoland Autonomous Council that administers the Bodoland region.

It was almost evening when the Winger dropped us off on the Assam side of the border at Jonai. From here, Pasighat is another 36 km. To get there we would have to cross the border and take another vehicle.

We stopped for a quick meal at a mud and bamboo hut that sold rice and curry, and then walked across into Arunachal. Once again, no one checked our Inner Line Permits we had taken so much effort to obtain.

From here, we booked another tempo, which as is the custom, picked up extra passengers – three girls. I think drivers in these parts hate wasting vehicle space. In less than an hour, we were at Hotel Aane – the local Adi tribe's name for the Siang – in Pasighat. Here, for the first time, our victory in the battle of ILP pass proved to have been worth the trouble. The permits were required to check in.

13

Pasighat

PASIGHAT IS THE OLDEST town in the 83,743 sq. km of Arunachal Pradesh. It was founded in 1911 by the British administrators who were looking at establishing control over the Adi tribe, then known as the Abor. There were at least two reasons for their interest: a growing Chinese push into Tibet, and a blank on the map between the Arunachal foothills and Tibet in which, it was said, there was perhaps the greatest waterfall in the world.

It was suspected then, but not yet known with complete certainty, that the Tsangpo was indeed the principal tributary of the Brahmaputra. Some doubts remained.

The Scottish writer and explorer Reginald Johnston, who later lived in the Forbidden City in Peking and served as tutor to the last emperor of China, Pu Yi, published an account in 1908 called *From Peking to Mandalay*. In it, he wrote:

> It may not be generally known that according to the Chinese authorities there are *two* rivers bearing the name of Chin

Sha Chiang. One is the Ta (Great) and the other the Hsiao (Small) Chin Sha Chiang, and *the 'small' one is the Yangtse*. In a first attempt to identify the Ta Chin Sha Chiang – which must obviously be a very great river – we are apt to be much puzzled; for we read of it as flowing through western Tibet and also as flowing into Burma through the 'Southern Ocean'. But the mystery is explained when we remember that the great river of southern Tibet – the Tsangpo or Yaru Tsangpo (literally 'Upper River') – used to be believed not only by Chinese but also by European geographers to be the main feeder of the Irrawaddy. We now know that the Tsangpo is none other than the main upper branch of the Brahmaputra; or rather we assume it from much circumstantial evidence. No European has yet followed the course of the Brahmaputra up to the point where it receives the icy waters of the Tibetan Tsangpo – which hurls itself over the edge of the Tibetan plateau and creates there a series of waterfalls that must be among the grandest sights in the world – but we now know, from the accounts of our native surveyors, the approximate position of the falls. The country between Assam and Tibet is unfortunately inhabited by tribes that are apparently hostile to all strangers.

Johnston was on point about the hostility to strangers.

In 1909, Noel Williamson, who had been the political officer at Sadiya since 1904, made a trip into what were then called the Abor Hills, up to an area the British called Kebang. He received an invitation to visit again, according to the contemporaneous account of Leslie Shakespear which was published in 1911:

This was done a year later, when Williamson and Dr Gregorson went into the hills, hoping in the friendly attitude of the tribesmen to be able to push up the Dihang river into the unknown hinterland and discover the supposed falls in that river which a former native explorer, Kinthup, reported in 1882 as existing. This Kinthup travelled down the Tsan Po from Thibet (*sic*), and was taken captive twice for periods of several months, but eventually reached a point north of the Abor country which he surmised must have been only thirty-five miles from the plains of Assam. He saw the falls near a place called Gyala Sindong but was constrained to return to Thibet. In March, 1911, both Williamson and Gregorson and their party came to grief, being treacherously cut down by Kebang Abors of the Menyong clan just after their arrival at a village, Komsing, only two or three managing to escape.

The warlike Abors are now known as the Adi, and Pasighat is the principal town in their area. The old town built in 1911 by the British has disappeared. The great Assam earthquake of 1950, which seismologists estimate was 8.6 on the Richter scale, changed the course of the Siang here. Like the old town of Dibrugarh, the old town of Pasighat too was swept away. My father, who worked for the Indian government and toured these areas from the late 1960s onwards, recalls visiting in the early 1970s and seeing remnants of the old town in the river.

Akshay and I took a walk around the town the morning after we reached. It was a place of scattered, nondescript buildings and run-down shops. Past the bazaar and out on a road that seemed like some kind of highway, we came upon a couple of restaurants advertising beef that looked like they would have made good settings for old kung fu films. Further down, there was a school at whose entrance was a curious cement tableau of various local worthies, none of whom I recognized, in traditional costumes. The figures were arranged in the form of a pyramid. At the apex of the pyramid, clad in his customary white dhoti, stood the very recognizable figure of Mahatma Gandhi.

We walked on to the Siang riverbank. It is a very pretty river, with cold, crystal clear water and blue hills pushing their heads in the clouds in the distance. After the Brahmaputra, though, it looked rather like a large mountain stream. The Siang, unlike the Brahmaputra, is not a river whose other bank you have to strain to see. It is only about 600–800 m wide near Pasighat, swelling to no more than twice that width in monsoon. By comparison, the Brahmaputra around Dibru Saikhowa, in full flow, is between 17–23 km wide.

Downstream near the river, two young Arunachali boys sat drinking cheap whisky out of a bottle. They looked like schoolkids. They offered us a swig, but both Akshay and I declined. It was 7.30 a.m.

Apart from the morning teatime alcoholics, we spotted a romancing couple and two girls sitting enjoying the view. The only other creatures we encountered by the river were two mithuns.

The mithun is the Indian bison. It is a powerful animal, usually black in colour with white sock feet. Despite its considerable size and weight – it is slightly smaller than the buffalo, but more powerful around the shoulders – it moves with a deceptively quick pace through thick undergrowth and up and down sheer hillsides.

We were walking on a mud track built on an earthen embankment with trees and bushes on both sides and the river beyond when two mithuns emerged out of the undergrowth. Our paths were going to intersect, so they waited patiently on the side of the road while we went past. Then they began walking behind us. I did not enjoy having them at my rear and was glad when after some time they decided to go back into the undergrowth on the other side of the embankment.

Further down we found ourselves at an intersection of a stream with the Siang. A truck was parked nearby and some men were loading it with smooth river stones. They told us we could walk upstream on the riverbed, which was mostly dry and full of stones that had been rounded and smoothed by the water. Getting back on to the road meant fording a bit of the stream that still had water in it, and climbing past a riverside village. It was a place of houses made of woven bamboo with tin roofs, and courtyards adorned with satellite television dish antennas.

The mud track gradually turned into a metalled road. At an intersection we found a tea shop, and walked in. It was run by a Gorkha family. They rustled up a fine breakfast of parathas and a sabzi, followed by tea with a doughnut-like Nepali sweet called 'mala roti' for dessert.

We had walked a few kilometres by then and so decided to take an autorickshaw back. Our driver turned out to be a man from the neighbourhood of old Pasighat, the town that had got washed away by the Siang in 1950. Remembering my father's story about structures visible in the river, I asked him if he had seen any parts of the old town in the riverbed, growing up. 'Ruins would show up in the winter when the water levels were low,' he said, 'and this continued till 2000, when flood waters swept away the last of it.'

Back in the new town of Pasighat, I met an old friend of mine from college. He was in charge of a government educational institution in Pasighat and was struggling to keep it functioning. There was only one teacher, apart from my friend, and neither of them had been paid their salary for nine months. There was no girls hostel but there were female students, because of which my friend had vacated his official residence to turn it into a makeshift hostel for them. The government had no money for staff salaries and basic infrastructure, but at the same time, things such as fancy dissection sets were being bought at extraordinarily marked-up prices. A box that might cost Rs 200, for instance, was purchased for as much as

Rs 12,000. A UPS worth Rs 1.5 lakh had been bought for ten times the amount. And so on.

The extent of corruption that he spoke of was staggering, even by Indian standards.

There was political unrest in the state at the time. The government of Chief Minister Nabam Tuki of the Congress was facing rumblings of dissidence. The government fell two months later when 21 of 47 Congress MLAs quit the party and switched over to allying with the BJP. The Speaker of the assembly, who remained loyal to the CM, had the state assembly locked up, so the governor, a BJP appointee, had an ad hoc session of the assembly conducted at a conference hall of a Guwahati hotel, at which the government was voted out.[18] A new government led by Kalikho Pul came to power. This government in turn was dismissed by the Supreme Court which was hearing a petition filed by the Congress Party. Pul committed suicide at his official chief ministerial bungalow, leaving behind a controversial suicide note[19] in which he named former ministers in the state and at the centre as well as certain Supreme Court judges, and mentioned the amounts in crores they had sought in bribes to swing decisions in his favour.[20] Despite efforts by Pul's wife Dangwimsai, there was no CBI probe into the matter. More was to follow. In February 2020, Kalikho Pul's son Shubanso was found dead under mysterious circumstances in Brighton, UK.[21]

This sequence of events had not yet begun to unfold when we were in Pasighat that day. My friend, who had not been paid his salary for nine months, responded to my angry criticism of the government's inefficiency and corruption by saying too large a section of the state's populace was coming to depend on government jobs, because of which staff salaries had become a big burden. No work got done because everything was everyone's job with the result that nothing was anyone's job.

The lack of governance showed even in the condition of the town's streets, in the daily power cuts, and a general administrative apathy that seemed to spread through the society and even the otherwise cut-throat private sector.

We came up against this in our attempts to withdraw money. The first ATM we found, a State Bank of India ATM, had its shutters down. We asked our way to an Axis Bank ATM. It too had its shutters down.

By and by we went to every ATM in town with the same result. We were eventually informed that the ATMs had shut for the weekend and would reopen some time on Monday. Since this was the state of affairs in the biggest town between there and China in the direction we were going, we thought it prudent to delay our departure until some ATM had been restocked and we had got enough cash in hand to take care of expenses for the trip up and down the Siang Valley.

The dysfunctional ATMs contrasted with the smoothly functioning places of worship all over the town. I spotted a gurdwara, Hindu temple, Buddhist temple, Donyi Polo Vidya Niketan with images of Goddess Saraswati and Bharat Mata at the entrance, and churches of various denominations.

Donyi Polo is a codified version of the old animistic nature worship of the Adis. The sun and the moon are its presiding deities.

Apart from religion and alcohol, popular culture seemed to revolve around television with some local twists. There were posters around town for an *Arunachal Idol* contest and a Miss East Siang pageant.

Football and cricket seem popular sports in the area. The footballers we saw in action were competent enough but it was the cricketers who caught my eye. There was not a single slow bowler in that lot. The idea seemed to be to hurl the ball as fast as possible in the general direction of the wickets. Sometimes it would bounce at half pitch, at other times it would fly at the batsman without a single bounce. The batsmen responded in kind, swinging their arms about and wielding the bat like a club. I was especially impressed by one particular batsman who, in response to a bouncer, brought down the bat from over his head in a downward motion. He missed, and so did the bowler. The ball swished past his ears.

Night fell quickly in Pasighat, and by 4.30 p.m. it was already dark outside. Akshay wanted to go out for dinner, so when the boy at the hotel asked us some time later what we would be having, we told him we would be eating out. He seemed surprised. We stepped out and realized why. The last of the shops was shutting down. The entire place was deserted and pitch dark. The only people about were heavily armed central security forces men. It was 7.45 p.m.

14

Damn Dams

THE SIANG UPRIVER FROM Pasighat is not navigable by boat. We started our drive up the Siang Valley in a hired taxi with a driver who turned out to be half Adi and half Haryanvi Jat. Like most people in Arunachal, he spoke Hindi with a penchant for ending sentences with 'hoga', which otherwise means 'it will be' but in Arunachal can mean anything from 'yeah' and 'all right' to 'I hope it's okay'. He also spoke fluent Nepali – the lingua franca of the mountain road drivers in these parts, as we later discovered.

The road out of Pasighat was smooth and wide and we were soon racing over a bridge across the Siang, out of town and up into the hills. The river gradually fell away. We climbed higher and higher. The road became a bumpy dirt track barely wide enough for one car, with sheer hill face on one side and the Siang, a ribbon of green and white, far below, on the other. Our progress was halted by a bulldozer parked across our path. There was dynamiting work going on ahead. A road crew was at work trying to widen the road. No one knew how long it might take before the road ahead of us was cleared for traffic.

Not that there was a lot of traffic.

One other Tata Sumo taxi, overloaded in the customary fashion of the place, groaned and came to a halt behind us. Later, another one pulled up behind it. Everyone got out from their cars to stretch their cramped legs. Only the two little goats tied atop one of the taxis were denied this pleasure.

We wandered around, smoked a cigarette, took a few photos, and then went back to check if there was any update on when the road might clear. There was none. We waited some more. Eventually, our driver, who had been sitting placidly on his haunches by the side of the road ambled over and said there was another way through the hill on the other side of the river by which we could approach Yingkiong, our intended halting place for the night, and the last town between there and China. It was a longer route, and there was no way to get to it except via Pasighat. We had a quick discussion and decided to double back and take that road rather than wait for what might be minutes or hours.

This other road was very much like the first. We bounced and rattled along the dirt track in the SUV. Dusk fell. We were still nowhere near Yingkiong. The only sensible thing to do was find a place to spend the night, and start off again in the morning.

We were in luck. Panging, one of the biggest Adi Minyong villages, was not far. Reaching there, we drove straight to the government Circuit House, the only likely place where we might find accommodation for the night. There did not seem to be anyone about. After some time, the caretaker, a short, friendly Nepali man, emerged. We would need permission from an officer who lived nearby, he explained.

Akshay and I went across to the officer's house. He was out for a walk. We waited at the gate. He came back after some time, looked

at our IDs, and agreed to allot a room for us at the Circuit House for
the night. It was with much relief that we went back there to drop
our bags and sleep off the weariness of the long and difficult drive.

In the course of the day, we had travelled a distance of
approximately 40 km in a straight line. That is the distance between
Pasighat and Panging on the map as the crow flies. The actual
distance on the curvy hill road is roughly 65–70 km. Adding to that
the distance we had covered going up and down the road on the
other side of the Siang, we had probably travelled around 100 km
in eight-and-a-half hours. That is also the approximate flying
time from Mumbai to Paris or Kolkata to Tokyo. Distance means
different things in different contexts.

Early next morning, at a tea shop that doubled as a ticket counter
for the Sumo taxis at the small market in Panging, we met an old
Adi man. His name was Oyar Gao.

Mr Gao was the secretary general of the Siang People's Forum,
an activist group at the forefront of the opposition to three
proposed power projects on the Siang river. A farmer, traditionalist
and follower of the Donyi Polo faith, he opposed the dams on the
Siang for a number of reasons. Sharp as the large knives everyone
in these parts carries, he reeled off the numbers of dams proposed –
168, according to him – the number already abandoned, and the
ones that were still in the fray. He traced the history of notions
about building dams on the Brahmaputra and its tributaries to the
Brahmaputra Board, a government body, in the 1980s. It was an
idea that he had opposed right from the start, he said.

All political parties had pitched for big dams, according to Gao.
Every chief minister of the state since Gegong Apang, the Congress
chief minister from 1980 to 1999, had cleared multiple projects.
None of them had seen light of day.

'We have seen off the flood control department, the Brahmaputra
Board and companies like Jaypee. I hear that now they are trying to
bring in Reliance,' he said.

One of his peeves with the distant powers in Delhi, and the ruling BJP state government – to which he did not sound altogether unsympathetic – was that they were busy worshipping the Ganga, but did not seem to realize that the Adis called the Siang 'Aane', which means mother and held the river in similar esteem.

The Adis had always resisted every invader, he reflected. 'This has always been no man's land,' he said. 'We had trade with the Tibetans and we used to extract tribute from people in the plains as far as Dhemaji.'

We were talking in Hindi, sitting on rough wooden benches in the misty morning. Gao spoke of the Donyi Polo worship of the sun, referring to it as 'Surya Devta', the Hindu name for the sun god. I asked him about a very contentious issue – the tribal love of meats including beef, and the Hindu worship of the holy cow. 'We did not have cows here, traditionally, we had mithuns,' he said. The mithun was a very important part of social and economic life. It was the animal given as bride price – the opposite of dowry, being a price paid by the groom's family to the bride's – and eaten at feasts. The cow was largely absent. 'Nowadays, young people eat cow, dog, anything,' Gao said with evident disdain.

We chatted some more before he headed off to his house. Akshay and I went for a walk around the village and found ourselves, quite by chance, walking past his large traditional Adi stilt house built of wood and bamboo on our way back. He was busy tending to his beautiful garden of numerous flowers that surrounded the house. We did not disturb him, and returning to the Circuit House, where we had been fortunate enough to get a comfortable room for the night, picked up our bags and resumed our journey for Yingkiong.

The road faithfully followed the course of the river. It was a hard road, but it was a lot better than the road that the earliest outsiders on this route had encountered a hundred years earlier. When Angus Hamilton, a member of the Royal Geographical Society and an adventurer in the old sahib style, travelled in these parts years ago, he complained of the entire absence of roads. In his 1912 book, *In the Abor Jungles, Being an Account of the Abor Expedition, the Mishmi Mission, and the Miri Mission*, Hamilton wrote:

> In addition to the dense vegetation, the region is distinguished by its rivers – at least four being quite large – and by what has hitherto been an entire absence of roads … Such pathways as did exist were mere animal tracks, while the best 'roads' were the chasms through which the rivers flowed. When the traveller was not wading waist-deep through these, he was crawling along narrow ledges cut out of the face of high precipices. Now and again he came to places where there was no ledge, while the path, such as it was, was continued by a rude gallery contrived out of the face of the cliff, or he found himself compelled to climb perpendicular cliffs with the aid of cane ropes.

Bridges in Hamilton's time in these parts often meant a single rope strung across a raging mountain river, which the traveller was expected to cross by a process somewhat like zip-lining. This mode of transport remained in vogue for at least half a century. In 1962, when war broke out with China, Indian soldiers were obliged to use similar 'bridges' at places.

Thankfully, getting around in these parts is now much easier, and the traveller only has to sit in a sturdy car, listening to music, while making painfully slow, bumpy progress at an average speed of approximately 10–20 km an hour. The scenery is still much the same as it would have been in Hamilton's day – dense vegetation and powerful streams – although virgin forest has given way to banana and orange plantations on the hills at places. In some of the villages, one could spot terraced rice cultivation being carried out. The population here is Adi, but we passed occasional pictures of crossed khukris – the Gorkha fighting knives – painted on rocks and trees, a sign of the Gorkha presence in this remote tribal area.

The first major village on the way is on the other side of the river. It is a village with a reputation – Komsing, where Williamson, the British political officer, had been cut down in 1911. To reach it, one has to cross a swinging cane bridge over the roaring waters of the Siang and climb a track through a forested hill. The hanging bridges tend to sway as one is walking on them, so good balance is important, and there are often gaps and holes in the bridge's flooring through which the foaming river below is visible. Careless travellers risk plummeting in.

We made our way gingerly across and began trekking up the hill. We had been told that the village itself was a couple of hours' march from the road, but we did not have the luxury of time to go all the way there and return. Yingkiong, the nearest place with hotels, was still a long way off.

The path was just wide enough for one person to walk. Branches of trees occasionally obstructed the path here and there. There did not seem to be any animal life about, but then, many Adis are fond of hunting, so animals here would be likely to keep their distance from humans.

We were walking in silence under the shadow of the canopy of trees through which very little sunshine filtered in, when we heard, of all things, a Mohammad Rafi love song in the maestro's own voice. The source of the unlikely sound was a mobile phone being carried by one among a small band of young Adi boys from the village who we soon came across. We stopped and exchanged hellos and asked them about the distance to the village, which here is measured in hours rather than kilometres or miles, and upon hearing that it was indeed a good hour and half away still, made our way back across the swinging cane bridge to resume our journey to Yingkiong.

The road winds up with the Siang far below. The water is green, flecked with whites where it crashes against rocks. It is a challenge for white water rafting enthusiasts, groups of whom sometimes arrive here to try their luck against the wild mountain river. We, however, did not see a single boat or raft of any sort in the entire stretch up from Pasighat.

Yingkiong announced itself by the sight of terraced fields of paddy dotted with the thatched roofs of huts. The town itself is built around its one main street. This is the section of the highway – if it can be called that – which passes through the town. The bazaar, where Adi women sell vegetables and chickens and the odd bottle of apong, sits by this road. So does the local branch of State Bank of India – with its ATM only open for a few hours on weekdays – as well as important government offices.

A board helpfully announced that the place is 141 km from Pasighat. This is a meaningless number. It took us the better part of two days to get from Pasighat to Yingkiong.

Choosing a hotel, though, took no time at all. There are two, and we asked our way to the nearest one. It was early evening when we reached Hotel Bap, just off the main road, located in a rough two-storey concrete building. There was no one behind the reception counter, or anywhere in sight. A television was on in the empty room, showing *Dilwale Dulhaniya Le Jayenge*, the Shah Rukh Khan-Kajol superhit from 1995.

Tulobai Thapa, the stylish young Nepali-speaking man who ran the place, soon materialized. Yes, a room was available. He showed us to the room with its two beds, the regulation mosquito nets, and an attached bathroom with piped water, buckets and mugs. It was all we were hoping for.

I was interested in learning more about the local view on dams and had worked my journalistic connections to find a number, but our phones had no signal since we left Pasighat. Nonetheless, borrowing a phone from a stranger, I managed to make the call. In the evening we met Vijay Teram, a lawyer who like Oyar Gao is also opposed to the proposed dams on the Siang. The power had failed, and it was quiet and very dark all around. The one candle in our room flickered, casting light on our intent faces.

The public hearings for the Lower Siang dam, one of three proposed on the river, had been cancelled thrice because of protests, he said. 'The fourth time, in 2012, they tried to intimidate us by bringing in paramilitary forces. So people burnt down the camp where the hearing was to be held, and the Jaypee (the dam construction company) camp ... After that, they have not come back,' Teram said softly.

The fields belonging to him back in his village would also be affected by the Upper Siang Stage-II dam, Teram told us. 'The decision is that whoever in the village sides with the government will be outcast. Our ancestors in the Anglo Abor wars fought for this land. We are not against development. We are for our land,' Teram said.

'They are coming and telling us, you will get compensation worth crores. People are saying our lands may be worth Rs 25,000 only, but it has sustained us for generations.' The issue for the local people was squarely about land, he clarified, not the environment.

In the past, the locals had had bad experiences with dam companies, as well as government officials, trying to buy off leaders of the anti-dam movement, and had subsequently chosen to have a loose 'leaderless' front of many organizations 'so the companies don't know who to buy off'.

A previous set of leaders had been paid Rs 40 lakh each and disappeared, Teram said. 'They can never come back to their villages, because if they do, they will be killed,' he said. He uttered the words softly, quietly, in a level tone, the effect magnified by the surrounding silence and the flickering candlelight. 'Justice here is

swift. Cases don't necessarily go to court, even for heinous crimes. I
am a lawyer. I know.'

He spoke of how the national news demonized 'khap panchayats',
the village-level organizations of north India infamous for enforcing
rules such as a ban on mobile phones for women.

Arunachal Pradesh has its own version of such organizations:
kebangs.

'It is a part of life. It is normal,' Teram explained. 'Here in the
kebang, there is a member from each household. Whatever the
kebang says is final.'

There was a conflict between the modern legal system and
these traditional village institutions, he said, but people in general
preferred to take their disputes to the kebangs rather than the courts
because decisions were swift and legal costs were minimal.

'The cost of justice delivery is borne by both the disputing parties.
It is the cost of the tea, apong and food consumed at the kebang.
Both sides get a chance to explain their positions, after which the
kebang deliberates and decides.'

The village elders were not literate, but they were often
knowledgeable and wise in other ways . He said, 'They know better
than you and me how to coexist with nature.'

They still followed certain superstitions though. He explained,
'For instance, we don't throw old clothes in the Siang because our
soul would go with them. We believe it is bad to kill a very big tree.
Before cutting trees, there is a ritual. People offer prayers to it. There
is acceptance of the supremacy of nature.'

Villages were self-sufficient in food grains. People reared
their own chickens, pigs and mithuns, and often grew their own
vegetables. They were not dependent on government handouts. The
population was generally healthy, and it was common for people in
villages to work in the fields till they were seventy or so, according
to him.

An Arunachal mountain stream on its way to meet the Lohit.
Photo: Akshay Mahajan

Dibang on a sunny winter day. Water levels of the river rise enormously after monsoon rains.
Photo: Samrat Choudhury

Siang riverside near Yingkiong.
Photo: Akshay Mahajan

The road to Tuting.
Photo: Akshay Mahajan

Apong-stop at a wayside bar.
Photo: Akshay Mahajan

Oyar Gao in a tea shop in
Pangin.
Photo: Akshay Mahajan

Crossing a hanging bridge.
Photo: Akshay Mahajan

The Ambassador car in
the Tuting monastery's
glass case. The monastery
is also sometimes referred
to as Yang Sang Pemako
monastery, Yang Sang
Chu being the name of
a stream that meets the
Siang not far away in the
sacred Buddhist realm
known as Pemako.
Photo: Akshay Mahajan

Pilgrims at Tuting gompa.
Photo: Akshay Mahajan

Inside the Tuting monastery.
Photo: Akshay Mahajan

The Siang river valley.
Photo: Akshay Mahajan

A man trotting through the forest on the opposite side of the Siang across from Tuting carrying the trunk of a tree on his shoulder.
Photo: Akshay Mahajan

A chorten behind Tuting gompa.
Photo: Akshay Mahajan

Inside a Sumo taxi.
Photo: Akshay Mahajan

Tekseng in his house in
Yingkiong.
Photo: Akshay Mahajan

Parshuram Kund, on the Lohit.
Photo: Akshay Mahajan

Babaji at the Parshuram
ashram.
Photo: Akshay Mahajan

Boatman Pal navigating in the waters near Dibru Saikhowa.
Photo: Akshay Mahajan

Pal's underage apprentice.
Photo: Akshay Mahajan

The floods had just receded a few days before this photo was taken, leaving a ravaged land behind.
Photo: Akshay Mahajan

Chapori cowherd.
Photo: Akshay Mahajan

Chapori life.
Photo: Akshay Mahajan

Fishermen at work on a
stretch of river between
Jorhat and Majuli.
The mouths of little
streams that flow into
the Brahmaputra are
favoured fishing spots.
Photo: Akshay Mahajan

Was the nature worship of Donyi Polo akin to Hinduism? Teram seemed to have a different view on the matter than Oyar Gao. 'A Shankaracharya had once come here. He said to me, "You are a Hindu, and I am a Hindu." I said no, I eat everything, I eat beef.'

He had also been invited by the largest and most powerful Hindu nationalist organization in India, the Rashtriya Swayamsevak Sangh, which was active in these parts, for a talk. 'I said I worship the sun but my Donyi is not your Surya Devta. You cannot be engulfing me.' He seemed to view the Hindu nationalist attempts at finding similarities as an exercise in assimilation by which the distinctive identity of his faith would be lost – and he clearly did not like the idea of assimilation on those terms.

The Adi experience in Arunachal was part of an ongoing tussle between various tribal communities across India wherein the RSS, which was working for Hindu consolidation against what it perceived as aggressive proselytization by some Muslim and Christian organizations, had been trying to draw animistic tribal religions into the greater Hindu fold.

It did not always go down well with the tribals, who had long suffered the denigrations of the Brahminical caste system with its obsessive food taboos, the exploitation of the business community – business was dominated by traders generally called Marwaris – and the unhelpfulness of a corrupt and opaque bureaucracy, whose face in these parts was the man from the plains of mainland India: the Bengali or Bihari babu.

15

Two Kinds of People in This World

WE FOUND A SHOP across the road from the Hotel Bap that sold some groceries, biscuits, cigarettes and other odds and ends. On one side was a 'restaurant' section that comprised a couple of rough tables, a wooden bench and some plastic chairs. An Adi family living in the rooms behind this place ran the joint.

Food was home-cooked, rice, dal and curries, simple and wholesome fare. Kokot, the owner's wife, informed us that the rice we were eating was from their own fields in their village 25 km away. 'We live here because of our children's education,' she said. This distant town was obviously not her first choice of residence.

The kind woman, who cooked only for us as we were her only customers, informed us as we were eating that 'Aings' such as ourselves, which meant outsiders, were known to be bad people. Her world was divided into Adis and Aings. The Aings were bad because they cheated the Adis when they ventured to faraway lands such as Assam, where they sometimes had to go for medical care.

Aing doctors looted the poor Adis, she said; her husband's brother had gone to Dibrugarh because he was ill and had been diagnosed with cancer. They had referred his case to a Guwahati hospital. The family had spent a fortune, two lakh rupees, on his medicines, and he had died not long after. Why didn't the Dibrugarh doctors just send him home if they knew he was not going to survive anyway, instead of putting them through all that?

And yet, she wanted her children – two girls and a boy, all in school – to go and study in the big bad Aing world, in those legendary cities of Delhi and Mumbai. She was a little worried at the prospect because her sister's son who had married an Aing – so she didn't consider all Aings bad, she clarified – had gone to Chennai to study hotel management. He had come back after some years because the people used to ask him if he was from China, and he didn't like it.

Akshay and I tried to console her by saying that even we felt quite lost and out of place in Chennai since neither of us could speak or read the local language, and Hindi was not popular down south, but she was not convinced. I had slightly better success cheering her up with stories of the taxi owners and drivers in Assam who had tried to rip us off. I told her it was because they knew we were from somewhere else, and new to the place. The Adi going there or to Mumbai or Delhi would doubtless face the same situation.

At the next meal, Kokot informed us that she would be leaving for her village in a couple of days to tend to her farm. There was a shortage of farm labour; they got some workers from Odisha or Nepal. Local labour was harder to get. Sometimes they just had to do all the work themselves.

At the following meal, another reason for the trip to her village emerged. It was the golden jubilee of her village school. There would be a big feast, and mithuns would be cut and cooked.

Meanwhile, her sister, the one whose son had married an Aing, had also arrived. From Kokot's story, I had assumed that the son had left his hotel management course in Chennai and fled. The sister asked us, upon hearing we were from Mumbai, 'Have you heard of the Oberoi Hotel?' She was very pleased to hear that we had. People in these parts did not know of it, she said, and it was hard to explain to them what a five-star hotel was.

Her son had worked at the Oberoi properties in Mumbai and one in Udaipur, which was one of the best hotels in the world. He had returned to Itanagar, the state capital, with his wife, who was from Odisha and worked with him, for the birth of their first child. When the child was a year old the couple would leave the baby with her and go back to work, she said. There was nothing in her account about Adis, Aings, or China.

16

Funeral Bar

IN THE EVENING, AKSHAY wanted to go out for a drink. We had bought a couple of bottles of white apong, and I said we could sit on the balcony and drink it. Akshay, however, wanted to socialize.

'I spotted a very local-looking place just down the road where people were sitting and drinking,' he said. 'It seemed to be the popular Yingkiong hangout.' He was keen on the authentic Yingkiong experience.

So we walked down, and indeed, it was not far. A few women were sitting on their haunches outside in the dark. A winding mud path led down to the courtyard of a hut with a sloping thatched roof. Some tables had been placed in this courtyard. There were candles on the tables. A long wooden bench and chairs lay scattered around the place.

Akshay marched in. I followed. 'Can we get alcohol here?' he asked a young man standing next to a table.

There was silence all around. The muffled sound of many soft conversations stopped. All eyes were on us. Akshay realized something was wrong. 'Is this a private party?' he asked.

'Tell them,' someone said in Hindi.

'It is a funeral,' the young man said.

We turned and fled. I was racing up the slope when I was overtaken by Akshay. 'I'm glad it's dark here,' he said as he passed me. 'Walk faster.'

I switched off my torch and quickened my pace.

It took us two bottles of apong on the balcony to recover from this mortifying experience. Neither of us had ever crashed a funeral before.

Getting apong is becoming relatively harder these days. Apong shops don't sell apong anymore. They sell cheap Indian-made foreign liquor, meaning rum and whisky made from a base of molasses rather than grains. The only brand of beer available in the Yingkiong market was Godfather Super Strong. The apong, a fine drink prepared from rice and a mix of herbs in a completely natural, organic way, is sold for Rs 100 a bottle on the street. Its place now is on the ground beside the vegetable seller.

There seems to be some shame attached now to drinking apong. Tulobai at the hotel had laughed at us when we asked where it might be available. People these days looked at it askance, he said.

The taste of apong is sweetish and the high is gentle. It is a mix of the alcohol high and the bhang high. If well made, it is one of the best drinks you can get anywhere.

It is doubtful that the Yingkiong youth would prefer it to cheap super strong beer, though. It's out of fashion.

Teenagers in Yingkiong are as fashionable and with it as their counterparts anywhere else. Jeans and tees with open check shirts over the tees is the regulation dress. Several of the boys rode past on gleaming 100cc motorcycles. The girls, who were mostly on foot, for some reason seemed to have a thing for bags designed to look like teddy bears, perhaps an influence from China or East Asia. Fashion is not my forte, but apparently it was a trend of the season.

The older women typically wear traditional handwoven wraps or salwar kurtas. Some sport jeans. The skirt is generally worn only by schoolchildren.

We also saw signs of an older world that endured alongside the modern one. An old man wearing a 'lengti' or loincloth that just about covered his private parts, and a sleeveless jacket for a shirt, walked past our hotel one evening. His hair was cut in a short bowl cut. He looked like he had walked out of an early British colonial photograph of an Adi man from a century ago.

The very distinctive bowl haircut used to be the standard hairstyle here then. It was done by placing the locks of hair against the edge of a dao or short sword, and hammered lightly with a mallet.

A lot of people outside the town still carry a dao. The old man was carrying one for his teatime excursion to the same tiny tea shop we had begun to frequent. I suppose it becomes habit after a time.

The spear is not so commonly carried, but we spotted an old man in a flowing red robe carrying a wooden spear with a mean metal tip, much like a javelin. He looked like a figure from an old Chinese kung fu film who had come to the market for his evening walk.

17

Into Terra Incognita

THE SIANG AT YINGKIONG is not a big river. It is perhaps half a kilometre wide, and the clear water flows with a roar between steep hillsides. There was not much riverside life apart from a construction crew digging for stones and a couple of Sumo taxis that underage drivers had driven down to the riverside for a wash.

We hitched a ride back to Yingkiong town, a couple of kilometres away, on one of these. The driver looked very young, perhaps fourteen or fifteen. The next day, during our drive to Tuting, further up the Siang valley, I asked the driver about this. He said there was a boy of thirteen driving a Sumo from Pasighat to Yingkiong. This is a stretch of road that would test the skills of professional rally drivers.

I enquired, though I knew the answer even before asking, about licences. The driver laughed. It was a silly question.

A lot of kids started working early in these parts, he said. He himself had started when he was fifteen. No one bothered about licences.

The driving test is quite comprehensive and severe, and it doesn't involve the government – the road itself is the examiner. If you fail the test, you are likely to die, along with your passengers. There is not a single traffic policeman on the entire stretch. Nor is any required; the price of traffic indiscretion being possible death, rash driving is rare.

The drivers ease the stress of the long, slow and strenuous driving by playing their favourite music. As soon as the overloaded Sumo taxi starts bumping along the single-lane mud tracks cut into the sides of tall hills, with cliff on one side and gorge on the other, the driver will normally pull out a USB stick and insert it into the music system. For the rest of your journey of eight or ten or twelve hours, you are likely to be treated to an assortment of his favourite hits at high volume.

On the drive out from Yingkiong to Tuting, which started at 6.30 a.m., our driver woke us up good and proper by first playing the collected works of the Punjabi popstar Yo Yo Honey Singh. He then worked his way through pretty much every 'item song' Bollywood has produced in its recent history. You may think you know your item numbers, but have you heard '*Naughty number one*'?

The drive to Tuting took us a straight-line distance of roughly 40 km as the crow flies. The actual distance on the winding road, according to Google maps, is 288 km. It takes more than twelve hours.

The Bollywood item numbers ran out at some point. For the remainder of our journey we were treated to the collected musical output of Nepal, starting with '*Resham Firiri*', a beautiful folk love duet with lyrics that make no sense … like love itself, I suppose.

Our co-passengers included a young Adi schoolteacher on her way to a school outside Tuting; a young Memba boy from a village called Mariong; a man from Uttar Pradesh; and a Khamba boy from Singa on his way to attend a relative's funeral. A couple of other men slept at the back, and said nothing to anyone through the marathon drive.

The road was a mud track for the most part, with countless little streamlets running across it. In some places it resembled a riverbed, with mud and pebbles.

We bounced along at the usual 20 km/h, listening to music. After about three straight hours of Nepali songs, the schoolteacher said she had had too much of the stuff. The driver turned a deaf ear to her complaint. The Memba boy took the opportunity to make a smooth move, engaging her in flirtatious conversation about the meanings of the lyrics. She played along, breaking the exhaustion of the seemingly interminable drive.

She clearly knew a thing or two about flirtation. In the morning, she had been on the phone with someone, calling him 'stupid' as a term of endearment, and exhorting him to catch up with the Sumo on his bike so that the two of them could ride together to Tuting. This was the sort of trip that the bikers with fancy bikes and gear we had met on the ferry across the Brahmaputra would call an expedition, but of course it could be other things to some of the locals – such as a romantic ride to office, for example.

Somewhere on the bumpy dirt track between Yingkiong and Tuting that is euphemistically called a road, as we rattled our way uphill, I discovered that the quiet, plain man from Uttar Pradesh sitting next to me was an agent of India's principal domestic intelligence agency, the Intelligence Bureau. We had got chatting because there was not much else to do to relieve the tedium. The scenery hour after hour was the same endless wilderness of forested hills rising sheer on one side, and sharp drop down to the faraway silver ribbon of river on the other. The groan of the engine and the endless stream of Nepali songs were the only sounds. The man started making what I thought was small talk about where we were from and where we were headed to. He spoke softly, but he was

insistently curious. What work did we do? Why were we going to
Tuting? What business did we have there?

I was more than happy to narrate my brief autobiography. Akshay
told his story. Then in turn we asked the man what he was doing in
these parts. Why was he going to Tuting? He worked there, he said,
and we enquired about the nature of his job. 'Have you heard of the
IB?' he asked. Indeed, we had.

The Intelligence Bureau used to be in charge of the security of
these areas, along with a paramilitary force called the Assam Rifles,
in the years when India and China were both stretching out towards
their remote peripheries until they collided in war in 1962. Since
shortly before that undeclared war, when Chinese forces cut through
Indian defences to advance deep into Arunachal, control had shifted
to the army.

The trouble had started over who originally owned the Tibetan
borderlands, from Aksai Chin in the west to Arunachal in the east.
Throughout history, these areas had remained outside the reach of
rulers in both Delhi and Beijing. In the case of Arunachal, what
little authority was sometimes exercised by outsiders was on the
edges, where the hills met the Himalayas and Tibetan plateau
in the north and the plains of the Brahmaputra Valley in the
south. Buddhism from Tibet had made inroads among some of
the northern tribes in the mystical lands known as the Pemako
associated with the eighth-century Guru Padmasambhava. There
were ancient pilgrimage routes and remote places of worship in
those areas, and the Dalai Lama's spiritual and political authority
extended to some pockets.

In the south, the tropical forests contained fading memories of
ancient Hindu kingdoms in the Dibang valley. There were legends
surrounding Tamreswari Mai, the temple of the copper goddess near
Sadiya renowned for its human sacrifices, which probably marked
the eastern limit of the ancient kingdom of Kamrup.

Between these two zones of civilization, such as they were, marked by the Hindu temples in the south and the Buddhist monasteries in the north, was fold upon fold of green hill rising towards the desolate Roof of the World. It was an area of wilderness. The tribes living in these wildernesses had lived in their own ways through the ages, protecting the secrets of their lands whose interiors appeared as a blank on the map of the world until the early years of the twentieth century.

The idea of the nation-state, and a new imagination of all frontiers as lines of control rather than zones of transition, gradually spread around the world during the late 1800s and early 1900s. The British colonial administration applied the new notion to India, creating a modern state out of a vast and disparate subcontinent threaded through with ancient linkages of culture and economy, but no political unity. After the modern countries of India and China emerged on the world map in 1947 and 1949 respectively, they began to extend the authority of Delhi and Beijing up to the farthest reaches of the lands that their maps showed as theirs. Cartography moulded destiny. The war of 1962, and the simmering conflict before and since, was perhaps inevitable. It arose out of things neither China nor India could control: the death of distance, and the concept of sovereignty that squeezed out old notions of suzerainty.

18

Test of Character

'WHERE WILL YOU BE staying?' the Intelligence Bureau man next to me asked. There were no hotels or guest houses. We would try our luck at the Public Works Department inspection bungalow, we said. We had no bookings and no idea what we would find. Our phones were out of coverage area. I had read somewhere, when we were planning our trip, that there was a PWD bungalow in Tuting and that it allowed travellers to stay if rooms were free. Tuting did not seem like a place that would be crowded.

It was pitch dark when we reached, around six in the evening. Like the rest of the Northeast, night falls early in these hills. There is no streetlight and few glimmers of light escaped the silent houses we crossed. The PWD bungalow itself was dark. We opened a creaking gate in the silence and, with my torch lighting the way, walked into the overgrown lawn. There did not seem to be anyone about. Then another torch began to move in our direction. A lean man of East Asian appearance asked us who we were and where we had come from. I realized with a start that he was wearing dark glasses in the darkness. He led us into the old Assam-type bungalow, our footsteps sounding like soft drumbeats on the planks of the wooden floor. His name, he said, was Combo – I later realized it was spelt Kombo and was the name of a place in Tibet as well as a village across the McMahon line on the Indian side – and he was the caretaker of the bungalow.

He asked us where we were from. Mumbai, we said. He did not speak any further, but simply asked us to follow him inside the building. We walked in silence through a verandah with tin roof to a large room with two beds. The man switched on the bulb and soon a faint yellow glow, like the illumination from a 'zero power' lamp, enhanced the surrounding dark and silence.

Kombo padded off wordlessly. The following morning he was back, in his dark glasses, to take us on a short trek. We climbed down the hill atop which the bungalow sits, past an army base outside which, in a forested patch, was half a plane, the remains of a cargo aircraft that probably crashed decades ago. The nearby airfield was an 'advance landing base' that had been used during the 1962 India-China war and was now being refurbished as tensions between the two countries grew. We walked on, through a jungle that led to a hanging bridge, passable only on foot, swaying over a gushing aquamarine river. It was the Siang.

The bridge is made of wooden planks tied together with woven bamboo. The structure is suspended from two iron cables, one on either side; it swings from side to side as people walk across.

We crossed to the other side and after walking through a forest, came to a little clearing that had fluttering Buddhist prayer flags and a small wood and tin shrine. Two big rocks lay piled next to each other, with a small gap at the bottom between them. Kombo told us the locals believed that only a person of honesty and integrity could pass through the gap. I figured I could pass the test on account of my small size if not my quality of character, and said as much. Kombo, however, insisted that size had nothing to do with it; character was what counted. So, with some trepidation – after all, I do not know if I meet the Buddha's exalted standards of morality – I lay down on the cold earth and wriggled my way through the gap.

It was Akshay's turn next. His frame is much larger than mine, and this test of character was clearly weighted against him. However, he gamely took the challenge. My worries that he might get wedged in there proved unfounded; Akshay's sterling character and hitherto undiscovered limbo dancing skills saw him slithering through the gap in the rocks in style.

Our satisfaction at having thus established our integrity and excellent moral virtues was short-lived. We were savouring the moment and recovering from our physical exertions when a small, lithe man trotted up the jungle track carrying the trunk of a tree on one shoulder. It was a log about 12 feet long and six or seven inches in diameter. He stopped at the clearing, and propped it up against a big tree. I tried moving it, and managed with great difficulty to only shake it a little. My backbone would probably have snapped in two if I tried lifting it, so I wisely decided to abstain from trying. Akshay merely looked at it and thoughtfully took a long puff of his cigarette.

We watched again as the man, who could not speak – he replied to Kombo's queries with smiles and communicated in gestures – lifted his load and trotted off again.

19
Dragon, Dragon!

THE SIANG IS NOW the principal cause of recurring tensions between India and China, as rumours repeatedly surface of Chinese plans to build dams on it, or divert it altogether, away from India. China has already built at least one dam on the river. In November 2014, the Zangmu dam in Tibet went into operation. *India Today* reported that the 'Zangmu dam, on which construction began in 2010, raised attention in India as the first major hydropower project on the middle reaches of the Brahmaputra, which has its source in Tibet, where it is known as the Yarlung Tsangpo.' The report added that three more Chinese dams on the river were in the pipeline. All would be 'run of the river' dams for generating power, meaning they would not halt the river's flow, the Chinese claimed, but the assurances did little to assuage misgivings in India.

The concerns are not environmental. India itself has long had plans to build 168 dams on the Brahmaputra and its tributaries, which would generate 57,000 MW of power. The construction of these dams would result in contracts worth millions of dollars: a powerful incentive to politicians and bureaucrats who would expect to get cuts. The narrative of the Chinese threat, driven by habitually suspicious security and intelligence officials, is thus amplified by business interests. Only the determined opposition of the local Arunachal tribes has kept the dams on the Indian side from being built so far, but fears of China stealing the river by diverting its flow are growing.

The basis of such fears lies in China's existing river linking project, called the South-North Water Diversion Project, which began in 2002. The project, according to *Raging Waters*, a book published by USA's Marine Corps University Press and CNA Corporation, a think-tank with Pentagon links, consists of three routes: the eastern, central and western. The authors, Nilanthi Samaranayake, Satu Limaye and Joel Wuthnow, say:

> The eastern and central routes focus on diverting water from southern China's Yangtze and Han Rivers, respectively, to the Yellow River in the north. These two routes have already been completed. According to China's official plans, the western route, still in its early planning stages, will concentrate on diverting the headwaters of three tributaries of the Yangtze (the Tongtian, Yalong, and Dadu Rivers, which are all domestic rivers on the Tibetan Plateau) to the Yellow River by 2050.

However, the authors, who had access to Chinese-language sources and experts, report that there is internal opposition and scepticism within China itself to the technical and economic feasibility of diverting the headwaters of the Brahmaputra, which anyway is not part of the project. According to Samaranayake, Limaye and Wuthnow:

Compared to the western route of the official South-North
Water Diversion Project, Chinese experts tend to be even
more dismissive of proposals to divert waters from the upper
Brahmaputra. CNA interviews suggest that the Chinese
government has given no serious consideration to these
proposals in recent years. In fact, a study commissioned
by the Ministry of Water Resources in 2000 reportedly
concluded that such plans would be neither necessary nor
feasible. Former minister of water resources Wang Shucheng
stated on at least two occasions that plans to divert the
Brahmaputra were not feasible. Thus, while China may
eventually give some consideration to such ideas, there is
no evidence to suggest that this is likely in the near future.[22]

Chinese dam-building, is, however, very much in the works.
Apart from the ones already constructed, the Chinese authorities
announced fresh plans in December 2020 to 'implement
hydropower exploitation in the downstream of the Yarlung Tsangbo
river', according to newspaper reports. The proposed location of the
project, at what is called the 'great bend' where the Tsangpo take a
U-turn before flowing into India, has caused concern on the Indian
side. Indian officials responded by announcing plans for one more
big dam of their own. The knee-jerk reaction misses an important
point. Although any upstream dams or diversions would harm the
river, it is impossible for China to actually 'steal' it. There are seasonal
variations, but by and large, most of the waters of the Brahmaputra
come from rainwater, not snow melt, and the contribution of glacial
melt to the Brahmaputra's total flow is very small. According to an
article in *The Hindu Business Line* by Nilanjan Ghosh of the Observer
Research Foundation, Kolkata, 'A very large component of the total
annual flow of Brahmaputra is generated in the southern aspect of
the Himalaya in India by tributaries from Buri Dihing in the East

to Teesta in the west.'[23] Ghosh further wrote, 'Data published by Chinese scholar Jiang and team show that the total annual outflow of the Yarlung River from China is estimated to be about 31 BCM (billion cubic metres) while the annual flow of Brahmaputra at Bahadurabad, the gauging station near the end of the sub-basin in Bangladesh, is about 606 BCM. These figures do not support the linear thinking that the flow in a river is proportional to its length inside a country.' In an analysis for the Observer Research Foundation, he has expressed some concern over China's latest dam plan, because it is 'located in the south aspect of the Himalayas, where the flow of the mainstream Yarlung is enhanced by the flow of another tributary Parlung Tsangpo'. Overall, his analysis of the flow data leaves little room for doubt that equating the Tsangpo with the Brahmaputra is misleading, at least as far as the volumes of water in the two are concerned.

There is, however, considerable popular suspicion that anything that happens to the waters of the Brahmaputra or Siang must be due to Chinese perfidy. While there are good reasons for being suspicious, the suspicion tends on occasion to slide into conspiracy theory.

In December 2017, reports began to appear in the Indian media of the waters of the Siang turning turbid and grey. The cause for it was not known, but as usual, suspicion immediately fell on China. 'Images show China may be using a secret tunnel to divert Brahmaputra water into desert,' a headline in an Indian online publication called *The Print* announced. The alarmist report, by a retired colonel named Vinayak Bhat, accompanied by low quality satellite images, announced that 'latest satellite imagery shows a massive new dam on the Brahmaputra river – Yarlong Tsangpo in Tibetan – with an underground tunnel that seems to engulf the entire water flow for almost one kilometre.' The images showed that 'The purpose of this project is possibly for diverting a portion of the Brahmaputra to the parched areas of Taklamakan desert,' the officer declared. He had an explanation for the darkening waters of the Siang. 'Satellite imagery shows that polymer resin adhesives are being sprayed by China all around this project area as a dust suppressant system,' he noted. He also saw, in the satellite images, stone crushers and cement plants at the site. The report was picked up by other media outlets and created a furore in India.[24]

The Chinese official media denied all this, and their experts advised India not to worry about Arunachal's environment, which they call South Tibet. 'South Tibet is the territory of China, which has the duty to preserve the local environment,' Hu Zhiyong, a research fellow at the Shanghai Academy of Social Sciences told the Chinese government newspaper *Global Times*. 'I have never heard of the project mentioned by the Indian side. It is hoped that the Indian side will not conduct unfounded speculation and reports,' Chinese foreign ministry spokesperson Lu Kang said in a written statement.

Two other Indian researchers, this time civilians, subsequently studied satellite images and discovered that there were indeed three new dams on the Tsangpo – and they had been formed by landslides following a series of earthquakes that hit the mountainous region through which the river flows in November. This matched the initial reports of the Indian government, which the country's Minister of State for Water Resources, Arjun Ram Meghwal, had mentioned earlier. 'There is a strong possibility that the colour (of the river's water) has changed due to natural reasons,' the minister had said. The retired colonel of military intelligence, who had seen dams, tunnels, stone crushers, cement plants and polymer resin adhesives in the Tibetan air, resolutely stuck to his story. However, two years on, with no such dam or tunnel in sight the matter was forgotten.

Such deep suspicion between the two Asian giants is fairly recent. The Indic and Sinic cultures have coexisted and influenced one another and all of Southeast and East Asia besides, through thousands of years, without ever coming into direct conflict. The high-altitude desert of Tibet and the Himalayan mountains were considerable barriers. Although the route over the mountains and through the Tibetan plateau represented the shortest route between the political and cultural heartlands of the two countries, even as late as 1951, Tibetan representatives of the Dalai Lama who signed away their country's sovereignty to China through the Seventeen Point Agreement travelled back from Beijing via the easiest route – by ship from Shanghai to Kolkata and then overland through Sikkim into Tibet on horseback.[25] It was the death of distance, made possible by modern transport and communication technologies, that led to the first tussles between the two countries.

When the territorial dispute between India and China first flared up during the 1950s, India and China had good relations, but new tensions were starting to show. The People's Republic of China had come into existence recently then in October 1949 when the Chinese Communist Party under Mao Zedong came to power after victory in the Chinese civil war between the communists and nationalist forces led by Chiang Kai-shek. The People's Liberation Army took control of Xinjiang in 1949, and Tibet in 1950. The following year, the Seventeen Point Agreement was signed between the Dalai Lama's representatives and the new government in Peking, now called Beijing, by which the Tibetans agreed, under duress, to 'return to the Motherland, the People's Republic of China'. The takeover of Xinjiang and Tibet, and the transition from suzerainty to sovereignty, eliminated the buffer states between India and China and brought them into direct contact with one another for the first time.

India, meanwhile, was also extending its reach into the formerly un-administered areas bordering Tibet – places such as Tawang, where an Indian expeditionary force under Major Bob Khathing of the Assam Rifles raised the flag in February 1951. Sometime in 1956, or possibly earlier, China began to upgrade a largely forgotten caravan trail through the remote high-altitude desert of Aksai Chin that linked Xinjiang and Tibet into a motorable road that later became a national highway. The road passed through territory that appeared, and still appears, on Indian maps as part of Ladakh, although the country's official map released in 1950 had left the border there unmarked. This road sparked off a dispute between the two countries. Meanwhile, a revolt against the Chinese had begun in the Khampa areas of eastern Tibet and spread from there to the Tibetan heartland including Lhasa. In March 1959, the Dalai Lama escaped to India. Relations soured further. The Indian and Chinese premiers, Jawaharlal Nehru and Chou En Lai, met in Delhi in 1960 to try and resolve the mounting differences between their countries. Chou offered a deal: China would drop its claim on the eastern section, meaning Arunachal and a small bit of Assam, if India dropped its claim on Aksai Chin. Nehru refused to entertain such a possibility, and the crisis escalated to war in 1962. Chinese forces swept across the McMahon Line into Arunachal facing little effective resistance.

The Karakoram and Himalayan mountain ranges form a massive natural barrier between Tibet and India along most of the 3,488 km disputed border between the two countries. That's a vast distance; it's more than the straight-line distance from Delhi to Hanoi. High mountain passes and valleys of rivers that cut through between the mountains are the only natural routes of travel in that forbidding terrain. They are also the natural paths for movement of armies. The Karakoram Pass in Ladakh marks the western extremity of such paths. The Dibang river valley in Arunachal Pradesh is the eastern end. In between these two, the Tawang tract adjoining Bhutan to its east, which used to pay taxes to the Tibetan administration of the Dalai Lama in Lhasa, forms one of the core areas of the territorial dispute along the entire length.

Trouble started there in September 1962 when a Chinese patrol crossed a stream called Nam Ka Chu and told the Assam Rifles men there to vacate their post. The Indian side began to bolster its defences by rushing in the army. The Chinese responded in kind, and a military build-up began on both sides. Statements about throwing out the Chinese and not giving away a single inch of Indian territory were made. Soldiers were rushed to the border. They landed there without even the basics, such as warm clothing. There was no supply line to many of those remote areas; supply was by air, through air drops in designated drop zones. The problems and lack of preparation were communicated up the chain of command. Unfortunately, an Indian civil and military leadership keener on managing domestic image than on military preparation tried to bluff and bluster its way through.

In reality, the Indians were putting on a show and hoping the Chinese would not attack immediately, allowing winter to come to their rescue. Internal political wrangling within the army and between the army and defence ministry worsened an already bad situation. When the Chinese attack came on 19 October with its main thrust in Tawang, there was chaos in the military. Defences crumbled in barely seventy-two hours. By 18 November, it was all over. Bomdila, south of the Se-la pass, had fallen, and the Indians were in headlong retreat. The Chinese were within easy reach of the important town of Tezpur in Assam on the north bank of the Brahmaputra. The civil administration there crumbled as officers fled. Indian generals considered withdrawal across the Brahmaputra, leaving its north bank to the Chinese.[26] The possibility of losing the entire Northeast, up to the narrow 22 km wide 'Chicken's Neck' corridor near Siliguri that connects the region to the rest of 'mainland' India, loomed large.

India learnt a hard lesson from that debacle; it now has four infantry divisions posted for the defence of Arunachal Pradesh, and fields missiles, battle tanks and fighter aircraft too. A new Mountain Strike Corps has been raised. Both sides are engaged in upgrading infrastructure along the whole LAC. China tested a new light battle tank in Tibet in 2017 and conducted live-fire exercises using howitzers. It is believed to have silos in the area holding missiles, including ones with nuclear tips. In February 2018, its military released images of its advanced J-10 and J-11 fighter aircraft on exercise in Tibetan skies. A month later, in March, the Indian Air Force landed its largest aircraft, the C17 Globemaster, at the newly refurbished advanced landing base in Tuting that Akshay, Kombo and I had crossed en route on our trek.

20
Culture Shocks

THE MORNING AFTER OUR trek, we walked down to the most spectacular building in Tuting – the local Nyigma Buddhist monastery. It is a new building set amid lawns and gardens. The foundation stone of the monastery was laid by the Dalai Lama in December 2003. When we reached, it was bustling with the activity of a school at the start of the day. Young boy monks clad in maroon robes filed into a large hall with low wooden benches on both sides of a central aisle at the end of which sat a large golden statue of a gently smiling Buddha. The chanting of mantras had begun; voices rose and fell in unison, filling the hall with the sound.

Nearby, there was a hostel and a school for juniors. More structures were under construction. The buildings were made of cement, but touches of the old Tibetan Buddhist aesthetic lent them a grace usually absent in concrete structures. The pillars, walls and ceilings inside the main hall were all hand-painted with intricate Buddhist iconography. The exterior was more sparsely decorated, just a few designs in maroon. Prayer flags fluttered all around us. Behind the hall, beyond a field, a few chortens were visible.

One rather curious inclusion amid all this was a white Ambassador car enclosed in a glass case. It sat near the main hall, with a photo of the deceased rimpoche of the monastery placed in front of it. We wondered about this, but were unable to find anyone who could explain its presence to us. A monk who I approached with the intention of asking the question said he was busy, and heading to the prayer hall.

There is not much to do after dark in Tuting except eat, drink or sleep; life starts at dawn and winds down at dusk. The following morning, we were having an early lunch when a man walked into the Tibetan mom-and-pop restaurant where we were eating. He saw us and immediately asked, 'Where are you from? What brings you here? What work do you do?' and so on. He was from the Intelligence Bureau.

In the evening, having nothing to do and no one to see, we went for a walk to the local Intelligence Bureau compound to catch up with our fellow passenger from the taxi ride. The whole place was dark and deserted. We were on our way back when we bumped into the man who had quizzed us earlier. There was nothing to do in the place, he said, so he entertained himself by taking long walks. Several of his colleagues kept busy with drinking, but this man did not drink alcohol. He also did not eat the meat here, because he was not sure if it would be halal. He had become a vegetarian except on the rare occasions when he would buy a live chicken, cut it himself in the correct way, cook it, and eat it.

He lived alone in the place. His family was back home in Uttar Pradesh. He did not want to bring his family to this distant outpost, and was eagerly waiting for his next transfer.

Coming to the Northeast had been a culture shock, he said.

The sloth and inertia of the vast government machinery for which he worked seemed to trouble him. He did not let on very much, but he said that a journalist at the ground level had a better chance of being heard in the corridors of power than an intelligence official at the ground level.

He was, however, able to solve one mystery for us. We had seen a State Bank of India ATM, but its shutters were always down. The ATM machine had arrived, the IB man informed us, but there was no generator and the quality of power supply in this place would not even light a 100-watt bulb. A few months had passed like this. A request had been sent to the state capital in Itanagar. At some point, months or years hence, the generator would arrive.

The bank itself, the only one in Tuting, had been closed for a couple of months before our arrival because an irate customer had beaten up the branch manager, the IB man said. The manager, who was from the mainland, had upped and left. Until his replacement finally bounced up the bumpy track from Pasighat, the bank had been shut.

There also used to be weekly helicopter flights to Tuting, the man said, but flights had been suspended after a helicopter went missing. An inquiry had been instituted. The report was awaited.

This state of affairs seemed rather sad to me until I had a chat the next morning with the cook at the inspection bungalow where we were staying. Gopal was an old timer in the place. His father, a Tamil man, had arrived in what was then the North East Frontier Agency or NEFA to work for the Public Works Department, married his mother, an Assamese woman, and settled down there. Gopal recalled the times when Tuting had no road connecting it to the outside world. The first road, the one we had used to get there, was opened only in 2000. Until then, supplies used to come by air, he said. Sometimes, during the rainy months, bad weather could stretch to long periods and flights were suspended. The whole town might run out of salt, sugar, oil or soap. They would have rice to eat; it grew in the nearby villages, but not in any great quantities. Terrace farming was not so widespread, and the use of weedicides and pesticides was unknown. The introduction of these had helped increase yields. The associated deforestation – the place used to be heavily forested all around, as opposed to thinly forested now – had caused temperatures to rise locally, Gopal told us. 'Earlier we would wear sweaters even in August,' he remembered.

Yet, he was nostalgic for one thing about the old, unconnected days – the town had been more cosmopolitan, in a way, and there was a sense of purpose as people came from far and wide to set up a functioning administration. The office staff came from all over India. The labour was mostly Nepali. By and by, everything had gone to local hands, and the old people from other places had left. This had not done any good for the administration, he complained. Many of the people from nearby villages who landed government jobs simply failed to turn up at work; they would go off to work in their fields or spend time drinking with friends.

We met one such man who claimed to work for the government's Department of Information and Public Relations. He was sitting outside a poky little shop when we passed by in the early afternoon. 'Come here,' he called out, beckoning us imperiously. When we walked across to him, we were subjected to the usual questions about where we were from and what we were doing in Tuting. When he heard Mumbai, he immediately launched into a long monologue about how he would soon be travelling to Delhi, how his flight tickets were booked, how he owned a car – a big car, no less – in Delhi, and it was coming to the airport to receive him, how he also had a flat there. He asked Akshay where his photographs were published. Akshay modestly named a few Indian publications, saying nothing of his international bylines, and said they sometimes published his work. 'Sometimes,' the man replied. 'When we want.'

I had had enough of his grandstanding and left, saying I was hungry and it was time for my lunch.

In the early evening, as dusk was falling, we had to pass the shop again. The Bollywood song *'Sohni de nakhre sohne lagde'* was blasting from a loudspeaker. Two evidently drunk men tottered about dancing outside. The man who had said he was from DIPR saw us and called out to us. We smiled and kept walking. 'Do you have photos like this in Delhi?' he yelled at us, waving a picture we could not see at that distance in the gathering darkness.

21

Halted by the Army

WE RESOLVED TO MAKE the journey to Gelling, the last point on the road before China – and the only sizeable village after Tuting on the Indian side – next morning. Gelling is literally the end of the road.

Finding information about how to get there proved to be surprisingly difficult. We tried our luck with Gopal and Kombo at the guest house, but they were not sure if and when there would be a vehicle to Gelling, and whether there would be a vehicle back. Even the man from the Intelligence Bureau was not sure. The man at the local taxi counter told us to be there at six the next morning, but would not issue us tickets; he said there would be a vehicle, but was reticent about details.

When we got there at 6 a.m. the next morning there was no one at the counter, and no vehicle. A man sitting at a nearby restaurant helpfully informed us that either the shared taxi to Gelling had already left or it had not arrived.

There was nothing to do except wait.

After some time, the Sumo counter man arrived. He asked the same man we had spoken to – who was the only visible person in the vicinity – whether the vehicle had gone. The man gave him the same answer. Thereafter, the counter man finally told us that the Gelling vehicle sometimes left from higher up the slope if it had already filled up. In other words, for the sake of his commission on two tickets, he had made us wait at a spot where we would either get left behind or get the worst seats.

We hurried up the slope and were just in time to see the vehicle depart.

Resigned to our fate, we went to have tea and breakfast. The Tibetan couple who ran the shop told us the Gelling vehicle usually started from there. Some days it would make two trips; some days, it would make none. There was also the problem of return. We would have nowhere to stay in Gelling, and would need to make quite sure that we caught the same vehicle on its way back – but there was no way to make sure except by physically occupying our seats, because no ticket bookings were taken. The man offered to drive us to Gelling himself in a couple of days, but our ILPs would run out by then. We had just one day left to make the trip.

The couple then said we could simply trek to Gelling. It was not very far. They did not know exactly how far, but there was only one road and it ended at Gelling. All we had to do was get on it and keep walking.

Getting there and back before dark – on foot – was not a feasible proposition. Anyway, we were out of options. We went back to the guest house, picked up our rain gear and hats and water bottles, and hit the road. We had not even reached the outskirts of Tuting when we were accosted by a small group of men, all from mainland India, who asked us who we were, what we were doing, where we were going, and so on. They said they were from the Intelligence Bureau.

We kept walking, so they fell in step with us while we answered their queries. Their suspicions had perhaps not been sufficiently allayed by the time the road reached the local IB office, but the men declined my invitation to join us on our little excursion. We left Tuting behind, and began our walk on the mountain road to Gelling.

It was a single track, as usual, but in better condition than the other roads from Pasighat onwards had been. The Siang kept us company, running steadily at the bottom of the steep hillside into which the road had been cut. It had the appearance of a green ribbon flecked with white. To our left, occasional mountain streams with crystal waters tumbled and rushed down the sheer slope, on their way to join the Siang. The vegetation all around was lush green, with a large number of banana plants along the roadsides, where they had probably been planted by villagers. We did not come across any of these people on the road. In fact, we did not come across any creature or vehicle for a while.

The first vehicle that came our way was a Bolero jeep. We thumbed it down, and the driver was kind enough to stop. He was a local road contractor on his way to inspect work on a new road being built to Singa, a place in the sacred Pemako pilgrimage route of the Tibetan Buddhists. He said he could drop us a little further down the road, from where he would drive off towards Singa. We gladly accepted.

We did not see any other people until he dropped us off, or after. We were again marching on with no idea of how much further we would have to go or how we would get there when a second vehicle, a small Chevrolet hatchback, came our way. We waved, and it stopped. The man in the driver's seat, wearing smart shades and stylishly dressed, looked like a local, and the owner of the car. The seat of honour next to him was occupied by a can of diesel. In the back seat, a shabbily dressed man sat by himself.

The owner agreed to drop us a little further down the road. We squeezed in at the back, while the can of diesel sloshed around importantly in the front seat.

The car owner was an engineer, and he was on his way to check on a small micro-hydel power plant that supplied power to Tuting. A member of the local Galo tribe, he had studied engineering in Hubli in Karnataka. Now he was the man in charge of this power plant. He offered to show it to us.

It was a tiny 25KW 'run of the river' plant built on one of the numerous mountain streams that flow into the Siang, and the building essentially consisted of one shed with a tin roof housing the generator.

The engineer wished they had bigger power plants. It was possible to build mini and micro hydel plants to produce enough power for the small towns and villages of Arunachal, he said, but the trouble was that the water level varied with the seasons. As water levels decreased, power generation became a problem. He blamed the low supply voltage in Tuting on this.

The water flowing freely, untapped, was like money flowing away, he said. The state needed funds and could become a developed state if it used the most abundant resource it had: water. It was possible now to do so without too much damage to the environment, he said.

He had nothing good to say of those who were protesting against the proposed dams. They were simply afraid of change and progress, he asserted. Why, they had even opposed the building of roads in these parts when the first roads were being built. The loudest protests were coming from those who had not got the most lucrative compensation packages, he said.

He scoffed at talk of dams bursting during earthquakes. No big dam in India had ever burst, he pointed out. Dams could be built to withstand earthquakes. People had even opposed the Bhakra dam in Punjab, he said. Look at how the lands irrigated by those waters had reaped a harvest of prosperity for generations. He was a true believer in the unalloyed benefits of technology and the transforming power of money.

We said goodbye to him and his assistants and resumed walking. We had walked perhaps a couple of kilometres without seeing another person or car when the sound of a large vehicle groaning up the track reached us. This time it was a Border Roads Organisation truck. We climbed in with two men in uniform who drove us in wordless silence to the village of Bona, 10 km from Gelling. Getting out, we stopped for a cigarette break at a roadside shop selling the usual knick-knacks: cheap biscuits from unknown brands, potato chips, dry cells for torches and slippers.

The man behind the counter was busy counting a fat bundle of hundred-rupee notes. He regarded us with the usual suspicion and proceeded to ask more questions than even the IB agents. The answers did not seem to satisfy him, but he eventually ran out of questions. We finished our cigarettes, filled our water bottles from a roadside tap and resumed our march.

After another kilometre or so of walking we heard again the happy sound of a vehicle coming from behind us. The morning traffic had been pretty much all in our direction, and everyone had given us a lift. This time it was a dumper truck. And in the cabin next to the driver, wearing his maroon robe, was the monk from the Tuting monastery who I had stopped to ask about the car in the glass case!

He stopped the vehicle, and asked us to get in at the back. We clambered up. The truck was loaded with fine river sand and bags of cement. Four scrawny labourers stood atop these bags. We joined them.

It was, by some margin, the bumpiest ride of my life. While going to the Lake of No Return on the Stilwell Road in Myanmar some years ago, I had bumped my head a few times on the roof of the Maruti Gypsy four-wheel drive we were in, as a result of being hurled out of the seat. This time there was fortunately nothing to bump one's head against even though I spent many long moments suspended in midair. Encountering a branch of a tree in one of those moments would have been unhealthy.

The road wound steadily up, as it had since Pasighat, with the Siang by its side.

At Gelling, we ran out of luck.

A convoy of army trucks was parked on the narrow single lane road in front of us. The dumper stopped. There was no path forward.

All of us got off to walk towards the village, visible less than a hundred metres ahead. An army man in battle fatigues called out to Akshay, and stopped him. He had spotted the camera. I went back to see what was happening. The soldier was joined in no time by a whole posse of others, all heavily armed and brandishing assault rifles. We were surrounded. The monk came to our aid. The soldiers were polite and respectful towards him, but they told him they would have to take us aside for questioning and could not let us pass.

The ridge of the hill facing us was the McMahon Line, the disputed de facto border. On the other side was China. The border wound a little further away to our right, where the river flowed at the bottom of the hill. There was no way down; up ahead, in the distance, we could see a waterfall, at the base of which was the last village on the Indian side, Bishing.

The soldiers, all strapping men from Maharashtra and North India, questioned us. The tone of questioning was aggressive; we were made to stand on the edge of the narrow road, with the Siang a ribbon far below us and a wall of soldiers around us. They demanded to see photos that Akshay had clicked. He had only taken photos of the scenery along the road, but they found even this to be suspicious, and forced him to delete several. They would not believe we were there to research a book. They also did not believe in the legitimacy of the Inner Line Permit we had taken so much trouble to get. They said they had not heard of any such office issuing permits in Dibrugarh and paid it no heed.

I demanded to speak to an officer. We could see, from where we were being questioned, that a tent had been put up in a nearby field where a Maruti Gypsy with the commanding officer's flag was parked.

The officers were busy in a meeting, we were told, but the appeal to higher authority had some effect. One of the soldiers demanded our ILP passes and walked off with them. The rest kept an eye on us; a flattering array of military might watching our every move. Eventually, a young lieutenant, looking fresh out of the National Defence Academy was called. He came with more soldiers and repeated all the questions the others had already asked. He was even more suspicious than the rest; he found my T-shirt, which had a camouflage pattern, to be odd. Where had I got hold of this T-shirt, he asked. I bought it from a clothes store, I replied. However, he would not believe such T-shirts were commonly available in shops everywhere.

We had told him we were journalists from Mumbai. I had showed him my press identification, which clearly said I was the editor of a newspaper there, and my other IDs such as driving licence and voter card. He seemed unsure of what to do; he could ask his CO but seemed to think that disturbing the great man would not be right for such a trivial matter. 'Put them back on the truck and send them back,' he told his men, and walked off, disregarding our pleas.

That was it. There was nothing we could do. Arguing with a truckloads of soldiers who clearly had nothing better to do than mill around us, after they had been ordered to send us back, was pointless. This was a place beyond mobile signals and possibilities of helpful phone calls. It was a place where the man with the gun was the law.

We waited while the labourers and the monk completed unloading the cement bags and sand, watching from afar the waterfalls we would be unable to visit.

The ease with which civilian authority is superseded by the military given the slightest opportunity is remarkable. The area we were in was a road in an Arunachal village, not a military cantonment, and there was no spike in military tensions with China at the time. We had the required government permits to be there. The army worked there, just as the Border Roads Organisation and other institutions of government worked there, and did not own the place any more than the rest of them did. The army men had seen our identification cards that said we were journalists, as well as driving licences and other documents. We answered all their questions, in Hindi, English and even some Marathi. We were two unarmed Indian citizens who had every right to walk on the street in Gelling village, and hardly launching an invasion. Yet they thought nothing of simply ignoring the ILP, the identification documents, and the press cards, and detaining us, preventing us even from simply walking around the village that was 100 m away and having a cup of tea there.

The nation's secrets are not out there on the roadside in Gelling. They are in computers in government offices in cities such as Delhi, Mumbai and Bengaluru. In today's world even free services such as Google Maps and Google Earth allow for sufficient resolution to see the topography of any area. Anyone who wishes to buy higher resolution satellite images can do so. The days of spies drawing maps are long over. If the military thinks it is protecting national secrets or vital installations by being suspicious of travellers, it should apply the same logic to people on the streets of Lutyens' Delhi, around North Block, South Block and India Gate, instead of doing so only in places like Gelling. That, no security force will be allowed to do, because then everyone, even the most ardent flag-waving nationalist, remembers that this is a democracy and not a military state. In practice, notions of equality, democracy and citizen's rights in India only extend to some communities – of the 'right' ethnicity, religion and linguistic groups – in some areas of the Indian mainland, at some times. It does not include everybody, and it certainly does not extend to all areas at all times. Akshay and I, despite checking the boxes for right ethnicity, religion and language, happened to be notionally in the wrong area at the wrong time.

There was a biographer of the Brahmaputra who got up to Gelling two decades before us. He wrote the only previous travelogue following the river. His name was Mark Shand. In his genial account called *River Dog*, Shand recalls reaching Gelling in an Indian Air Force helicopter. 'In minutes, Yatish, Bhaiti (his dog) and I were tucking into tea, lemonade and ginger biscuits while the three soldiers stood to attention behind us, moving only to fill up our glasses,' he wrote. He was plied with food and Contessa Rum and given an escort to hike up to the ridge of the hill which is the McMahon Line, from where he could peer into Tibet.

Like Shand, none of the people who indulge in flag-waving from the comforts of their big city offices and homes will ever have to experience ordinary life in a remote border area. Even if they visit such a place, it will not be on the back of a dumper truck – it will be as a valued guest of the government or military, probably in a helicopter. The same jawans who grilled us and blocked our way would then stand at attention, call them 'Sir,' ferry them around and bring them tea and meals, not moving except to fill their glasses and plates. The 'nationalists', secular or religious, like the valued international guest, would leave with the cockles of their hearts warmed by the hospitality, scenery and apparent firepower, all at their service.

22

Reincarnating Lamas and Evangelists

O N THE WAY BACK, sadder than we had arrived – we had made a grueling journey so far, for so long, only to be turned away at the last stop by the army – we stopped for tea at a roadside shack and bonded with our fellow-travellers. The labourers were two Bengali boys from Tripura, one Bengali boy from Silapathar in Assam and a local Adi man. The driver of the truck was from Odisha. The monk did not say where he was from but told us he had spent thirteen years before coming to Arunachal in a place called Bylakuppe in Karnataka, which is a major centre of Tibetan Buddhism.

He was all praise for South India. It was a peaceful place where they did not have bandhs every two days, he said. This obviously contrasted with life in Northeast India, where there were so many different groups calling bandhs that sometimes one only discovered a bandh had been called on finding oneself stranded during a journey.

It was, however, not bandhs that I wished to discuss with him. I had finally found the opportunity to ask him about the Ambassador

car in the glass case at the monastery in Tuting. He was reticent. It
had belonged to a guru in Bylakuppe and had been brought here to
keep him in memory, he said, before walking off.

It was an unsatisfying explanation. Why bring it here of all
places and all the way from Karnataka, 4,000 km away? We were
still mystified. One of the Bengali boys finally explained that the
deceased monk was expected to be reincarnated and come to Tuting.
The car, in a fine example of planning for the future, was being kept
ready for his reincarnation.

There was a moment of silence at this revelation. Then the
driver of the truck, L.V. Sobro, started to tell the story of the old
days, when there were no roads in the region for cars or any other
vehicles. Sobro was a plains tribal from Gopalpur-on-sea on the
Odisha coast. He had arrived in Arunachal in 1984 as a labourer for
the Border Roads Organisation. The road to Gelling from Tuting
was being cut out of the hill by hand; he had worked on cutting
this road on which we were now standing. Tuting itself was a dot,
not quite on the map, and isolated from everywhere else except for
the walking paths and the airfield. Sobro quickly realized that the
physical labour would do him in. He could cook, and made himself
useful cooking meals. His food was good. The boss appointed him
as his personal cook. It was an easier life, and one that allowed him
the opportunity to learn driving – he spent time in the cabins of
trucks and learnt by observing, he said.

After some time, tiring of the chores of cooking and cleaning and
wanting to experience a little more freedom, he angled for a driver's
job. He got one, but driving on these roads is dangerous even for
veteran drivers. Soon after, being still inexperienced, he met with
an accident. His truck rolled down a cliff. He and the helper were
trapped inside, badly wounded but alive. They would have bled to
death but for an army convoy that happened to be passing by. Sobro

and the helper were rescued. It took him a year to recover from his injuries.

During this time, he went back to cooking. As he recovered, he wondered about his options. Driving paid a better salary – Rs 250 a month plus rations – and there was the lure of the open road. He realized that even with the risks involved, he preferred the driving job. During his year-long convalescence he had also met a Bengali woman and married her. He now had responsibilities; he needed the money. He went back to driving. They had a son, who had grown up and was now studying in Silapathar. 'We cannot afford to send him to the big cities,' he said.

Sobro had an interest in the history and culture of the area. He remembered that when he first arrived in these parts in 1984, he and the BRO labourers would come across local tribesmen who wore only a 'lengti' or loincloth made of a single large leaf. '*Chalte chalte dhoti change ho jata tha*,' he said – the loincloth could be changed during the course of a walk. It was easier than shopping for clothes, and free. All anyone had to do was spot a good replacement growing nearby, pluck it and wear it. Regular change of the leaf was necessary because it would dry and shrivel up.

Salt was a luxury item then, and only the richest could afford it. Dal and cooking oil were hard to come by. Soap was a rarity. But the locals had managed; the banana plant and the mithun had sustained generations. Life had improved greatly for people in recent years, said Sobro. He was not sure where it was all going, but so far, so good.

They dropped us back near the monastery. We returned to the guest house in Tuting and found it abuzz with activity. A party of preachers had arrived from Along, a town west of where we were, in Arunachal. They had the room next to ours. The place was resounding with loud cries of 'Praise the Lord!' and 'Hallelujah!'. It turned out that Gopal, the cook, was a Christian, and the preachers were his guests.

Next morning we were awakened by more shouts of 'Praise the Lord!' and 'Hallelujah!'. The sounds, clearly audible through the thin wall, rose to a frenzied crescendo. After some time they stopped and the group of preachers walked past our room to the dining room where tea and breakfast were being served. I joined them there. Introducing myself, I asked the man next to me what title I should address him by. 'You can call us Evangelist,' he replied.

The evangelists had arrived to do what their title suggested. They were all local Arunachali tribals affiliated with a church in Kerala in south India. The three men and three women had driven up from Along and would be doing some preaching and healing before returning the day after.

Before breakfast, everyone stood around the table and prayed. I did not catch the muttered words. Then the evangelists burst out in a final round of 'Praise the Lord!' and 'Hallelujah!' before we all sat down to our tea and biscuits.

23

Breakdown

WE LEFT FOR YINGKIONG on our return journey after the customary puri-sabzi breakfast at Niamtso, the little Tibetan shop we had been frequenting during our stay in Tuting. Warm goodbyes were exchanged all around. Akshay gifted Kombo his National Geographic jacket. Our Sumo taxi arrived, and we had the back seat all to ourselves – a luxury, except that now without the insulation of tightly packed bodies, we were tossed around on the bumpy road like clothes inside a washing machine. The driver, a teenager as usual, set a scorching pace. He raced along at 30km/h or so, a tremendous speed on that road, before making a long halt at a rare intersection on the road for, he said, a change of vehicles, needed for reasons he would not explain. The change eventually didn't happen, and having wasted a good hour or so, we got back on our way. We had gone only a short distance when a lone man carrying a gun flagged us down. He passed his old 0.22 rifle through the window to me, and then clambered in. He said he was a local hunter who hunted wild dogs, wild cats, wild hogs, and the occasional deer in the forests around us.

We were making good speed – perhaps too good – when suddenly there was a loud noise. The driver got down to investigate, then climbed back and drove on, more slowly now, with the noise continually getting louder. We stopped again on the outskirts of a village called Migging.

It turned out that two struts of the suspension had broken. It may have been knowledge of such a possibility that had driven the aborted mission to change vehicles.

The driver took out his tools and proceeded to take off the wheel. He hammered the suspension with a crowbar in a vain attempt to push the intact part of the suspension to the middle, where it had broken. Hours passed. Not a single vehicle had passed us in either direction since our halt at the intersection where we had waited for the change vehicle that didn't materialize. We discussed our options.

Two of the passengers wanted to push on at any cost, with or without the suspension. One was a local boy who had a job interview the next morning in Yingkiong. The other was a schoolteacher from Bihar who taught at the Tuting Kendriya Vidyalaya. He was on his way home for vacation and had reserved train tickets from Dibrugarh.

Another man, who had worked as a local guide taking trekkers to Singa in the holy Pemako, advocated returning to Tuting. It made no sense to push on only to be stuck at some even more awkward spot on the road, he said. He recalled one time he had got stuck during a trek with a party of foreigners. They had got snowed in due to unseasonal snowfall. He was carrying a satellite phone and they had managed to call in a helicopter for rescue. Their travails had not ended when they returned to Tuting; the local IB crew and police had descended on them, and harassed them for money as their permits had expired. The fact that this was due to an emergency made no difference to the policemen's aspiration to make a quick buck.

Akshay and I looked at one another. This was the last day our Inner Line Permits were valid. Pretty much the entire IB office in Tuting had met us by this time, and asked us the same questions over and over.

And here we were, stuck on the road.

We were still considering our options when a vehicle came along. It was a cement truck groaning up the road, heading towards Tuting. We decided to hitch a ride, rather than wait in hope. The driver and his assistant kindly let us into the cabin, which had a bunk behind the driver's seat.

We were really out of travel luck that day. This truck too suffered a flat tyre just before Tuting. We eventually got a ride on a Sumo coming up from Yingkiong, and returned to the guest house only by nightfall, as we had the first time, exhausted after a hard day of travelling, with no progress made.

Kombo seemed neither surprised nor happy to see us. He neither smiled nor frowned. His one good eye remained hidden behind his dark glasses. 'You could have tried staying at Migging,' he said, before leading us back to the same room we had left that morning.

24
Yingkiong Again

THE NEXT DAY, WE left the guest house again with me muttering a few silent prayers for better travel luck. It was around 6.30 in the morning and we were having breakfast when a tipsy man reeking of alcohol came and asked us, yet again, the same litany of questions about who we were and what we were doing there. He was also from the local Intelligence Bureau office, the shop owner informed us. By this time, we had probably met the entire and fairly considerable staff of the IB in Tuting.

The journey back to Yingkiong was largely uneventful after that, except that we had another drunk man in the seat with us at that early hour. Morning drinking is clearly a thing in these parts; we had also seen those kids in Pasighat drinking at 7 a.m.

The Sumo dropped us on the wrong side of the Siang, across from Yingkiong. A thin, steep, gravelly path led down to a long hanging bridge across the river. Laden as we were with backpacks and bags, a misstep on the path looked dangerous, perhaps deadly.

The bridge is maintained by a local committee that has put up notices exhorting people not to beat up the staff 'without reason'. The condition of the bridge constituted good reason, in my opinion, but Akshay and I were more likely to be at the receiving end of a beating right then. The staff regarded us, like the IB men and the soldiers, with suspicion. We heard some muttering. Their suspicions, however, were different. One man asked if we were from a 'dam party'. No, we said, we were travellers. They did not seem to believe us.

The walk across the bridge lay before us. We could see the bridge swinging as people walked across. The river roared and raged below. The flooring was of wooden planks, but there were plenty of gaps where a plank had fallen off and not been replaced.

'Last smoke?' said Akshay. He did not specify what 'last' meant, and I did not ask. We had a smoke and prepared ourselves for the crossing.

It was a very cautious walk with our loads on our backs. This is a relatively busy bridge, and a long one, perhaps 300 m or so, and we found ourselves in a line with people before and behind us, and the bridge swaying under our feet. To make it more complicated, there was traffic in both directions. We had to march at roughly the same pace as the others – a challenging task, since they were all locals, used to this sort of bridge, and mostly unencumbered with luggage.

It was with a sense of acheivement that we made it across. A few Sumos were waiting there, and we got a ride on one back to the relative comfort of Hotel Bap. It felt like the place had grown between the time we left and came back. Our eyes, now accustomed to Tuting, saw Yingkiong as a big town with facilities. A major one was a functioning ATM. It was being loaded just as we reached the place, and a queue had already formed outside. We joined the queue. As soon as the shutter went up, the queue dissolved into a scrum. Everyone rushed inside at once. There everyone huddled in close contact watching the first person pull money from his account.

One woman in the crowd handed over her ATM card to a man she seemed to be acquainted with, told him her pin within easy earshot of everyone, and walked off to buy something. Another woman, who had arrived with her dog, left the crowd to put a packet of biscuits in its mouth. Her place in the non-queue was secure; the community of ATM-withdrawers moved a smidgen to fit her back into the crowd when she returned.

25

The House with the Mithun Heads

AFTER WITHDRAWING MONEY AND getting a bit of rest, we decided to walk across to the house next to the hotel that had caught our eye during our previous stay at Yingkiong. While our hotel was an ugly, featureless concrete structure, the house next to it had character. It stood tall on stilts atop a small mound in the middle of a patch of open land. The walls were woven cane and adorned with rows of mithun skulls. The roof was corrugated tin sheets. A TataSky dish antenna sat in the courtyard.

We decided to try our luck with talking to the owner of this very interesting house. It was early evening, around 4 p.m. The gate at the bottom of the little hillock that led to the house was open. We walked in hesitantly and with slow steps went up the curving path to the verandah in front of the house. An old man with the traditional bowl haircut was sitting there. He looked at us and said nothing. I tried speaking to him in Hindi. He did not respond. I tried Assamese. No response. There did not seem much point in trying any of the other languages I knew. We regarded each other in silence. The man motioned towards the gate. An awkward silence followed.

I looked in the direction the man had motioned. There were two small concrete structures with tin roofs at the edge of the courtyard. A bulb was on in one. It seemed to be a bathroom, and there was somebody inside. The man seemed to be suggesting that we should speak to whoever was in the bathroom.

We waited. The awkward silence grew. Dusk fell.

Then the bathroom door opened and a beautiful young woman clad in a little wrap, freshly bathed, a towel around her head, walked out. We were standing at the bottom of the steps that led into the house. We got out of the way as fast as we could. She did not look at us, and walked past.

'Let's go,' said Akshay. After our previous Yingkiong experience of fleeing from a funeral after marching in and demanding drinks, we were both primed to run away quickly from any cultural misunderstandings.

We turned to escape. Just then the gate opened and a man wearing a hat walked in. We were stuck. I feared for a moment that, given the language barrier, we might have some difficulties explaining our presence here, especially if the woman had been discomfited by our unexpected presence, and our heads might be added to the mithun skulls on the trophy wall.

The man came and looked at us. We had come from Mumbai and were looking to speak to the owner of the house, I told him in Hindi. He replied in the same language, asking us to wait. I heaved a sigh of relief. A minute or two later, he gave us places to sit on his bamboo verandah. He was the owner of the house, he said, and his name was Tekseng.

Tekseng was 74. He had lived in Yingkiong most of his life. His family was from Simong, an old and powerful Adi village in the hills above Yingkiong.

'Our elders used to fight all the way from here to Tibet,' said Tekseng. 'They used to enforce boundaries between the Khambas and the Membas from Gobuk to Singa and up to Bishing,' he added, naming villages in the surrounding hills.

The Khambas, also called Khampas, are a Buddhist community from the Kham region in eastern Tibet that inhabits both sides of the disputed border between India and China. The Membas are very similar, being also a Tibetan Buddhist community that inhabits both sides of the border. The two tribes seem to have had ancient differences that, according to Tekseng, needed the peacekeeping forces of their neighbours, the Adis – who are also divided into warring clans such as the Panghi, Padam, Minyong and Gallong – to enforce territorial boundaries.

Leslie Shakespear's account of a British expedition to these areas in 1912 confirms some bits of Tekseng's boast. It was an expedition with 100 soldiers of the 8th Gurkha Rifles and porters carrying supplies for twenty-four days that went up the Dihang – as the Siang was also known – to survey its course. He wrote:

> Rain and mist interfered with survey work, and the Naga coolies were greatly exhausted with marching. However, this party did make a dash and got some distance beyond Shimong, which was found to be, with its sister village of Karko, a sort of barrier between Thibet and Assam; these two strong villages on either side of the Dihang allowing no Thibetans to pass south and no Abors or Assamese to pass up. From here a broadish, well-defined trade path led towards Thibet, trodden by hundreds of laden yak bring commodities to Shimong, whose inhabitants distributed the same through the northern Abor clans.

The yak caravans are long gone. The border that was once permeable has hardened into an impenetrable wall. Shimong still exists, but the days of its former glory are only a receding memory in the minds of old men like Tekseng.

He seemed unsentimental about those times. They were hard times.

There used to be fights over salt, he recalled. It was a rare and precious commodity. The Tibetans used to export it – rock salt. The Adis and their Khamba and Memba neighbours would barter it for rice.

The trade routes were closed off after the India–China war of 1962. Tekseng was then a young man. 'The Chinese forces had reached Gelling,' he says. 'I did not run away. I took a rifle and decided to stay and fight.'

He went and presented himself at the camp near the local school where the Indian soldiers were stationed. 'They were cooking goat meat and rice, and drinking alcohol out of hollow bamboo mugs,' he recalled.

It seems a strange thing to remember about a war, but then, the Chinese did not push ahead down the Siang valley; they poured in through Tawang in the west, and down the Dibang valley in the east. Here in Yingkiong there was no fighting.

This was the last frontier town on the Indian side, Tekseng said. 'Between here and China there was no town.' In 1962, it does not sound like it was much of a town. 'There was no road here,' he said, 'only a walking track to Pasighat.' It was a long walk of many days.

The town's development started after the war. 'In 1969, Yingkiong became a gram panchayat,' Tekseng said. 'From there the change started'. It was not all positive change in his opinion. Democracy, after all, has its perils. 'I support one person, you support another … from there the quarrels started.'

However, he wasn't happy with the pace, 'There has been development. But the kind of facilities in Mumbai, Delhi, Kolkata, Guwahati … where will you find such facilities in the jungle here?'

It sounded strange coming from a man who from all appearances – the house, and his own person – was a traditionalist, but Tekseng said he favoured development. 'We especially need roads,' he averred.

But his support for development did not extend to dams. 'My head gets hot thinking about it,' he said. 'We heard that the ministers took money and allowed the dam companies.' According to him there should be a proper kebang meet to deliberate on the matter, and bring clarity on how much land would go under water if the dams were to be built, and who would get what kind of compensation. Some compensation money had been paid, he had heard, but it never reached the people who would be affected.

Apart from events in the state, Tekseng also kept track of national and international events on TV. He followed the news in four languages, he said – English, which he understood but did not speak, and Hindi, Assamese and Nepali, all of which he was fluent in.

He was unhappy with an issue in the news. The Opposition had been criticizing Prime Minister Narendra Modi for his frequent foreign travels. 'It is important now to make friends with other countries and do business with them,' he said.

The Bharatiya Janata Party is known to be a Hindu nationalist party. Tekseng, however, was a follower of Donyi Polo, and quite far from being any kind of fundamentalist. 'There is a Donyi Polo temple here. While crossing it, I blow my car horn. When crossing a Ram temple, I do the same. Crossing a mosque, I do the same. Crossing a church, I do the same. God sent all the great men and women to help the world. They are all avatars,' he said.

He was not exactly a nationalist either. When he started his schooling in 1952, they never sang the national anthem, 'Jana Gana Mana', he recalled. 'We used to sing the Assamese state song, "*O mor aponar desh*".' These areas were in Assam at the time. There was also an Adi anthem, a salutation to Donyi Polo. 'Jana Gana Mana' came later, and Tekseng was not quite happy with it. 'In "Jana Gana...", they have mention of Punjab, Sindh, Gujarat, Maratha, Dravida, Utkala, Vanga, but no mention of us. Should we go to China?' he asked with a dry laugh.

I thought of telling him that when the song was written in 1911, the map of India looked quite different, but it seemed like an unnecessary interruption.

He concluded our long teatime conversation with a reflection on the wealth of Arunachal. Surveyors had found oil under the ground, he said. There was also other mineral wealth that could be used to make cement. 'There are also a lot of ancient fossils under the ground. People keep finding them,' he said. So, indeed, they do.

Later that night, we were having dinner at Kokot's when she asked us if we would be interested in buying an egg – a dinosaur egg. Someone in her village had found it. If we were interested, she could ask for it and it would arrive in a day or two.

We had no plans to start a Jurassic Park. We declined the kind offer, and the following morning, started off down the hill for Pasighat, and across the vast Brahmaputra to Dibrugarh.

SECTION II
Brahmaputra, Upper Assam

26

Dibrugarh

DIBRUGARH TOWN ITSELF STILL has something of the sleepy feel to it that Guwahati used to have years ago. There are still a lot of Assam-type houses with their sloping tin roofs. Traffic has increased here, as everywhere else, but roads still have the chaotic mix of cars, buses, bikes, cycle-rickshaws, pedestrians, cattle, dogs, that are typical of towns in the plains of India. There are also little minivans that substitute for local buses.

The town, whose edges are a roughly half hour drive from the centre in any direction, is ringed by tea gardens. Dibrugarh was, and to a substantial degree remains, the heart of Assam's tea trade.

The town was built by the British colonial administrators as a military garrison and district headquarters in the 1800s. The name is probably derived from the river Dibaru, with the ending 'garh' signifying fort. It was a fort on the bank of the river Dibaru; the word Dibaru itself is from the Dimasa language, with the word 'di' meaning water. The Brahmaputra flowed further away, around half a mile from the town. Over time, the town expanded. And a channel of the Brahmaputra began to flow into the Dibaru, making it a braid of the Brahmaputra.

The first commercial tea garden of Assam was a garden in Chabua close to Dibrugarh that was set up in 1837, soon after the territory had come under British rule. That was also the year a Major Griffith undertook an expedition through the area up to Sadiya. He noted in a report published in the *Asiatic Journal* that, 'The greater part of Muttock, which I had thus an opportunity of seeing, may be characterised as capable of producing tea, the soil being in almost every instance of that yellow colour, hitherto found to be so characteristic of the tea localities.'

The land was known as Muttock because of the Motok tribe that dominated the area, though Griffith's expedition also took him through lands inhabited by the neighbouring Mishmi tribe. The suitability of the Motok lands, then an independent kingdom, the adjacent Ahom territories, and the Singpho tribe's lands further east, for tea cultivation, was also reported by Charles Alexander Bruce, first Superintendent of Tea Culture, and prompted the annexation of these territories to British India.

Apart from tea, Dibrugarh's growth owes something to an attack on a British garrison at Sadiya in 1839, which formed the East India Company administration's easternmost frontier outpost at that time. The local Khampti tribe rose in revolt and killed the British political agent, Major White, and the troops in the garrison. Sadiya was temporarily abandoned, but the strategic need to position military forces and establish an administrative headquarters in Upper Assam became a priority for the Company Raj.

Dibrugarh consequently became headquarters of Lakhimpur district in 1842. At the time, it was a place of dense jungle and grasslands with tall elephant grass.

The town's population, thirty years after it had been established as district headquarters, was enumerated in the census of 1872. There were 2,774 people in the town, and another 1,096 in the military cantonment. The total came to 3,870.

It grew rapidly in subsequent years with migration from various parts of Assam and India adding to the numbers. The lands of Upper Assam had been depopulated due to years of war with the Burmese, who took large numbers of men and women away as slaves. Those who could escape, fled. When tea gardens were set up, plains tribals were brought in from what is now Jharkhand, West Bengal, Odisha and Telangana to work as labour. Marwari businessmen and Bengali babus came. Assamese families from the old Ahom capitals of Sivasagar and Jorhat moved to the new town. And of course, there were the British sahibs at the top of the social ladder.

You won't find many signs of the old town they built any more. It no longer exists. Most of it is now under the Brahmaputra.

There was a great earthquake in 1950. The river changed course, swallowing old Dibrugarh. The demise of that town contributed to the growth of its neighbour, Tinsukia, which escaped major damage and became the centre of Upper Assam's tea and oil industries until Dibrugarh got back on its feet.

The town has now fenced itself off from the river. A high earthen embankment, as tall as a two-storey house, runs along the riverside, separating the houses, shops and offices from the river. There are still people living on the narrow strip of land on the wrong side of the embankment, though.

Akshay and I took a morning walk through one of those riverside villages with their bamboo houses topped with tin roofs. The rituals of daily village life were being lived out by its winding path, too narrow for two people to walk abreast. The path led to the riverbank where, in one place, a group of women were busy washing clothes in the river. About 50 m downriver, a group of men sat chatting.

They were mostly bare-bodied, clad only in shabby lungis. One old man among them, dark, thin, scrawny, called out to us, 'Where are you from?'

He was speaking in English, with a slight Assamese accent. English is the language of education in modern India; it is also, usually, the language of the middle and upper classes. His appearance, however, was at odds with this. We answered his question, and in turn asked him to tell us about himself. He said he lived there, and had once had a job. The memory of that seemed to make him uncomfortable. Dismissing us with a curt 'Okay, thank you' he walked away to resume his perch by the river.

27

On Board the Akha

RIVER ISLANDS DOT THE Brahmaputra along its length. There are several around Dibrugarh. They are only accessible by boat – or helicopter. Getting to them and back is no easy matter.

One bright autumn morning, we boarded a houseboat called the Akha to visit some of these islands on a stretch of the river upstream from Dibrugarh in the direction of Pasighat. The Akha is a mobile clinic. It is a large wooden boat made by local carpenters from Dhola in Tinsukia under the supervision of a boat builder named Kamal Gurung. It is 22 m long and 4 m wide and houses a basic OPD and lab apart from the crew's living quarters, kitchen, bathrooms and toilets. The engine that drives it is a 120-hp truck engine.

It was built on site at Maijan ghat near Dibrugarh. Work was completed in June 2005.

The initiative was the brainchild of Sanjoy Hazarika, author of several books, founder-director of the Centre for Northeast Studies and Policy Research at Jamia Millia Islamia, and International

Director of the Commonwealth Human Rights Institute. Earlier, no services, including healthcare, reached the people who lived on the 2,500 or so river islands on the Brahmaputra, and Sanjoyda ('da' means 'elder brother' and is the customary way of respectfully addressing male seniors in Assam and Bengal) had decided to do something about this.

I happened to know Sanjoyda and wrote to him asking if Akshay and I could spend some time on the Akha. He put me in touch with Dr Bhaben Bora, the doctor who ran the boat clinic. Yes, said Dr Bora, we could go with them on a round ... but a round meant several days on the boat, and there was no coming back once we set off. Life on the boat was not going to be very comfortable, he warned. Were we up for it?

We were not big on comfort.

Boarding the boat by a couple of wooden planks, each about six or seven inches wide, we tottered across with our backpacks.

The boat was of two storeys, and divided into two sections by a sort of deck area. The bow section on the upper storey had the pilot's cabin right up front, followed by a cabin for the two nurses on board and a small lab. The lower storey had the area that served as OPD and medicine chest and doubled as a sort of sitting area during the day and a sleeping area at night. There were two cabins for the two doctors, Dr Bora and Dr Juganta Deori.

The stern section of the boat had the engine and the crew's living quarters. The only crew member with a cabin was the pilot of the boat, who slept in his cabin up front.

We put down our backpacks in the OPD-cum-sitting-area below the deck, and climbed back out. Everyone who had a job to do was busy with the tasks to complete before the voyage. The doctors and nurses were checking medicines; the crew was busy loading the last of the supplies, including bottles of drinking water. The waters of the Brahmaputra are muddy in most stretches, unsuitable for drinking without proper filtration.

Eventually all checks were done and Sanjay, a young man from Dhemaji on the north bank of the river, knocked out the peg to which the Akha was tied by a thick rope, and pulled anchor. The planks were pulled on board. The Akha's engine roared to life. The pilot, a dark, stocky man with red paan-stained lips who Dr Deori called El Capitan, pointed the prow of the boat with its holy tulsi (basil) plant in a tin away from the shore and towards the horizon, where the water met the sky.

People settled down in their places. We sat on two plastic chairs on the deck, staring in silence at the river with its seeming infinity of swirling waters and sandbars. After some time, tea was served. Dr Bora, a slim, bespectacled man in his forties, who had been busy organizing his work, joined us.

The Akha provides mainly maternal and child healthcare, antenatal and postnatal care, and assists with child deliveries, apart from its OPD services, Dr Bora explained. It also carries family planning kits and provides advice on the subject.

He lamented the lack of coordination that is an affliction of the behemoth of Indian government. 'They don't ask people at the ground level what is required and when. They just hammer things down. Look at these leaflets,' he said, pointing to a bundle. 'This is meant for creating awareness about Mission Indradhanush (a national vaccination programme) which is starting today with our visit. The awareness material should have been distributed at least a couple of days before our visit. What is the use of sending it with us? It is a waste of money.'

Even medicines reached them close to expiry dates, he said while pointing to a big box that was barely two months from expiry.

'Where we go, if a child dies after taking a medicine, they will beat us up or kill us. No one can reach in time to save us. It would take at least four to five hours,' he said.

The life of people on the 'chars' or river islands, and the 'chaporis' or sandbanks adjacent to the river – which often become islands, depending on the seasons and the water levels – was hard, Dr Bora said. There was an unending, elemental war between land and water in those islands. In winter, the waters would recede and land would grow, often making it possible to walk from one char to the next. With the rains, the tides would turn, and water would overpower land. The river would submerge whole islands, sweep away crops and cattle and houses and sometimes people.

'The geography of the chars and chaporis keeps changing,' said Dr Bora. 'I have seen a char that we will be visiting shrink due to erosion. The land gets eaten away.' People consequently had to move house every few years.

The main occupations of the char-chapori dwellers is farming and rearing buffaloes and cattle for milk. They live isolated lives, cut off from the shores of the great river because many people cannot afford their own boats. To get to the mainland, they need to hire boats. According to Dr Bora, 'One trip from a char to the mainland and back can cost anything from Rs 500 to Rs 1,000. They can't afford it.' It is a strangely isolated existence.

No government services had reached these people from 1947 till 2008, when the Akha began its first trips with assistance from the state's rural health mission.

The other doctor on board, Dr Deori, had said little in all this. I asked him about his work and how he had come to find a job here on this boat. He said, 'I worked for twenty-two years in government jobs and in tea gardens. It gave me no satisfaction. I did it to bring up my children. This is giving me satisfaction,' he replied.

A tough, powerfully built man with distinctly East Asian features, Dr Deori looked much younger than his sixty-nine years. He had taken up the job with the Akha after his retirement, and enjoyed the work and the outdoorsy life it entailed.

His surname indicated that he was probably from the local Chutiya tribe, but he avoided using the word, with its multiple meanings, while talking of his tribe … and I maintained a diplomatic silence.

'Our tribe is from around Sadiya,' he said. 'The place was called Kundil, after the god Kundil Mama.' Long ago, the priests in all the 'devalayas' or holy places in Kamrup used to be Deoris, Dr Deori said. 'All of them eventually became Brahmins and adopted the sacred thread.'

He launched off on a long discussion about the history of Assam and how the many warring tribes came to be assimilated into an Assamese identity over the centuries. We were still talking about this when the Akha reached its first stop, Bali chapori.

28

Chars and Chaporis

THE SHORELINE OF THE chapori was a mass of river sand, not much higher than the surrounding river, with tufts of grass here and there. Further inland, the sand turned to soil on which more grass and the odd tree grew.

The population was a mixed one, an ongoing example of braids of identities merging and forming. The men were mostly Biharis; the women, Assamese. Singh was a common surname, but everyone spoke Assamese.

Like Dr Bora had said, subsistence farming and buffalo herding were the main occupations.

A small medical crisis occurred on deck as the first few patients streamed in. Most were women carrying babies for vaccination, with other slightly older children in tow. Only one patient was a man – a buffalo herder, who came in with a cut that needed a tetanus shot. This was administered, but the man fainted. As both doctors turned their attention on him, I recalled Dr Bora's dire prediction about what might happen if a patient died.

A drip was quickly set up and the man recovered consciousness. He began to smile sheepishly, embarrassed for having passed out.

It emerged that he had not eaten a single morsel of food since dawn, when he set out with his buffaloes. It was afternoon and the hot sun beat down mercilessly on the treeless, arid land. A drink of clean water and a biscuit set him right.

The task of vaccination resumed. It was late afternoon by the time the last of the women had left with their children. We were starving. The crew had been at work in the galley, preparing a simple but very tasty lunch of rice and chicken, and we set upon it with gusto, before raising anchor to push on upriver.

By 4.30 p.m., it was sunset; the river was lit in an orange glow, mirroring the sky above.

The Brahmaputra is too dangerous for large boats to navigate in the dark. A night halt had been planned at the next inhabited chapori. As the Akha reached this small island in the gathering dusk, Sanjay, the deck hand, leapt ashore to secure the boat and pull out the wooden planks that would serve as the gangway. The medical staff and crew filtered ashore. The pilot, El Capitan aka Chacha, emerged with his lungi drawn up over his knees, a small fishing net in one hand and a torch in the other, and set off into the darkness. The pharmacist, Atul Das, followed.

I followed after some time to see what they were up to.

They had gotten down to their knees in the muddy waters of a little rivulet that flowed from the island into the river. Das was holding the torch while Chacha threw the net in close to where the rivulet met the river. They checked the net to see what they had caught after each throw, and tossed the contents into a bucket. They seemed to be gathering a good catch of little fish.

We returned to the Akha.

Night away from the world of electric lighting and cars and human habitations is a deep oasis of darkness and quietness. The river gurgled. Sometimes there was a small splash; perhaps a jumping fish or maybe a bit of earth falling into the river. The crew spoke in low voices.

For dinner we ate some of the small fish that Chacha had caught, with dal and rice. As usual, it was an excellent, fresh and honest fare that was better than the bland Indian food in five-star hotels.

After a bit of sitting out on the deck looking out into the darkness, it was time to turn in. Mattresses were rolled out on the floor of the OPD, and mosquito nets tied. Sleep in these parts is difficult and dangerous without the mosquito net. Nor is sleeping outside, or on land, a safe option. Apart from mosquitoes – the deadliest creatures in the world barring humans and microbes – there are also snakes about.

By 10 p.m. it was lights out. I was up at a little after 5 a.m. the following morning. Most of the crew was already busy. Chacha and his fishing partner Das had gone out fishing. Sanjay was rustling up a cup of tea.

On a sunny day, morning on the river is a beautiful time. The greyness of misty dawn slowly warms with the glow of the sun. The whorls and eddies ripple and shine. The fog slowly disperses.

The morning light allowed us to have a better look at the island where we had spent the night. It was grassland, but at a higher elevation than the previous chars and chaporis we had visited. In the distance, we could see a few scattered trees. Then, silhouetted against the morning sky, I saw a woman clad in a saree, cradling a baby in her arms. She was walking towards us.

More women and children followed. They were all coming to the Akha.

This was Mohmora (the name means 'dead buffalo') chapori, a seasonal river island with a mixed Bihari and Assamese population.

People had been leaving this place in recent years because the river was cutting in, eating away the land. It was a process we witnessed with our own eyes. At the edges of the river, every now and then, a mass of dry sand would crack and topple into the water with a splash. The Akha set sail after a couple of hours. It was a relatively short journey upriver from there to our next stop, Aisung chapori.

The only other craft we had seen until now on our journey was the odd wooden dugout canoe of small size with one or two figures paddling or poling with bamboo poles, seemingly from nowhere to nowhere. Once, we spotted a larger boat fitted with a motor, its makeshift bamboo awning covering a cargo of cattle. Dr Bora advised us not to take any pictures of that boat as it went past; the men on it were probably smugglers smuggling cows, who may have felt threatened by us. The cow is holy for many Hindus and illegal traffic in cows can be dangerous for those who ply this trade. This in turn makes them likely to resort to fight or flight if they feel they might get caught.

As we approached Aisung, the river traffic increased a little. Instead of a dugout canoe once every hour or so, we now saw three or four in an hour. The men in the dugouts looked different too. They were more East Asian in appearance – members of the Mishing tribe.

The Mishing are closely related to the Adi tribe who inhabit the Siang valley of Arunachal Pradesh, further upriver. They share similarities of language and religion, and their own legends speak of an ancient journey down from the Arunachal hills. They are a river people – the only tribal group in the upper reaches of the Brahmaputra valley with that tradition.

Also called Plains Miris in colonial records, they have probably intermixed with other communities and tribes in the plains over the centuries. They are a good looking people, combining in many instances the best of East Asian and South Asian features.

At Aisung, we came upon a beautiful white sand river beach with a number of wooden rafts tied to stakes on the island. The land itself looked green and fertile, unlike the sandy chaporis we had been visiting so far. The grass was thick. The trees grew almost all the way to the riverfront. There was thick undergrowth from which massive buffaloes with curving horns would occasionally emerge, peacefully grazing.

We anchored there. The crew disembarked and got to work erecting a tent. Some Mishing women began to arrive, dressed in colourful traditional wraps, holding their babies. Some men too filtered in, including a few who rode in on motorcycles.

Aisung looked in every way like a picture postcard of an unspoilt island, pristine, pretty, rugged and raw.

Akshay and I went for a walk along the riverfront. A group of boys around seven or eight years old were having the times of their lives running around on the rafts. Fleet footed, they leapt lightly on the loosely tied logs and ran across to dry land. We went ponderously across, stepping on the bobbing, rolling logs with caution and barely managing to make it across.

These rafts were the trunks of trees. Each log was at least six feet in length and often eight or ten inches wide. Some rafts had as many as forty such logs. These were the trunks of what must have been great trees, probably hollong. Now they were on their way down the Brahmaputra from where they grew, in the forests upstream.

One of the men on our boat had worked the timber trade earlier. The trees came from Arunachal's reserve forests, he told us.

In the evening, after the day's work was done, I talked to Dr Bora about this. There was no chance of timber smuggling reducing, he said. Everyone benefited from it – the villagers who worked as transporters or loggers, the saw mill owners, the forest officials who took the bribes to look the other way, the police, local politicians and even sections of the local media.

The people involved in the trade at ground level are oblivious to the larger environmental costs. Where they live, in and near the wilderness, the thing about trees is that there is no dearth of them. Cut one and there's always ten more. Moreover, they also regrow, even if it takes years.

The concern of the man who is working transporting logs down the Brahmaputra is more immediate than climate change. He wants some money to afford his basic requirements of life. I remembered our first river guide on the banks of the Brahmaputra in Dibrugarh. Mr Smuggler, the timber 'businessman', was probably employing many such men. He also did it for the money. It was the business he knew, and it paid for his whiskey and his children's education. People further up the chain, such as the police officials and politicians, were also getting their cuts. Everyone needs money, and saying no to easy money is hard.

There is an organized timber mafia, just as there is a drug mafia, a coal mining mafia, a sand mining mafia, a limestone mafia, and even a fish mafia, in Northeast India. These mafias control the businesses. They bribe government officials and local politicians. They also allegedly contribute to election funds. Governments and officials come and go, the system goes on forever.

Winter is logging season in the forests. The trees are cut, transported to river beaches and stacked. As water levels rise with the rains in monsoon, the stacks are tied into rafts and floated downriver. It's a very old business – centuries old, dating back to before the colonial period. At that time, logging was legal. A lot of people, such as the builders of the pagoda we had visited on our way to Parshuram Kund, had done very well out of it.

A Supreme Court ban in ordered in 1996 has had no adverse effect on the business. The evidence is visible in 'before' and 'after' satellite images that show reserve forests across Northeast India as shrinking patches of green.

The hollong tree, with its beautiful straight trunk rising to heights of up to 150 feet, is especially popular with loggers.

My ruminations on Arunachal's forests floating down the Brahmaputra were interrupted by picnic preparations. The Akha was anchoring at Aisung for the night, and the crew proposed a feast.

A feast in the upper reaches of the Brahmaputra valley and up in the neighbouring hills means 'gahori' or pork. Everyone contributed money and two of the crew members set off for the Mishing village to get fresh pork. Chacha set off with his fishing net down the pristine river beach, past the parked rafts, to get some fresh catch. Sanjay, with Dr Deori in the role of chef, got to work preparing a 'khorika'.

Khorika is a very typical Assamese style of preparation. It is a barbecue made out of bamboo placed over a wood fire. The bamboo has to be cut into thin, strong skewers sharpened at the ends. This takes some skill and time to accomplish.

The fire was roaring and the khorika ready by the time Chacha returned with his catch of 'puthi' and other small fishes. These were quickly cleaned, salted and placed on the bamboo skewers for roasting.

The feast around the campfire on the island, with the bright stars above and the dark river beside, was excellent. The menu comprised pork curry, rice, dal, vegetable curry and roasted fish. Our condiments were fresh lime and 'jolokia', the lethal local chilli.

The chillies in this part of Northeast India are some of the hottest in the world. They include the variety called bhut jolokia, meaning 'ghost chilli', which vies for the title of the hottest chilli in the world, along with the bird eye chilli from neighbouring Meghalaya and its cousin the Naga raja mirchi. The ghost chilli is said to have the capacity to turn its eaters into ghosts instantly. Basically, you simply jump out of your skin when you bite into one. I wouldn't scoff at the possibility of such an occurrence; there are credible reports, including one published in *The Telegraph* of London, of a bhut jolokia burning a hole in a man's throat. The same report helpfully mentioned that, 'A ghost pepper measures 1,000,000 on the Scoville scale, and is 400 times hotter than Tabasco sauce.' Folks who use it with their daily meals do so with caution. They are also likely to find Tabasco bland and tasteless.

The bhut jolokia needs careful handling. Touching it and then rubbing the eyes or other sensitive areas is sure to produce a hellish burn. Eating it means feeling the heat kick in slowly and last a good twenty minutes or more.

Next morning, barely an hour after the customary early start, the Akha made its first mainland halt since leaving Dibrugarh. Some supplies needed restocking, and there was a market a couple of kilometres from the riverside at this place called Balijan. A small ferry, a 'bhut-bhuti' of a kind locally known as 'fighter' had also pulled up at the ghat where the Akha made its unscheduled halt.

Akshay and I disembarked there and set off with our backpacks on a trail that took us through a couple of sandy riverbeds with ankle- to knee-deep water, into a tea estate also called Balijan, and through it to the market on the other side. I was trailing Akshay by a good distance and ended up chatting with a passenger who had disembarked from the 'fighter'.

He was a schoolteacher at a local government school near the tea estate. He said he had an MBA degree and had worked in sales for a pharma company in Kolkata, but had returned to his family home here in Assam after his father passed away. His father had also been a government schoolteacher.

The path turned into a pucca road. We left the school and the schoolteacher behind and reached an intersection where an autorickshaw was parked. By this time, a man on a bicycle, skinny and dark and wearing tattered clothes, had attached himself to Akshay. He tried quite unnecessarily to help us load our backpacks into the autorickshaw. Then he asked the autorickshaw-wallah in Assamese why he had agreed to take us to Chabua, the nearby tea town, for only Rs 150, and asked him to delay us. I turned towards him and told him I understood Assamese. He was unabashed at having his attempted scam caught and began to beg – not from me, but from Akshay – for Rs 10. We asked the autorickshaw-wallah to start driving. He reluctantly let go of the auto when it started moving.

Our journey had been full of such attempted scams. The idea of 'greed is good' had permeated to the grassroots, but the idea that extortion, scam and entrepreneurship are not synonyms was still to reach everywhere.

29

The Ahom Hardliner

IN THE EVENING, RELAXING over drinks at the Dibrugarh house of our friends Millie and Masood after our little voyage, we met a curious character.

Atul Buragohain was born in a village near Dibrugarh and grew up there. He was eighty-six when we met. His features are distinctly East Asian, though he is dark-skinned. He was sporting a straw hat, and kept it on even inside the room at night.

His early memories are of World War II. He remembers a fighter plane falling out of the sky and crashing in a farm at the edge of his village. It was an American plane, he said, and the pilot survived. He recalled, 'The trains used to be full of American and British soldiers.'

For many people and communities in India's Northeast, the Second World War was a period of awakening; it was when the affairs of the world came to impinge upon their ordinary lives in remote hills and valleys that until then had stood largely outside the accelerating currents of history. British, Indian and American forces clashed with the invading Japanese army and Netaji Subhas Bose's Indian National Army in Nagaland and Manipur in the terrible and famous battles of Kohima and Imphal. A Chinese Nationalist force under the American General Joseph Stilwell was stationed in Assam, and helped build the legendary road from Ledo in Assam to Kunming in China that bears Stilwell's name. The US Air Force planes flew sorties over Arunachal and across what pilots called the 'hump' of the eastern Himalayas into another part of China.

In those days, the Brahmaputra river had not yet been bridged. Troops had to be ferried across by boat. Giant rail ferries carried train wagons with war materials across from Amingaon to Pandu near Guwahati.

The river and Dibrugarh town were then about two miles from their present location. ' ... 1950 was the great earthquake. The DC bungalow, SP bungalow, government school, planters' store ... all used to be near the riverfront. They just sank into the water,' said Buragohain. 'The riverbed came up in some places, and you could cross over to the north bank by stepping on rocks. If you took a hollow bamboo, stuck it in the ground and put a flame to the tip, it would light up like a torch. Gas was coming out of the ground.'

Dibrugarh at that time was the premier town in Assam, and was connected with Kolkata by a steamer service that had first launched in 1856. It had built its fortune with tea and oil, both of which had been discovered in the vicinity during colonial times.

Mr Buragohain had an interesting account of how the British found tea in the area. 'Jenkins sahib gave a sip of tea to the Singpho chief or Gam who took the sip and said "phalap". Jenkins asked what phalap was. The chief replied it was what they called "the drink". Jenkins asked where the leaf could be found. The chief replied that it grew in the forest near their village. Then the British collected samples and sent them for testing. It proved to be tea,' he said.

The Jenkins sahib of this story was a Captain Francis Jenkins of the East India Company, chief commissioner of Assam, who had surveyed the area first in 1831–32. His claim to primacy was disputed by a Captain Charlton, who also laid claim to having been the first Englishman to establish that tea was indigenous to Assam. However, both of these gentlemen visited Assam years after Major Robert Bruce, who had come up to these areas in 1823. The tale of a British officer discovering tea in Assam after meeting a Singpho chief called Bessa Gam is usually told with Bruce, not Jenkins, in the role.

The Singphos and their neighbours, of course, knew they had 'phalap' all along ... but it didn't quite become tea until the sahibs took to it, and made a product of it.

According to Mr Buragohain, 'The Assamese then were independent-minded. The locals refused to work for the British, so they imported labour from Bihar, Jharkhand, Bengal, Andhra ... before that they had brought Chinese workers. The Chinese were the babus until the Bengalis became babus.'

British accounts present a starkly different version. Leslie Shakespear wrote in his history of these areas published in 1914, 'The people now met with in Assam are a peaceful, almost effeminate race, in no great numbers, addicted in large measure to opium-eating, and not disposed to diligent labour; whence the necessity for importing the great number of coolies from India required to work on the tea gardens.'[27] The truth, as is often the case, probably lies somewhere in between. The low population was a numerical fact, recorded in censuses. The opium habit was indeed widespread. However, the reason locals did not want to work on gardens probably lay in economic factors. The historian Jayeeta Sharma, in her book *Empire's Garden*, wrote, 'Given abundant land availability, it was quite logical that most Brahmaputra valley peasants should not have been overly attracted to wage labour as a way of life.' The locals had their own fields to look after.

Tea garden work, to this day, continues to be done by the descendants of the 'coolies' Shakespear refers to. The 'imported labour' of Buragohain's account from the tribes of central India are now known as the 'tea tribes' in Assam. A lot of other kinds of manual work, such as farm labour, construction work and driving cycle rickshaws, is done largely by Bengali and Bihari labourers, including an unknown and unknowable number from the other side of the Bangladesh border, which has been a contentious issue in the state's politics for decades.

By this time, we had moved into our second round of drinks, and Mr Buragohain was warming up. 'Most of the Assamese now were Bengalis before they became Assamese. Bhattacharjees, Chakrabortys, Baruas are converts to Ahom. So are Boras, Saikias, Hazarikas … all these were titles given by the Ahom kings. But we are the real Assamese!' he declared. The 'we' that Mr Buragohain was referring to was the Ahoms. 'Warren Hastings (a British governor general of India) took this model and gave titles too, which also became surnames … such as Dewan, Patowary and Choudhury,' he went on.

His account of history was an interesting one.

The fact of the matter is that the Ahom dynasty was established by a group of men from the Shan hills of Myanmar and adjacent areas in what is now Yunnan province in China. A prince named Siu Ka Pha or Sukapha had migrated from there through the jungles and hills with a band of followers in the early years of the thirteenth century. The *Assam Buranji* of Harakanta Sarma-Barua (his full title was Sarma-Barua Choudhury Sadar-Amin), published in the Assamese language in a volume edited by Professor S.K. Bhuyan in 1930, traces Sukapha's lineage to Lord Indra:

> At some time in the past, Swargadeo meaning Indra dev, taking refuge in Jachinfa or Saraswati, made up his mind that on earth there are many Chandravanshi and Suryavanshi kings, I am the king of gods, but my children don't have a kingdom on earth therefore I will send them the means to become kings.

The means which the divine engineer Vishwakarma presented Indra with was called the Somdeo. This, Indra presented to two brothers, Khunlung and Khunlai, who he then sent down from heaven to earth by means of an iron chain around AD 568. They established their rule in the kingdoms called Mung-ri-mung-ram and Mung-khu-mung-jai (associated with Mong Mao, a Tai state corresponding roughly to today's Dehong Dai Autonomous Prefecture of Yunnan in China[28]). Their descendant Sukapha, with the magical Somdeo, 1,080 people, two elephants and 300 horses, was the one who, according to the *Assam Buranji*, came across the Patkai Hills on India's border with Myanmar to the lands where he established the Ahom dynasty in 1228.

The new arrivals married into the local tribal communities, such as the Barahi, which were eventually integrated into an Ahom identity. Other local groups such as the Motoks and their cousins the Morans were given positions in the new administration. The Kachari, Khampti and Miri tribes were similarly included. In the early days of Ahom rule the king was assisted in his duties by his two deputies, called Buragohain and Borgohain, who were selected from among the Ahom nobility.[29] Both of these titles still exist as surnames, as in the case of the man we were meeting, Atul Buragohain.

Nitul Kumar Gogoi has written in his book *Continuity and Change Among the Ahom* that the Ahom King Pratap Singha, about 400 years later, created two new designations of Borbarua and Borphukan, which he translates as Secretary General and Governor General. The Borbaruas were generally selected from families belonging to the Moran, Kachari, Chiring or Khampti tribes, he says. Naga and Miri tribals also won positions. So by and by, all major local ethnic groups were included in the Ahom administration.

The kingdom had a system of unpaid or 'corvee' labour. In this system, each adult male between the ages of fifteen and fifty in the Ahom kingdom who was not a noble, priest or slave was called a paik. The paik had to render free service, civil or military, to the king, in lieu of which he received a small parcel of a little over two-and-a-half acres of land called 'gaa mati' for cultivation. In this system, which matured during the reign of King Pratap Singha in the early 1600s, paiks were organized into larger units called 'got' and 'khel'. There were designations and titles up the administrative hierarchy. A person who commanded 20 paiks was called a Bora. One who commanded 100 paiks was a Saikia. The commander of 1,000 paiks was a Hazarika. The commander of 3,000 was a Rajkhowa. The Phukan commanded between 4,000 and 6,000 men. The Baruas were deputies to the Phukans.

There were also professional specializations. So for instance, the medical corps were commanded by Bezbaruahs. Two councils of six Phukans each reported to the Borbarua and Borphukan, who were directly under the king. The highest ranking officers in the Ahom king's administration alongside the Borbarua and Borphukan remained the Borgohain, Buragohain and Borpatrogohain. All these official designations, or titles, have survived as Assamese surnames. You can meet Boras, Hazarikas, Saikias, Baruas, Phukans and all the rest – except Paik – long after the Ahom administration that gave them the titles is gone. Although about 90 per cent of the population were paiks, that surname however cannot be found anywhere in Assam.

These were the people – practically all Assamese – that Mr Buragohain was calling 'converts from Bengali'. It was not meant to be a compliment, and was unlikely to be received as such. There has, for more than 100 years now, been a tension between the two identities.

The Bengali and Assamese identities are linguistic identities based on languages that have common roots. The dialects of the two languages spoken in the lands along the downriver sections of the river, Lower Assam, both emerged from a common language, Kamrupi Prakrit, less than 1,000 years ago.

Despite many similarities in language, religion, food and culture, chauvinists on both sides are often keen to emphasize differences. The Assamese, being smaller in numbers and fearful of Bengali migrants, tend to be more sensitive about protecting their separate identity. There is also more awareness of the linguistic differences between the two languages in Assam. The average Bengali in West Bengal, used to hearing and speaking 'standard Bangla', is likely, for example, to find both Sylheti, which is considered a Bengali dialect, and Assamese, difficult to comprehend. This ignorance is partly a function of the state's politics. Identity politics has never been mainstream in Bengal, unlike Assam, which has a storied history of 'jatiyotabadi' meaning 'race-based' politics, with the race in question being defined in linguistic terms. Bengali politics has always been predominantly ideological, and was dominated for decades, until recently, by the Left, which sneered at politics of religion and ethnicity. Even now, the political contest is mainly ideological, between Hindu nationalism and Indian secularism with a Bengali flavour.

I glanced across at Millie, an Assamese whose surname is Hazarika, to see how she was dealing with the blow from Buragohain who was sitting in her living room telling her who she was. She was grinning from ear to ear.

The Ahoms, Mr Buragohain reiterated, were the 'real Assamese'. They had their own cultures and traditions, he said. He was clear that they were not Hindus. 'Hinduism is not a religion. Hindu means people who live by the Sindhu river,' he pointed out.

'I am not a Hindu,' he declared. 'I don't like Hindu culture.'

I enquired about his Hindu first name, Atul. He was not happy with it.

'Somebody gave me that name, I didn't choose it,' he replied. 'We are Tai people. Our people are spread all over Southeast Asia. We still have cultural linkages.'

Exchanges and interactions had begun between the Tai peoples of various countries, he said. It was a fairly recent thing.

He was not especially proud of his own Assamese heritage. 'Assamese is a link language, like Nagamese,' he said. The different indigenous tribes of Assam all had their own languages, he pointed out, just as the different Naga tribes had theirs.

The dream he cherished was of some kind of Tai homeland with its capital at Ruili in Yunnan province of China … coincidentally a spot associated with the ancient original homeland of the Ahoms, and with the fugitive chief of the United Liberation Front of Asom, Paresh Baruah, who judging from his surname and his Motok family origins was also a 'convert to Ahom' by Buragohain's standards. The ULFA, founded in 1979, has been fighting an insurgent campaign to separate Assam from India since then.

The Chinese government seems to be encouraging the idea of Tai unity. The community in China is called 'Dai', and has its own autonomous areas in Yunnan bordering Myanmar, the Dehong Dai and Jingpo Autonomous Prefecture and, just south of it, Xishuangbanna Dai Autonomous Prefecture. Mr Buragohain showed us an invitation to a conference of Tai peoples. 'Someday, China will take all this,' he declared. Tibet, he added, had always been part of China.

Mr Atul Buragohain had spent his life carrying that name, speaking Assamese, surrounded by Hindus, and living in India, the land of his birth, whose passport he carried. Yet, he had apparently rejected all of these, and the process of acculturation and assimilation over centuries by which his ancestors had gone from being 'pure Tai Ahom' to being Assamese.

30

ULFA

WE DROVE UP TO Tinsukia a couple of days later. It is the only city in Upper Assam that rivals Dibrugarh, but it is a poor rival. Walking around that town brought about a rare consensus among all of us in barely five minutes: It was a bad idea to be walking around Tinsukia. In fact, it was probably a bad idea to even be in Tinsukia.

It was early October, but still sweltering hot. Rubbish law strewn on the streets. The roads were a mess and the traffic was awful. The town itself seemed a haphazard outgrowth of architecturally ghastly constructions. Overall, the immediate impression was of a town in the badlands of north India's Gangetic plains, not the Brahmaputra valley.

The heart of the town was a pond, its waters green with age, in the middle of which stood a little platform with a statue of a fierce-looking man with East Asian features carrying a sword. A wall ran around the pond. Outside, the chaotic traffic honked its way past vegetable vendors who sprawled on the ground, their wares spread before them.

The gate that controlled entry to the pond and the small green area around it was locked. The three of us – Millie, Akshay and I – speculated on who the statue might be of. In Assam, statues of fierce-looking men with swords tend to be of either the Ahom General Lachit Borphukan or the Koch General Chilarai. This was too far upriver to be Koch country, so the Ahom General seemed more likely.

It turned out to be neither. The statue was of a local king, Sarbananda Singha, a king of the Motok tribe that inhabits the area, who had got that pond dug. This pond, Tinkunia Pukhri, was once at the heart of the town of Bengmara, which, under Singha, became capital of a new Motok kingdom in 1791.The establishment of the Motok kingdom came after a period of sustained revolt against the local empire of the day in that part of the world – the Ahom empire. This local hero, Sarbananda Singha, was one of three rebel leaders who carved out their own territories by overthrowing Ahom rule in their own areas of influence following what is remembered in Assam's history as the Moamaria rebellion, a revolt by members of the Mayamara Vaishnav sect to which most Motoks belonged.

We drove out of the town a short way upriver for lunch at a fancy highway dhaba named after the road: NH 37, for National Highway 37. The road took us past tea gardens and a little town called Makum. It's another of those things about Assam – the nondescript often hides remarkable stories.

The name Makum is apparently not derived from any of the numerous local languages and dialects; it is derived from 'ma-kam' meaning golden horse in a Chinese dialect, Cantonese. The town was built and inhabited by a Chinese population that migrated from areas around Hong Kong, Macau and Canton to work in the Assam tea industry mainly in the first half of the nineteenth century following the East India Company's annexation of Assam after the Anglo-Burmese war of 1826. They were, as Atul Buragohain had said, the first babus (clerks) on tea estates.[30]

The Makum they built had the usual things any town needs – shops, houses, restaurants, temples, a school – all run by the local Chinese. It was a proper Chinatown in rural Upper Assam. Its residents were on their way to becoming Assamese Chinese and Indian Chinese when the army of Mao Tse Tung invaded neighbouring Arunachal Pradesh and distant Ladakh in 1962.

As the People's Liberation Army took Tawang and rapidly advanced down the mountains towards Assam, the Indian government of Pandit Jawaharlal Nehru moved to intern the Chinese residents of Makum. The war, which lasted barely a month, was close to its end when they were put on a train to an internment camp in Rajasthan. Many of them remained there for years; about half were eventually packed off back to China.

Few signs now remain of the Makum Chinese community. The local Chinese temple fell into ruins, and the Chinese school became a Hindi school. There is still a China Patty or Chinese street in Makum, and a few Chinese families somewhere in the little town, but they do not advertise their presence.

The tea gardens, all peaceful and green around us, hid their own tales of conflict. They were caught up in the crossfire of a different war.

The places we were passing through now were the heartland of the once powerful armed insurgency of the United Liberation Front of Asom. The ULFA used to run its parallel administration in these parts during the 1990s. The group's fugitive commander, Paresh Baruah, is from a village just off the Assam Trunk Road we were driving on, a place called Panitola between Dibrugarh and Tinsukia.

During the days when the insurgency was raging, the ULFA used to serve extortion notices to businesses in the area demanding money. Tea companies had the difficult choice of paying up and playing nice with the armed militants, or staying on the right side of the law and Indian government by refusing.

At least in the early days of the insurgency, many tea companies chose to pay up. Their decision was influenced by a murder.

Somewhere on the stretch of road that we were driving on, in April 1990, an industrialist named Surrendra Paul, brother of the famous London tycoon, Lord Swraj Paul, was shot dead by suspected ULFA cadres. He had come to the area to inspect the gardens and operations of the Assam Frontier Tea Company, of which he was chairman. He was on his way back to Dibrugarh when some men stopped his car. One of them knocked on the window next to Paul. He apparently rolled it down and asked, 'What is it?'

The man pulled out a handgun and shot him dead.

Three local ULFA men – Jugal Kishore Mahanta, Saurav Gogoi and Pradip Gogoi – were directly implicated in the murder. The police case also named the organization's top leaders, its chairman, Arabinda Rajkhowa, and its armed wing commander, Paresh Baruah.

Mahanta and the two Gogois were acquitted in 2005 for want of proof. Proof of ULFA militant involvement continued to elude the police for twenty-two years, from 1990 to 2012, when Rajkhowa was also acquitted.[31]

Shortly after Paul's shooting, in June 1990, the ULFA called a meeting of tea industry leaders at a tea garden near Dibrugarh. A deal was struck by the ULFA Dibrugarh unit chief Tapan Datta at gunpoint. Tea companies would have to pay 'taxes' to the militant group. The money was to be reckoned on a per kilo of tea basis or on acreage of the estate, and for the larger companies, it ran into crores.

Hindustan Lever Limited, the Indian subsidiary of the multinational Unilever, owns several gardens in the area from where it produces tea for brands such as Brooke Bond and Lipton. One of its estates, Doom Dooma India, refused to pay. This meant their manager could be shot dead anytime. Pressure mounted on the Central government to do something; the government put the Indian intelligence agencies at work on airlifting the tea garden managers out immediately. On 8 November 1990, a secret evacuation flight was organized from a World War II airstrip near Doom Dooma, with support from the army and Aviation Research Centre, a wing of intelligence agency RAW, the Research and Analysis Wing.

Those were turbulent times politically for the country. Two days later the Central government of Prime Minister V.P. Singh fell as the Janata Dal split, and a new government led by Prime Minister Chandra Shekhar, with the Congress' support, came to power. One of the significant things it did was dismiss the Assam government of Chief Minister Prafulla Kumar Mahanta of the Asom Gana Parishad and launch a military operation, Operation Bajrang, on 27 November 1990 to clear out the ULFA, which was finally declared an unlawful organization. The shooting started in earnest on both sides.

In the midst of all this, Tata Tea chose to deny payment, and stay put.

As a result, the ULFA's pressure on Tata Tea increased. Their argument was that companies operating in its areas would have to pay them as a way of paying back the people of Assam, from where the companies were making money. Tata Tea responded by increasing its outreach and social welfare activities in the tea garden areas, arguing that it would help the people of Assam directly. It was as good as its word.

The ULFA backed off.

Things might have continued in that vein if it were not for a kidnapping carried out, not by the ULFA, but by another of the numerous armed militant groups in Assam at that time.

In 1993, militants of the Bodo Security Force, an armed outfit fighting for a state for the ethnic Bodo minority to be carved out of

Assam, kidnapped Bolin Bordoloi, Tata Tea's regional manager, and held him for ransom. Bordoloi was not just a tea company honcho; he also happened to be the son of one of the greatest icons of modern Assam, Gopinath Bordoloi, who was the leader of the state during the crucial years leading up to Partition, and its first chief minister.

Bolin Bordoloi's kidnapping sent shockwaves through the country.

The Bodo group demanded USD 15 million to release Bordoloi.[32] The Congress government of Chief Minister Hiteswar Saikia in Assam came under enormous pressure to secure Bordoloi's safe release. And the Tatas refused to pay up.

The government, in desperation, let loose the police on relatives of the Bodo Security Force leader Ranjan Daimary – the man who would later become head of the National Democratic Front of Bodoland. His actress sister Anjali was picked up by Assam Police.

Meanwhile, Tata Tea discovered an underutilized resource – a doctor named Brojen Gogoi who worked for the company in Assam. Dr Gogoi happened to know the ULFA Chief Paresh Baruah well. The ULFA and the Bodo Security Force, though fighting for ultimately contradictory goals – the Bodos sought to split Assam in half – shared good relations dictated by necessity. The Bodo militants received arms and training from Burmese insurgent groups such as the Kachins, and this was mediated by the ULFA. Therefore, they were dependent on ULFA's goodwill.

Negotiations began for Bordoloi's release. Under the ULFA influence, the Bodos publicly climbed down from USD 15 million (around Rs 45 crore then) to Rs 5 lakh, which they said was the cost of hosting their unwilling guest. Privately, however, it is possible that different deals were being struck.

The ULFA Chief Paresh Baruah, in an interview in 1997, said, 'In 1993, Tata Tea's regional manager Bolin Bordoloi was abducted by the Bodo Security Force and our information suggested that the Tatas indeed paid around one crore rupees to the BSF.'

This episode sparked off another in a chain of events. Baruah said that when they heard the Tatas had paid the Bodos, 'We got in touch with Tata Tea and said if they could pay the Bodos, why not us? To which Bolin Bordoloi himself said, "Please get in touch with our head office. We cannot decide on these matters here. We are small fries."'

Now the hard bargaining between the ULFA and Tata Tea began. According to the ULFA chief:

> On Bordoloi's advice, I spoke to their managing director in Calcutta, not once but several times. I also wrote a letter dated December 12, 1995, making a formal demand for money. The managing director suggested that I should meet senior Tata Tea officials and discuss the whole matter. He said the money paid to the BSF was because of the threat to Bordoloi's life, but the ULFA, if it had the good of Assam at heart, should not ask for big money and disrupt Tata Tea projects in the state – projects that would benefit the people. We then decided to meet – and Bangkok was where we met in early 1996. S.S. Dogra, Bordoloi, one South Indian gentleman, whose name I have forgotten, and Bora were there.

The ULFA asked for money or communications equipment in their Bangkok meeting with the Tata representatives. The Tatas said they couldn't give either. Finally, a deal was struck on medical assistance; Tata Tea would ensure free specialist medical care for people of Assam. Naturally, this included the ULFA's cadres as well, as it soon emerged.[33]

On 23 August 1997, a woman with a newborn baby was arrested at Mumbai airport. Days earlier, she had checked into the city's famous and upmarket Jaslok Hospital for her delivery. She had registered at the hospital under the name Bonti Baruah. It turned out that she was ULFA's culture secretary Pranati Deka. Her husband Chitrabon Hazarika was ULFA's finance secretary and one of its top leaders.

Deka's arrest led directly to the Assam government gunning for Tata Tea. Prafulla Mahanta was again chief minister and having been fired once courtesy pressure from the tea industry, he had a point to prove. Assam Police knew of Tata Tea's Dr Gogoi's links with the ULFA. It transpired that he had personally escorted Pranati Deka to Mumbai. The police sought his arrest. Tata Tea said he was on a study tour in the US. Ratan Tata met Chief Minister Mahanta to sort out the matter, but it didn't end there.

Dr Gogoi was arrested and charged with being a member of the ULFA. Evidence that the good doctor had been spotted in the company of ULFA members in Geneva surfaced. Tata Tea was accused of aiding and abetting the ULFA. The company's managing director, R.K. Krishna Kumar, sought anticipatory bail in Mumbai. Dogra, the general manager who had been part of the delegation that met ULFA leaders in Bangkok, was arrested.[34]

At this stage, the big boys of Indian industry got involved. The cast of characters expanded to include some of India's most celebrated industrialists and a legendary general. Ratan Tata roped in fellow Parsis, the millionaire industrialist Nusli Wadia and former Indian Army Chief General Sam Manekshaw, among others, for help and advice. Unbeknown to him, someone – not from the Central government, according to the then Home Secretary K. Padmanabhaiah – was tapping Wadia's phones. The phone recordings got leaked to *The Indian Express*.[35]

The Assam government let out that there was now enough evidence against Ratan Tata to warrant a charge of conniving with those waging war against the state. This was in the days before 24/7 news television, and much before the celebrated interrogator Arnab Goswami, who happens to be Assamese, arrived on the scene, otherwise several Very Important Persons might have exploded in puffs of outrage on national television. Nonetheless, it led to major headlines and waves in the corridors of power all the way across the country, from Guwahati to Delhi to Mumbai.

The big industrialists roped in the big lawyers. Ram Jethmalani, Arun Jaitley and Raian Karanjawala came on board as Tata's crisis management squad. This was reported in detail by *India Today* magazine in an article by Swapan Dasgupta.

Over in Bangladesh, where the ULFA chief – whose insurgent movement had picked up alongside the same student agitation directed against alleged illegal Bangladeshi migrants that propelled Prafulla Mahanta from university student to chief minister – gave an interview from his secret hiding place. He had wound up as a 'guest' of the Bangladeshis. Among other things, he accused Mahanta of going after the Tatas for pretty much the same reason that the ULFA had gone after them. Mahanta had personally asked the Tatas for money before the assembly elections, and they had not paid him, Baruah alleged.

Tata Tea, meanwhile, leaked information about its collaboration with the Intelligence Bureau, which had been in the loop on the company's dealings with the ULFA for several years. The company's public relations machinery kicked into action. The Tatas cried that they were being singled out, even though every tea company in Assam was paying militant groups, and they were not. In response, the Assam government widened its probe to include other tea majors, who now fell into a panic.

The battling parties reached Delhi to seek support from the Union Home Minister, Indrajit Gupta of the Communist Party of India. The veteran communist, it is believed, chose to side with the industrialists who were allegedly 'helping' the ULFA in cash or kind; he was accused of this by Chief Minister Mahanta.

The United Front government of Prime Minister I.K. Gujral, which was propped up with external support from the Congress, collapsed a couple of months later, in November 1997, over a controversy related to another extremist group. The Congress withdrew support over the issue of M. Karunanidhi's Dravida Munnetra Kazhagam party's alleged support to insurgents of the Liberation Tigers of Tamil Eelam, the group that had assassinated Rajiv Gandhi. The DMK was a part of the Gujral government, and the Congress had demanded the party's ministers be dropped from the cabinet.

Krishna Kumar's bail was contested by the Assam government, and the matter went to the Supreme Court. Jethmalani, Jaitley and Soli Sorabjee represented the Tatas. The court let him off on a technicality. After that the matter slowly died down. No big name wound up in jail. If any deal was done between the contending parties, it has remained out of public view.

The ULFA was already past its peak at the time all this was happening. Its firepower and influence had reached their highest levels between 1990–92, when it ran a parallel administration in the state with the collaboration of several senior police officers, lawyers, journalists and politicians. The blowback to its murderous excesses, which had started with the dismissal of Mahanta's government and Operation Bajrang in November 1990, had destroyed much of its fighting capability. Assam's wily Chief Minister Hiteswar Saikia of the Congress had engineered a split in the militant outfit, inducing a large group to surrender in April 1992. This group came to be known as 'SULFA' or Surrendered ULFA – and it became an armed militia in its own right, one that operated with the tacit backing of the state. More army operations had followed including one in 1995 called Operation Golden Bird that was organized in coordination with the Myanmar army, targeting insurgents on both sides of the India–Myanmar border. In 2003, the Indian army backed the Royal Bhutan Army in an operation to drive out the ULFA from its bases in Bhutan.

The last straw for the ULFA and several other militant outfits in Northeast India came in December 2008, when elections in Bangladesh brought Sheikh Hasina of the Awami League to power. She reversed her predecessors' policy of allowing the militants to function from safe havens in Bangladesh. A large number of top leaders including ULFA's Chairman Arabinda Rajkhowa were nabbed and handed over to Indian agencies. Only one key militant, Paresh Baruah, escaped. News filtering out from Indian agencies said he had managed to find covert Chinese protection in Yunnan near that country's border with Myanmar. It is perhaps a coincidence of history that this was the area from where the first Ahom king, Siu Ka Pha or Sukapha, and his band of followers, according to the *Assam Buranji*, had come.

31

On the Tea Estate

ASSAM'S TEA INDUSTRY CENTRES around the colonial era tea plantations that can be found across Upper Assam, and in parts of Cachar. Life on these tea estates has always been lived in a bubble, physically near but in every other way distant and distinct from the surrounding lands. In the colonial era, it was a world of chhota hazris and bada sahibs, a place with a vocabulary and a lifestyle of its own. 'The ordinary routine of a day is, up at five, chhota hazree (small breakfast) at five-thirty, work until eleven, when hazree is served, afterwards rest until two o'clock, followed by work until five-thirty or six, bath and dinner, and a final adjournment to the verandah, where, reading, smoking, a chat if there is anyone to talk with, over the result of the day's work, until nine-thirty, bed time, brings the day to a close.' This was a day in the life of George Barker, a British tea planter in Assam, published in his account of plantation life in 1884.[36]

Many of the gracious bungalows built in the architectural style peculiar to colonial Assam, which came to be known as Assam-type, still stand. They were usually built a little like the local 'chang ghars', on stilts a few feet above ground level – a necessity of the flood-prone landscape. Life in them, and on the tea plantations around them, still retain remnants of the old colonial aura. A day in the life of the planter still has elements of the colonial lifestyle.

Akshay and I went to stay with his wife's relatives Raj and Runtun at their bungalow on a tea estate near Doom Dooma. They were gracious hosts, and the house itself, an old Assam-type bungalow with sloping tin roof, was very impressive. Everything about it was massive. The guest bedroom we were in had an attached bathroom and study. These seemed so vast to my Mumbai-apartment sensibility that I felt like I was going for a morning walk when I went to the loo. The study overlooked the front lawn, which was the size of two tennis courts.

Inside, everything was wall to wall carpeted. The ceilings were high. Even the shower in the bathroom was at something of an altitude. The water came down like a waterfall.

The house had its own silent, obsequious and highly efficient service staff of eighteen including gardeners and cooks. Service was by ringing a bell, which in keeping with the times was now an electric one. You could press the bell, and a servant would appear like a djinn ready to obey your command. The number of servants in the days before electricity and piped water exceeded the present tally, but not by much. There were paani-wallahs who carried water, punkah-wallahs who fanned the sahibs with hand-fans, a gorukhiya or cow-herd and a couple of stable-hands to look after the horses. These are gone but the rest of the staff – the khidmatgar or butler, the khansama or cook and his assistants, and the chowkidars, sweepers and gardeners – are still around. The horse-wallahs have been replaced by the car-wallahs, meaning drivers.

Ringing the house from all sides are big old trees, and then, the tea estate proper, which has its own factory and a golf course for the sahibs. The tea garden itself consists of neat rows of trimmed tea bushes stretching far into the distance, where on a morning you might see lines of women plucking two leaves and a bud and putting them into the cane baskets on their backs.

The entire set-up is a throwback to the days when the planter and his memsahib would have their chhota hazri on the front lawns, waited on by servants. The custom still survives.

Raj himself fits the burra sahib role well. He comes from an old political family. There were black-and-white photos in the vast covered verandah of one of his grandfathers, a veteran politician, with India's first prime minister, Jawaharlal Nehru. Both his maternal and paternal grandfather knew Nehru, who had been their house guest during visits to Assam.

At least on the surface, things have not changed very much in the tea estates from the days of the British Raj. It is a different world outside though, and the time warp is wearing thin. Ideas of democracy, equality and workers' rights have penetrated to the furthest reaches. The old Indian of the working class who was bound by hierarchies – of caste, gender and age – no longer exists. In his/ her place is an aspirational creature, a person of impatience who's up for hardscrabble and the occasional little scam to get ahead.

I expressed a desire to speak to Raj about the tea business, but was advised that this was not a good time to be having the conversation. There was some tension in the business; the tea labourers were demanding a big bonus and the managements were resisting. With state elections due in Assam, and the ruling Congress government facing a stiff challenge from the BJP, the whole issue had become politicized. The labourers, whose lives have been rife with exploitation for generations, were getting restive. Slogans of 'murdabad,' meaning 'death to', had been raised. There was a possibility that things might turn ugly.

When things get ugly in these situations, the ugliness is inhuman. The death slogans are not merely slogans. People do get killed. Masood, our friend in Dibrugarh, had recounted one such incident. A manager of a tea estate, who had a reputation for being cruel and a bully, had been killed by his workers in an outburst of rage. According to Masood's florid account, the man's body was then cut into little pieces, cooked and eaten.

Tea company managements, after their difficulties with insurgency, have been struggling with increasing costs of production, competition from emerging markets and newly popular drinks. They complain of declining revenues. Their golden age was the pioneering days of planter raj in the nineteenth century, when the tea trade was expanding around the world and finding avid customers everywhere.

The difficulties then were different.

The first eight boxes of souchong and pekoe tea bound for London left Assam in 1838. At that time, there was only one experimental tea estate run by Charles Bruce near Sadiya. Then and until decades later the wooden chests had to be carried, on elephant back or by bullock cart, down to the nearest river ghat. There the chests would be loaded onto country boats to sail downriver, down the Brahmaputra to Calcutta, a journey that took over three months before the advent of the steamer. From Calcutta the tea would travel in sailing ships around the Cape of Good Hope to London. The ship journey, before the Suez Canal was inaugurated in 1869, used to take another three months at minimum. Altogether, it took about six months for tea from Assam to reach the tea-drinker in London.

When steamships and the Suez Canal shortened the journey to little more than a month in the 1870s, old hands complained of boredom. George Barker, the grouchy author of *A Tea-Planter's Life in Assam*, wrote:

> These days of the Suez Canal have discounted travellers' adventures, and reduced the possibility of risk and accident to a minimum. The average old Anglo-Indian, with memories still clinging to him of the journey around the Cape, lasting over a period of one hundred days, thinks no more of journeying backwards and forwards between England and India than any ordinary Londoner would of an excursion to Margate (75 miles from London) by river steamer.

After arriving in Calcutta, an Assam planter in the 1880s would typically spend a few days in the city buying whatever supplies he might want, and possibly hiring a 'khidmatgar' or butler for himself. Then he would embark upon the final leg of his journey by train from Sealdah station to Goalando ghat in today's Bangladesh. It was a journey that took a mere eight or nine hours. From there, he would take a steamer upriver towards Dibrugarh.

The journey of the tea labourers was much more grim. Typically, these men and women of tribes such as Santhal, Oraon, Telanga and Munda, often fleeing famine in their traditional homelands – unfortunately not a rare occurrence in those times – would be lured to Calcutta by 'coolie-catcher' agents who are still remembered in tea garden songs for having painted false pictures of lives of plenty that awaited the workers in Assam. Then they would be stuffed onto steamers like human cargo, and sent on the long journey. In a world before antibiotics or a cure for malaria, disease inevitably took its toll.

Getting in or out of Dibrugarh, even from as far as London, is now a matter of a few hours by air. Plantation life is still nonetheless considered somehow remote and distant. The managers and their families seem to view the remnants of the colonial lifestyle as one of the compensations for living far from the big cities. Not that they are missing much. The usual gadgets around which so much of urban life revolves – the computer, the television, the mobile phone and the motor car – are all present in the tea planter's bungalow. The internet is a bit slow, but there are other joys. There's no traffic to beat on your way to work and the food and drinks are farm fresh and cheaper, or even free.

Wanting to know more about the tea business, I reached out to Manoj Jalan, the owner of a reputed tea estate on the outskirts of Dibrugarh. The first topic that came up for discussion when we met was the giant bungalows, by which I was much impressed. Mr Jalan said the planter lifestyle came with a legacy, about which there were 'perceptions'. 'If the legacy of a plantation is that there are big houses, you don't expect planters to break them down,' he said. Basically, his position was that the old houses were part of the plantation's heritage and they obviously could not and should not be demolished.

The comfortable heritage of the planters' life contrasts sharply with the heritage of the tea garden labourers, who still live in slovenly habitations on the edges of estates and earn a pittance. They used to be paid below legal minimum wages on some estates until the 1990s. Things have improved somewhat, but poverty, illiteracy, alcoholism and disease are still rife in the tea labour colonies.

Poverty eradication would take time, Mr Jalan said, since the planet has over five billion poor people. 'The question is, is the community progressing?' he asked rhetorically. The fortunes of a large community are tied to an industry, he pointed out, and their fortunes depend on the fortunes of the industry. The industry's fortunes are facing a downturn, according to him. 'Go to any beverage mart. The space for traditional tea is shrinking.'

Tea businesses were diversifying in response. His family had been making little forays into the tourism business; tea estates and bungalows made for picturesque holidays. He saw good potential for tourism in Assam. 'Myanmar gets one million foreign tourists a year. Assam gets 26,000,' he said. 'We are four hours away from Myanmar by road. Similar people, similar landscape.'

He could have made an even more stark comparison with Thailand, which got 35 million tourists in 2017. Bangkok is three-and-a-half hours from Guwahati by air; so is Mumbai. The Assam landscape is similar to that of inland Thailand. As for the people ... the Tai Ahoms were Tais before they became Assamese.

32

Interview in a Dying Language

I HAD HEARD OF one village of speakers of a Tai language other than Ahom that still existed somewhere in the vicinity of Digboi, the place where the first oil well in Asia became operational in 1890. We asked Raj and Runtun. They had a friend they call 'IQ' – his name is Aikyo – who turned out to be a Tai with connections in the community. He knew of the village. Even better, he knew someone who knew someone who knew the headman of the village.

We set off for this place the next day. It was near Margherita, a town built by the British circa 1884, but named after an Italian queen because the engineer building the first rail link in those parts, the Dibru Sadiya Rail, happened to be the Italian Roberto Paganini.

The village, we had been told, was near the Dihing river. The road was a good two-lane highway with electricity poles on the side painted with the name of the All Tai Ahom Students' Union. Every ethnic community across Northeast India inevitably has its own representative organization, and often, its own student union.

These organizations mark off their own areas of influence and act as pressure groups. They also typically feed into larger ethnic organizations that are like federations of the smaller ethnic groups.

Traffic was thin. Apart from occasional cars and bikes, there was public transport – big autorickshaws, overloaded with people sitting front, back and everywhere. The surrounding landscape was flat river valley with paddy, betel nuts trees, bamboo groves and palms. The houses were mostly of woven bamboo mats with thatched roofs. Here and there, evidence of change showed itself in the form of cell phone towers and solar panels.

We reached the village in the early afternoon. It was a quiet place of houses on stilts with sloping roofs. The headman's house reflected his stature. It was a large concrete structure on concrete stilts and with a painted tin roof, unlike other more ramshackle structures that stood on wooden poles. The headman, a thin old man with East Asian features, was expecting us. He had also called two of his friends, both in their seventies, bespectacled and clad in lungis and shirts, in a style common in Myanmar, to keep him company during the interview. We all sat down in the living room.

It is one thing to find a village that has fifty speakers of an almost extinct language, it is quite another thing to hold a meaningful conversation with these speakers of said vanishing language.

Akshay and I beamed at them. They smiled back at us. We folded our hands in greeting. They did the same. There was nothing more to be done, expect plunge into the conversation. I launched off in my mix of broken Assamese, Hindi and English. They replied in what sounded to me like chaste Assamese and bits of broken Hindi and English.

Their people had come from the land of Siam, now called Thailand, the headman said.

'Nine tribes came here from Siam … their names are … '

There was a pause.

'Nine tribes … Kha mung, Thu mung … '

Another of the old men piped up, 'Tha mung!'

'Khu mung, Thu mung, Tha mung,' I muttered.

'Not Tha mung,' the headman said.

'Not Tha mung?'

I looked at my notes.

'Three tribes … ' I began.

'Not three, one tribe.'

'One tribe?'

I looked sheepishly at my notes.

There was a moment of silence. We went back over the names again. It transpired that two of the names were different names for the same clan … and they were clans, not tribes.

The listing resumed. Names came from around the room. 'Chao lik,' one of the men said. 'Chao hai,' said another. Then they paused. I counted the names out out loudly. This sparked off a mini conference in the Dialect of Very Few Speakers. Another name was proferred. I thought it sounded like 'Kem jo'. I repeated it. Yes, it was Kem jo.

Proceeding thus, with great difficulty, we reached a count of eight. '*Kitna hua abhi?*' one of the old men asked in Hindi. I told him. We were still a clan short, and by this time I didn't care what its name was. The old men, however, had plunged into another mini conference in their language. Akshay and I sat silently not understanding a word. Eventually there was a pause; I took quick advantage of it.

'Okay so nine clans came, then what?' I asked.

They had a written language, the men said, and this immediately sparked off yet another conference in the dying language. We waited. Eventually I had had enough. I cut in with my next question.

'So when did your people come?'

'1700,' said one man.

'1800' said another.

Neither of them said anything more. This time there was no conferring. I looked at my notes in silence. There was a pause. Eventually Akshay spoke up.

'Why did they come here?'

This time there was a clear answer. Their people had a battle with the Chinese, the headman said, in which they were defeated. They dispersed after the defeat. Some went to Siam, where he claimed they had set up the Siam kingdom. Others went as far as Cambodia, Laos, Vietnam and Malaysia. And some had made their way up to Assam.

The story bore resemblances to historical accounts of the Tai kingdom of Nanchao in Yunnan, although the time period did not match; Nanchao had collapsed in 937 AD.

I asked if they understood Thai.

'Yes of course,' he replied.

Thais had visited their village, he said. They had met Thai groups at Bodh Gaya, where everyone went for pilgrimage, and they had kept in touch.

'I am planning to visit Thailand soon,' one of the men said.

I asked if their people and the Tai Ahoms were same. No, the headman replied, they were a little different … like the Assamese of Upper Assam and the Goalpariyas.

It was an interesting example. The Goalpariya language is somewhere between standard Bengali and standard Assamese.

The old men had warmed up to the theme of Thailand. Chiang Mai, he said, was a place associated with their people. It was a place of meeting, signified by a pole struck into the ground. They were Tais and Suryavanshis, he said. This sounded strange, but only for a moment. There were Hindu kings all across Southeast Asia centuries before the first Tai Ahoms had made their way into Assam.

I enquired about their language. Did the young people speak it?

'The younger generation understand the language but don't speak it properly ... like your Assamese,' he replied, and they all laughed loudly at my Assamese. 'Youngsters are more interested in learning English. They want to study in English-medium schools. But we have started teaching our language in the village school.'

There was a process of cultural interaction with other tribes of the region, and other religions such as Hinduism, over a period of time, they explained. In this village, people had retained their culture, language and religion. There were a few Tai Khamyang people in Jorhat and Golaghat too, but they had largely become assimilated into the Assamese mainstream.

'There is now a process of cultural revival among the Tai peoples,' the headman said.

There were other Tai groups too in Assam, he added. The Tai Khampti, Tai Phake, Tai Aiton and Tai Turung were there, apart from the Tai Ahoms. With the Khamptis, they have relations of marriage. The Tai Phake are in the same general neighbourhood as them, on the banks of the Dihing river. The Tai Aiton and Tai Turung are in Karbi Anglong and Jorhat.

By then it was late afternoon. We broke for lunch. The dining table was in a room at the back of the house, at a higher level than the sitting room. It had to be approached by a small flight of stairs. The food was simple and tasty ... rice, dal, fish and a vegetable dish. Spices were minimal. Flavouring was by herbs.

Our kind hosts then offered to walk us around the village and up to the temple. It was a Theravada Buddhist temple, sleepy and quiet. There was not a soul in sight as we entered the building compound. The structure itself was a simple building with wooden flooring and walls made in the typical Assam style, with wooden frames and ikra reed interiors covered by a plaster of mud. A statue of the Buddha sat on a pedestal at the end of the hall. We all sat in silence for a few minutes. It was a quiet, peaceful moment.

33

Sivasagar

A SSAM GETS ITS NAME from the Tai Ahom dynasty that ruled a kingdom which gradually grew into an empire over a long reign of six hundred years starting in 1228. They were originally speakers of a Tai language like the old men we met. They also had their own religion. Over the centuries, they had gradually become Hindus and speakers of Assamese. At some point, Brahmins 'discovered' a genealogy for them, making them Indravanshis (descendants of Indra) rather than the customary Chandravanshis (moon kings descended from Krishna) or Suryavanshis (sun kings descended from Rama). But the kings, until almost the end of the dynasty, had names in their own Tai language apart from their Hindu names. The kingdom they had established was, for long, ruled from capitals in the vicinity of the town we were visiting next, about 70 km downriver from Dibrugarh.

Sivasagar today is a small, sleepy town in Assam's Brahmaputra valley, around 12 km from the river. In centuries gone by, this town and the areas around it were the centre of Ahom power. The monuments here bear testimony to a grand past. The centre of the town is dominated by an artificial lake called the Siva Sagar or Sea of Shiva that gives the place its name. The Shiva Dol, a temple to the God of destruction in the Hindu trinity, stands on a slight elevation next to this. There are two smaller accompanying temples, the Vishnu Dol and the Devi Dol, to Lord Vishnu, the preserver, and Goddess Durga, the warrior goddess and slayer of asuras, respectively.

A line of listless beggars sat with small mounds of uncooked rice in front of them on the narrow pathway that leads into the temple complex. The main temple itself is a tall ridged dome of over 100 feet. Inside, a few seemingly bored priests stood around. We walked past them into the damp, dimly lit sanctum sanctorum. A black stone Shiva lingam, the phallus of Shiva that is a symbolic representation of the male principle, stood next to a natural hollow in a rock the sides of which had been covered in white marble. Akshay and I bowed our heads and joined our hands in a namaste. A temple priest who was watching us invited Akshay to dip his hand into the moist hollow of the rock, which he called a yoni – a Sanskrit word for vagina, in this case a representation of Goddess Shakti, the feminine energy. I did not receive the same invitation.

Despite its name, the yoni is the dominant feature in this temple. Assam was and remains, along with Bengal and Odisha, an important centre of the Shakta tradition of Hinduism, in which Shakti, the divine female energy of the universe, has primacy.

The construction of the temple was begun during the reign of a Bor Raja or chief king who was not a king – it was Queen Phulesvari, one of the wives of the superstitious Ahom monarch Sib Singh, who held the title. Edward Gait, in his *A History of Assam*, wrote:

Sib Singh was completely under the influence of Brahman priests and astrologers; and in 1722 he was so alarmed by their prediction that his rule would shortly come to an end, that he not only made many and lavish presents for the support of temples and of Brahmans, in the hope of conciliating the Gods and averting the threatened calamity, but also endeavoured to satisfy the alleged decree of fate by a subterfuge which greatly diminished his prestige in the eyes of his people. He declared Phulesvari, who assumed the title Pramatesvari (one of the names of Durga) to be the 'Bar Raja' or chief king; made over to her the royal umbrella, the Ahoms symbol of sovereignty; and caused coins to be struck jointly in her name and his.

Phulesvari, a former temple dancer, was a zealot of Shakta Hinduism. Gait further wrote:

> She was even more under the influence of Brahmans than her husband, and in her consuming zeal for Sakta Hinduism such as often distinguishes neophytes, she committed an act of oppression which was destined to have far reaching and disastrous consequences. Hearing that the Sudra Mahants of the Vaishnav persuasion refused to worship Durga, she ordered the Moamaria and several other Gosains to be brought to a Shakta shrine where sacrifices were being offered, and caused the distinguishing marks of the Shakta sect to be smeared with the blood of the victims upon their foreheads. The Moamarias never forgave this insult to their spiritual leader and, half a century later, they broke out in open rebellion.[37]

Phulesvari died in 1731, upon which the king married her sister and declared her Bar Raja with the name Ambika.

The Shiva and Vishnu Dol were completed around 1734. Next to these, a large bamboo tent had been erected, and a loudspeaker was blaring. It was live music and the lead singer was good, with a raw, folksy command of tune. A group of worshippers sat watching the performers on stage. The band consisted of two semicircles, one each of men and women, who sat facing one another. The circle of singers, men clad in dhotis and women in saris, was belting out Krishna bhajans in Assamese, in tunes reminiscent of Bihu. One man who had matched his dhoti with a funky T-shirt was dancing some Bihu moves. The lead singer would occasionally stand up from his place in the circle to croon with the mic in his hand. It seemed like a song without end; it went on and on in a hypnotic way. We might have remained there, pleasantly mesmerized, but we had places to go and things to do.

34

Old Ahom Capitals All in a Row

WE LEFT TO EXPLORE some more sites associated with Ahom history around Sivasagar. All the capitals of the Ahom kingdom from the first one in 1228 to the last one that preceded the arrival of the British were within a few kilometres of here. Only Jorhat, the last capital, was further downriver.

Charaideo was the first Ahom capital. It was set up by the founder of the Ahom dynasty, Chaolung Siu Ka Pha.

Nothing remains of it now, except a number of burial mounds called maidams, rather like the pyramids of the Egyptian pharaohs, but hemispherical in shape and made of earth and brick in a style similar to those in Korea. These mounds were raised over the graves of the kings along with some of their belongings. The belongings are long gone. Grave robbers have long since burrowed into the maidams and decamped with their contents.

A man chasing cows from the gate of the burial complex was the only person apart from us that morning when we reached

Charaideo. He took a break to go into a little office and emerged with two tickets before resuming his cow herding. We walked into the complex with its tall trees and its grassy mounds like hills. A few goats grazed on them. Apart from these and the odd cow that had slipped past the gatekeeper, we saw no creatures for a while. Then we spotted a man scything the grass high up on the tallest of the maidams, at the top of which a small, ruined brick structure was visible. We made our way up towards it.

The place was quiet and peaceful and lonely. From atop the tall maidam, the view across was the countryside, trees, hills. At the base of the maidam, there were the remaining fragments of a wall that had once enclosed the area. The outline of the wall was in the shape of an octagon; it was a shape with some special, mystical significance, perhaps an aspect of Taoist influence that had slipped in via Mong Mao, the old Tai kingdom in Yunnan which was the ancestral home of the Ahoms.

Only one of the small maidams was built with a gate leading into it. We went in. It was cool and damp and empty inside.

At the edge of the complex is a beautiful, overgrown old lotus pond. The trees crowd around, leaning over it. It is a place that speaks of an ancient grace. It brought to mind a Zen garden, and inspired us to try our instant haiku skills. The sky was overcast and a few drops of rain had begun to fall. We managed 'Raindrops on the lotus-leaves, pitter-patter,' over one cigarette, before the growing numbers and intensity of the raindrops forced us to flee.

Outside, nearby, a new concrete gateway has been constructed, leading to a new building. The gateway announced, in a Tai script followed by English and Assamese, 'Yunnan to Patkai to Che-Rai-Doi'. That is the route Siu Ka Pha and his band are believed to have followed.

According to the *Assam Buranji*, Siu Ka Pha had with him 2 elephants and 300 horses, 2 nobles and a band of 1,080 people. But according to Gait, Siu Ka Pha had with him 2 elephants and 300 horses, and a following of 9,000 people of whom 8 were nobles. The band wandered about the hilly country of the Patkai for thirteen years from AD 1215 before arriving in Khamjang, believed to be in the Kachin state of today's Myanmar. Some Nagas attempted to resist his advance towards what is now India across the Pangsau Pass but ' ... he defeated them and perpetrated frightful atrocities on those whom he captured. He caused many of them to be killed and roasted, and forced their relatives to eat their flesh,' according to Gait.

Siu Ka Pha and his men then set about conquering the surrounding tribes and establishing their kingdom.

For a long while, the Ahoms followed the practice of cutting off the heads of rival kings and burying the heads under the steps of the royal temple at Charaideo so that they might walk on it whenever they entered the temple.

Apart from the heads of kings of neighbouring tribes such as the Chutiyas, the head of an early Muslim invader was also added to this collection. His name was Turbak Khan and he invaded the Ahom kingdom in April 1532 with a force of 1,000 horses, 30 elephants, an unknown number of foot soldiers as well as artillery, a new technology of war at the time.The invaders from Gaur, corresponding to modern Bengal, were initially successful. At this, some Ahom women, led by a legendary warrior princess named Mula Gabharu, took to the battlefield and died fighting. Eventually the tide turned against the invaders. Turbak Khan's forces were routed and he died on the battlefield, and his head was duly despatched for burial at Charaideo. Many of his soldiers were captured, and they remained in Assam. They are said to be the progenitors of the Assamese Muslim population now known as Goriyas, a name derived from Gauriya, meaning 'people of Gaur'.

Shortly after this, the victorious Ahom king, Suhunmung, was assassinated by a servant who crept into his bedroom and stabbed him in his sleep – apparently at the behest of his son, Suklenmung, who then ascended the throne and moved the Ahom capital from Charaideo to Garhgaon, about 15 km away.

'Garh' means fort, and the Ahom capital established in 1540 is said to have been surrounded by an earthen fortress wall. A detailed description has survived from the account of a Persian writer named Shihabuddin Talish who accompanied the Mughal invader Mir Jumla more than a century later in 1662. Mir Jumla was a Persian from Isfahan who came to Golconda to work in the diamond business there. He wound up becoming a favourite general of Mughal Emperor Aurangzeb – during the war of succession that had followed the death of Shah Jahan, Mir Jumla had led Aurangzeb's army against his elder brother Shah Shuja, pursuing him all the way to Dhaka. Shah Shuja fled to Arakan in today's Myanmar, the area associated with the Rohingyas, with the remnants of his army and a large treasure. There he was possibly put to death by the local king. Aurangzeb appointed Mir Jumla governor of Bengal.

Mir Jumla soon came into conflict with his new neighbours, the Koch and Ahoms, who had been engaged in fighting one another for some years previously; under their great general, Chilarai, the Koch had defeated the Ahoms and sacked Garhgaon. However, after the deaths of Chilarai and his elder brother, the Koch King Naranarayan, their kingdom gradually split into two due to succession issues between their descendants. Eventually, one of the two Koch kingdoms, Koch Behar (or Cooch Behar), fell under the rule of the Nawab of Dhaka following civil war between them.

After Shah Jahan's death, when civil war also broke out in the Mughal empire as a battle of succession erupted, the Ahoms, taking advantage of the situation, advanced into Kamrup and took Guwahati before plundering their way down to Dhubri and beyond. The western Koch kingdom, which had been under the Nawab of Dhaka, declared independence. When the Mughal war of succession ended, Mir Jumla, who had now become the new nawab in Dhaka, set about recovering these lost territories. His victory over the Koch was swift. He then advanced against the Ahoms with a fleet of large warboats on the Brahmaputra, called ghrabs, commanded by Portuguese and Dutch officers. The Ahoms fled, with King Jayadhwaj Singha himself abandoning his capital and heading east to Namrup. Nawab Mir Jumla entered Garhgaon and occupied the raja's palace.

A description of Garhgaon from the time survives in Talish's *Fathiya-i-Ibriyya*:

> The city of Garhgaon has four gates of stone set in mud, from each of which to the Raja's palace, for a distance of three kos, an extremely strong, high and wide embankment has been constructed for the passage of men. Around the city, in the place of a wall, there is an encompassing bamboo plantation, two kos or more in width.

The king had an audience hall called Solang Ghar, which greatly impressed Talish. It was made of wood and stood on pillars. 'Probably nowhere else in the whole world can wooden houses be built with such decoration and figure-carving as by the people of this country,' he wrote. It was decorated with mirrors of brass that dazzled the eye.

The wooden structures have long since disappeared. Along the side of the road to Garhgaon is a ditch, a remnant of the medieval moat. The road passes through an unremarkable gate into the precincts of the old town in which nothing of the old remains except a small four-storied structure of sandstone made during the reign of King Rajeswar Singha in 1752 at the site of the old wooden structure that so impressed Talish. 'The fort and the royal complex were badly damaged and disfigured due to procurement of raw materials from the monument by the locals for building their houses,' the Archaeological Survey of India's note on the structure laments.

Inside, the building is absolutely bare. The stone itself is defaced with the usual graffiti of unknown names and loves that manage to find their way onto every such structure. A few couples sit on benches in the lush green lawns. The ambience is peaceful, even rustic ... a far cry from the times when it was the centre of royal intrigues and the target of invasions in which thousands of men on either side died.

Legend had it that there was a tunnel that led from this palace to the Talatal Ghar, an underground palace of three storeys above which the four storeys of another palace, the Kareng Ghar, stand. The Talatal Ghar and Kareng Ghar together constitute the Rangpur Palace. This was the centre of Rangpur, barely a kilometre away, where the Ahom capital had moved to from Garhgaon around 1702.

The Kareng Ghar is far bigger than the Garhgaon Palace. Rusty old iron cannons greet visitors near the entrance. The structure, a pavilion of sorts with large open terraces that lead down into chambers whose brick walls have turned green with the moss of the ages, is as bare as the Garhgaon Palace. Arched doorways lead into a succession of empty rooms and out into the lush green grounds. The underground section, the Talatal Ghar, has been sealed off; people were said to disappear into its secret tunnels.

Jintu, our driver, perhaps pleased at finding travellers interested in visiting all the Ghars, decided to show us yet another 'ghar' of more recent provenance near the Kareng Ghar. It was labelled a 'Jadu Ghar', which means 'house of magic', although the term is more likely to be used for museums. It was a small concrete structure. Inside, stuffed into glass cases and strewn around the floors, was a completely random and eccentric collection of objects. A dead bat hung from a thread near a ventilator. Daos and spears poked out from behind doorways. A dead kitten in a formaldehyde jar sat not far from another jar that claimed to contain the ashes of Assamese cultural icon Bhupen Hazarika. There were completely ordinary-looking eggs in a basket for no reason whatsoever. And a rusty old, massive, wicked sword labelled 'bali dao' which from its appearance looked like it was designed to decapitate humans or large animals. There was also, near the sword, a Remington typewriter.

The man who had let us in had disappeared. We were left alone in the place, and departed after wandering around this strange Jadu Ghar for a while, not knowing what eccentricity had led to its creation.

The roads by which we left themselves had a bit of history.

Close to Garhgaon there is an old Ahom road called the Dhodar Ali. It is a road with a past. Built during the reign of the Ahom king Sutaphaa or Gadadhar Singha in the late 1600s, it was apparently named 'dhodar' after the lazy opium addicts who were pressed into constructing it. This road, which runs close to the border between Assam and Nagaland, used to mark the boundary of British-administered territory in the mid-1800s before the adjacent Naga Hills, then independent, gradually came under British rule.

One other significant Ahom monument was on the way back to Sivasagar, and we dutifully paid our respects there as well. It was the Rang Ghar. This sports pavilion of the Ahom kings was built during the reign of Pramatta Singha between 1744–50. From here they used to watch buffalo and cock fights, wrestling matches and other such gladiatorial contests held in the grounds in front of the pavilion. Just to make sure you get this about the place, the government has helpfully constructed life-size cement statues of buffaloes fighting and wrestlers locked in combat, in larger than life size. There's also a cement spotted deer, standing as though grazing contentedly on the real grass.

Cement statues of animals are a thing in Assam, Akshay had noted. From the moment you land at the Guwahati airport you are greeted by cement animals. Rhinos are especially popular, but there are plenty of cement elephants and buffaloes too. The reason for these cement zoos is not clear to me; after all, there are often real elephants, tame ones, even on the roads of Guwahati. The sides of the roads have plenty of real buffaloes everywhere, including all around the Rang Ghar in Sivasagar. It's easy to tell the real buffaloes from the fake. They are not allowed to taste the grass in the hallowed precincts where their cement compatriots graze.

35

The Pir from Baghdad

THE AREA AROUND RANG Ghar is a predominantly Muslim neighbourhood. Oddly enough, we didn't spot any Muslim habitation anywhere near one of the most important sites associated with Islam in Assam, the dargah of Ajan Fakir, on the banks of the Brahmaputra 26 km from Sivasagar town.

Ajan Fakir, whose original name was Shah Miran, came to Sivasagar from Baghdad via Ajmer and Delhi in 1630. Along with his brother, who had also made the epic journey, he settled down in Garhgaon. Shah Miran married a local Ahom woman, said to be from the nobility. He came to be known as Ajan Fakir because he used to sing the azaan, the Muslim call to prayer – a new thing for Islam in Assam, at the time. He also composed songs that still survive to this day. They are known as zikrs and zaris.

The narrow, potholed road to the dargah led away from Sivasagar through paddy fields and villages. There were no cars apart from ours. Cattle, goats and chickens wandered around as if they owned the road – which they did. Our driver, Jintu, was terrified of the chickens … or more accurately, of the owners of the chickens. The villages we were passing were 'Dom' or fisher folk villages, and Jintu informed us that these people were 'most danger'. He had, however, used the same expression earlier for the Nagas, who inhabit the hills in the distance behind the old Ahom capitals, and for the Muslims around Rang Ghar. He seemed like a man given to extolling the violent tendencies of neighbours.

Jintu's particular fear of chickens came from his fear that he would accidentally run over one of the creatures. The 'most danger' Dom villagers would then surround the car and demand compensation, saying the chicken would have laid eggs and the eggs would have turned into hens and those hens would also have laid eggs, and so on … in other words, the price of a single chicken was potentially infinite.

It was a strategy of extortion that might indeed be employed successfully on the lonely road lined by paddy fields and the Dikhow river. After Jintu's exposition, we looked at chickens crossing the road with far greater alarm. I caught myself wondering, for perhaps the first time in my life, 'Why do chickens cross the road?'

We saw little of the 'most danger' owners themselves. There were a few villagers on bicycles and the odd man sitting in a ramshackle little village shop. They looked peaceful enough, in their relaxed attire of lungis and vests, cycling lazily or lounging around. The shops sold only a few odds and ends – cheap biscuits, cigarettes, salt, sugar, pulses and such. The villagers wouldn't need to buy too many things from shops anyway. Paddy grew all around and was plentiful. Fruits and vegetables too grew all over. There was no shortage of cattle, goats and poultry. The surrounding rivers and ponds had fish.

The necessities of life did not seem very hard to come by here.

The villages had a concept of nightlife too, Jintu warned us. This involved getting very drunk on local brews or 'Indian-made foreign liquor', and getting into brawls. In other words, it was just like Delhi or Gurgaon.

Fortunately, we managed to make our way to Ajan Pir's dargah without running over any chickens.

At the site of the dargah itself is a little village. The Brahmaputra runs about half a kilometre away, across an open grassland that fills with water during the monsoon. The land gives way sharply to the river; there is a fall of four or five feet. A strip of land is visible in the distance on the other side, a dark line of trees on the horizon. The sky was blue flecked with puffs of white. The water reflected it. It was deceptively calm. Only the water hyacinths floating down showed just how fast the river was at this point.

We walked closer to the edge. The rains had not quite ended. The river was brimming. Up close, we could hear it swirling and gurgling. It looked a muddy brown, muscular and strong.

The dargah itself is a white, domed structure with a gate and fence that was festooned with ribbons of many colours. It was completely empty the afternoon we reached. We had to open the latched gate and let ourselves in. There was not a soul in sight.

After washing our hands and feet at a tube well, we went in. It was silent, serene. We paid homage to the pir and were on our way out of the grounds surrounding the dargah when we encountered the first villager – an old man clad in a dhoti who asked us for money in the pir's name. I gave him all the change I had, seven rupees, and he went off happy.

I found it strange that the dargah of one of the earliest and most celebrated men associated with Islam in Assam should be deserted. Jintu said people normally visited in January when the Urs of the saint is held and there are lines of cars. The rest of the year, it seems, the pir is left to rest in peace in his grave by the Brahmaputra.

Maidam, Sivasagar.
These are tombs of former
Ahom monarchs.
Photo: Akshay Mahajan

Tea garden path, Upper Assam.
Photo: Akshay Mahajan

Ghat in the morning,
near Guijan.
Photo: Akshay Mahajan

Returning travellers,
Aisung chapori.
Photo: Akshay Mahajan

The boat clinic.
Photo: Akshay Mahajan

The Brahmaputra at
sunset, Biswanath.
Photo: Akshay Mahajan

Riverside funerary ritual.
Photo: Akshay Mahajan

Dr Deori (left) and Dr Bora.
Photo: Akshay Mahajan

A fishermen's camp en
route Dibru Saikhowa.
The fishermen spend
months out on long
fishing trips.
Photo: Akshay Mahajan

The river crossing
by ferry.
Photo: Akshay Mahajan

Boys playing on a raft, Aisung chapori.
Photo: Akshay Mahajan

Carefree boyhood on a
chapori.
Photo: Akshay Mahajan

The jungle road to
Bordumsa.
Photo: Akshay Mahajan

Feral horses of Dibru Saikhowa.
Photo: Akshay Mahajan

Bogibeel bridge under
construction near
Dibrugarh.
Photo: Akshay Mahajan

Fresh catch at the ghat.
Photo: Akshay Mahajan

Masks at Samaguri satra, Majuli.
Photo: Akshay Mahajan

The Kalia-daman
sequence depicts Krishna
slaying the serpent.
Uttar Kamalabari Satra,
Majuli.
Photo: Akshay Mahajan

Radha arrives for the play.
She's actually a boy dressed
up for the role.
Photo: Akshay Mahajan

Sattriya drummers playing drums called khol.
Photo: Akshay Mahajan

At the memorial of Azan
Pir near Sibsagar.
Photo: Akshay Mahajan

Kareng Ghar, an old
Ahom palace, at Garhgaon
near Sibsagar.
Photo: Akshay Mahajan

An abandoned Assam-type house.
Photo: Akshay Mahajan

Inside the antique
departmental store, Doss &
Co, in Jorhat.
Photo: Akshay Mahajan

36

Spiritual Jorhat

DRIVING OUT FROM SIVASAGAR towards Jorhat we crossed, without noticing, a bridge that spans a stream called the Namdang. It is a bridge more than 300 years old, and is carved out of stone. Construction those days didn't have to contend with pilferage of cement; the bridge remains in regular use. It is now part of National Highway 37. Barely 60 km further downriver along the south bank of the Brahmaputra is Jorhat, the last Ahom capital. This was where king Gaurinath Singha, battling the Moamaria rebellion led by the Motoks, shifted his capital in 1794 shortly before his death. His dynasty's rule effectively ended in 1817 with the Burmese invasion of Assam, and the British annexation that followed their victory over the Burmese in 1826. The beginning of that end had been heralded by 1794 itself, when the first British forces led by Captain Thomas Welsh of the Bengal Army, responding to his entreaties, had arrived in Jorhat to restore King Gaurinath Singha to his tottering throne.

Jorhat today is a largish town that sits at a safe distance of some 15 km from the river. Remnants of the old Ahom era remain in the form of key roads whose names end with 'Ali', such as Gar-Ali and Na-Ali, and water tanks called 'pukhri', with names that often indicate who it was constructed by or for. The British district town, with its usual administrative offices, court and police station, is still a living presence. There's also an antique departmental store called Doss & Co which opened in 1901. It claims to be the first departmental store in what is now Northeast India. It is still housed in the original building, and retains the air of a place that belongs to a century long gone. The products it sells make a few reluctant concessions to the present age, but the displays and shelves are all vintage early 1900s.

About 16 km outside the town is the burial place or 'maidam' of the great Ahom General Lachit Borphukan, now designated 'National Hero Lachit Borphukan Maidam'. The maidam itself has the appearance, like the ones around Sivasagar, of a grassy mound or hillock. A statue of the general stands outside. He had died within a year of his famous victory at the Battle of Saraighat, a naval encounter with invading Mughal forces led by Rajput king Raja Ram Singh of Jaipur in 1671.

The Rajasthani connection remains strong in today's Jorhat, thanks to the presence of a vibrant Marwari business community in the town. We were having dinner in a small roadside fish and rice restaurant in a busy market area when we saw what seemed to be a religious procession involving members of this community. Shouts of '*Ek, do, teen char, babaji ke jay jay kar*' attracted our attention. Two men with multicoloured flags passed by first, followed by a couple of men laying down a mattress of some kind on the bustling road. This was for a man clad in white dhoti and sleeveless banian-type T-shirt who proceeded to prostrate himself on the mattress before getting up. The mattress would then be moved a few feet ahead, and the cycle repeated. The rest of the procession consisted of the cheerleaders raising the slogans, and the rear was brought up by women clad in saris with the 'ghoonghat' drawn demurely over the head covering the faces.

Religion, spirituality and magic of all kinds seem to be thriving in Jorhat. There was a big hoarding right at the heart of the town, across from Doss & Co, that proclaimed the astrological services of a certain 'Dr Sri Sri Ghosh'. It appeared from his hoarding that Dr Sri Sri Ghosh began by promising to cure cancer, diabetes, brain haemorrhage, eczema and a large number of all the other ailments known to medical science till that point. His qualifications for this, proudly advertised, were gold medals in various occult disciplines. He also had talents in solving problems beyond the mere bodily. He could apparently sort out issues of business, money, romance, and so on. Basically, he was the answer to all of life's problems.

We went looking for him. His office turned out to be a shop in a new mall next to a store selling computer accessories. A bored salesgirl stood behind a counter selling a wide range of good luck charms. Dr Sri Sri Ghosh's product line was truly secular in the Indian sense of the word, encompassing all faiths. The shop stocked everything from rudraksh necklaces to Turkish evil eye beads and Islamic wall hangings with 786 written on them. There was even a poster with Chinese lettering, perhaps of Buddhist or Taoist provenance. The good doctor himself was sadly not at hand. He had been called away to Tinsukia. His website proclaimed that he was available everywhere from there to Guwahati. His travels must keep him quite busy.

Not far from Jorhat town is a very different kind of magical space – an old and hallowed counterpoint to the new shopkeepers of spirituality. This is the Dhekiakhowa Bor Namghor, a place of worship associated with the most revered of Vaishnav saints in Assam, Sankardev and his disciple Madhavdev. It is said to have been established by Madhavdev around 500 years ago. The current structure is a modern concrete one, with the familiar cement animals – a pair of elephants in this case – at the gate. Inside the spacious building is a hall where visiting devotees light earthen lamps, of which there is row upon row. In one corner is a lamp larger than the others, that holds a pride of place on a stand of its own. Legend has it that this lamp has been burning continuously since it was lit by Madhavdev in 1528. Reincarnation is a reality of life in India. The body of the lamp may not be the same one that was lit in 1528. It doesn't matter; the spirit is the same. It is the same lamp.

The faith and culture that lit the lamp burns brightest today in a river island in the Brahmaputra roughly opposite Jorhat. This is the island of Majuli, the centre of the Vaishnav sect established by Sankardev and Madhavdev. Getting there is a matter of taking a ferry across from Nimati Ghat, a half hour drive from Jorhat – when transport is available.

In the countless variety of mostly religious festivals in India, there is only one secular festival that diverse groups in various parts of the country love to celebrate. It is called 'bandh', which means shutdown. As the name suggests, it is a day on which shops and markets are shut, taxis and private vehicles go off the roads, schools see negligible attendance, and many or even most government officials in departments other than police, hospitals and a few other similar 'essential' ones squeeze in at least a half holiday. It used to be particularly popular in Bengal and across Northeast India where any group with a letterhead and the wherewithal to send out a press release was likely to be able to call for a successful bandh. In the world before coronavirus in which we were travelling, something of the habit remained. As news would spread that some group with a tough-sounding name – using 'Liberation' in the name really upped street cred in Northeast India – had called a bandh, a quiet joy would ripple through the citizenry. People would complain about how they would have to skip office or stock up on vegetables, before proceeding to enjoy a rare holiday spent doing absolutely nothing.

We woke on our appointed day for heading to the river island of Majuli to find there was a 'Bharat bandh' that had been called by central trade unions in Delhi. Assam has never been ruled by Left-wing parties. It has not had a strong trade union movement outside the tea industry for decades. The main political parties in the state have long been the Congress and Asom Gana Parishad, to which list the BJP is the recent addition. This, however, did not get in the way of the bandh's success; there was no public transport in sight. We managed to call a tourist taxi through an acquaintance of Akshay's. The vehicle arrived to ferry us to the Nimati Ghat – the name is a corruption of 'naya mati' meaning 'new earth' – on the banks of the Brahmaputra. Getting there was no trouble on the empty roads; the trouble was that the ferry ghat was also empty. A few men were hanging around on the stationary ferry that served as the ticket office. They told us that there would be no ferries to Majuli that day. We were stuck.

We were still waiting, discussing our options, when a police jeep with a posse of men brandishing AK-47s raced in. It was followed by a Toyota Innova with a flag on the bonnet from which a man, obviously an important person in these parts, emerged. 'MLA,' our driver told us in an undertone. The man walked down, while talking on his mobile phone, to the same stationary ferry where we had been told there would be no vehicles for Majuli. Chairs magically appeared on the deck for the man to sit. Cups of tea were served. On Akshay's urging, I walked gingerly past the armed guards and went to have a chat with him. He turned out to be a senior police officer on his way to Majuli. He was helpful. Yes, he said, we could hitch a ride with him.

A neat and well-maintained police ferry boat quietly drew up. We joined the officer and his group of guards. A priest from one of the monasteries in Majuli, who like us had been stranded at the ferry ghat, was the only other passenger.

The officer was on his way to inspect security arrangements for the planned trip of Assam Chief Minister Sarbananda Sonowal to Majuli, his constituency, the following week. Majuli would be declared a district on that day. 'Development' was coming to the island.

Our first view of Majuli was as a line of green on the waters of the river that stretched to the horizon. A few boats came into view as we got closer. The ghat itself was a sleepy place with bamboo shacks in which a few men sat around doing nothing. We joined them for a while. It seemed like a good place to slow down and drop our city-bred rush.

By and by, a large diesel autorickshaw ferried us to our hotel, which was a bamboo hut. Even the floors of the verandah and the one room were made of bamboo. The walls were interlaced bamboo. The ceiling was bamboo over which there was a thatch roof. Only the bathroom had a cement floor.

The furniture, such as it was, was bamboo. The beds were made from bamboo and there was a cane table. For amenities we had electricity and running water in the bathroom. There was a ceiling fan in the bedroom.

The hut stood on stilts. Below it and all around us was a wetland. Looking down through the gaps between the bamboo slats of the floor, we could see water and weeds. We were pretty much a part of the landscape. This was very pretty, but the flip side to this was that the floods had just receded and the place was alive with insects. Every evening, after dark, switching on any light would draw tens of thousands of insects until the light was darkened by teeming insect bodies. We learnt to keep our lights off from dusk to well after nightfall. Nightlife comprised dinner and reading in bed under the mosquito net. Tucking in the mosquito net carefully was a task of critical importance, one that needed to be done with attention to detail, because it would mean the difference between peaceful sleep and a night-long battle.

Sunset and sunrise in the hut were beautiful. At sunset, the sky would turn many shades of mauve and orange. In the silhouetted trees lining the road across from the water surrounding us we would spot silhouettes of birds flying in to nest. The still water would reflect the scene.

Quiet, dark nights would give way to mornings awake with silent stirrings. Kingfishers would swoop in from the trees, flashing towards the surface of the water to vanish with a little fish in the mouth – or not. In the green wetlands and grasslands surrounding us, there was the white of egrets. Ducks and pochards swam through paths amid the water plants. Sometimes, a rare human form could be seen in the waist-deep water.

Majuli is an island in more ways than one. Its charming rural life of picturesque villages set amid wetlands and paddy fields, and its Vaishnava monasteries with their timeless traditions, are surrounded by the rising tide of urbanization and crony capitalism in Assam. The island itself is being eroded, physically, by the very river that gave it birth. Chunks of its earth are being eaten away by the Brahmaputra. Its land area has shrunk from a maximum estimated at 1,256 sq km to about 515 sq km now. Entire villages have been forced to move time and again as the river has swept away the land. Some monasteries, known as satras, have relocated four or five times during their years of existence to escape the land-eating, course-shifting river.

The oldest of the existing satras date to around AD 1600. The first one, which is said to have been established by the founder of the Ekasarana Vaishnavite movement in Assam, Srimanta Sankardev, at a site marked by a bilva tree – and hence called Belguri – was swallowed up by the river in the distant past. The Kamalabari satra, which was established in an orange or 'kamala' garden in Majuli in 1595, is still around. So is a branch of this satra, the Uttar Kamalabari Satra, which dates to 1655.

It was around lunch time on a sunny afternoon when we got to Uttar Kamalabari. A line of people – men on one side, women on the other – sat silently on the floor on the verandah around the central hall of the satra. Inside, a priest was droning on. We joined the men's line. After some time, people came by and silently placed banana leaves in front of every person in the line. Then a handful of sprouts was handed out on every leaf, followed by a banana each. No one touched the food. We all sat waiting for the priest to finish his long prayers.

After this lunch, it was time for the cultural events. The satras are renowned as sites of culture. Srimanta Sankardev's Vaishnavism had powerful elements of song and dance that have been passed on through the centuries in these satras. There is music, known as 'gayan bayan', and theatre, known as 'bhaona'. Songs called 'borgeet' for which the lyrics were composed by Sankardev himself are still sung more than 450 years after his death.

The language of those songs is Brajabuli. It is a now-extinct literary language that has words of Maithili, Bengali and Assamese. The language is believed to have emerged in the fourteenth century. The first poet in the language whose renown has survived into the present is Vidyapati of Mithila, modern-day Madhubani in Bihar, who died in 1448.

In those times, Brajabuli would have been a convenient link language for people from what are now Bihar, Bengal, Assam and Odisha to communicate in. The dominant languages of these states are related to one another; they emerged from the same roots. In the fifth century the lingua franca of the common people in these areas is believed by linguists to have been a form of Prakrit called Magadhi Prakrit. This gradually split into different languages.

An eastern dialect of Magadhi Prakrit called Kamrupi Prakrit existed in the ancient Kamrupa kingdom which spanned what is now Assam and north Bengal and parts of what is now Bangladesh. This is the oldest kingdom of these areas known to history.

The eastern boundary of the Kamrupa kingdom according to the Yogini Tantra, a sixteenth century text, was the river Dikshu which is variously identified with the Dikrong or Dibang rivers in Upper Assam and Arunachal. The western boundary was the Karatoya river. There is now a river of this name in Rajshahi division of northern Bangladesh, but there is no river in the vicinity that corresponds to old descriptions of the original Karatoya, which must have been a quite considerable river, other than the Teesta and the Brahmaputra itself. The entire Brahmaputra Valley was part of Kamrupa. It was a kingdom that lasted almost a thousand years before gradually falling off the map by the thirteenth century.

There is still a living memory of that ancient kingdom, which survives as a district of Assam. There is also a Kamrupi dialect which sounds like something between standard Assamese and standard Bengali. It has lovely folk songs, many of them odes to Lord Krishna. From the Kamrupi Vaishnava tradition to the Vaishnava tradition of Majuli, there is a continuity.

The satra itself is a unique feature of the Eksarana or Mahapuruxia tradition of Vaishnavism that traces its origins to Sri Sankardev, the great fifteenthth-century Bhakti saint from Nagaon. In Majuli, a cluster of these satras has survived, more or less intact, to this day, with their ways of life and traditions that hark back to a very different world. Each satra has its own unique features. Several are custodians of cultural traditions that have nigh disappeared from the wider world outside.

Uttar Kamalabari, a monastic satra, is known for its music and dance. We were fortunate to catch a performance enacted inside the satra's prayer hall which is called 'namghar'. It began with a group of men clad in white dhotis, white kurtas and white turbans, doing a performance in which they played drums called 'khol' and cymbals, while singing and dancing – a sample of 'gayan bayan'.

There was a break before the next event, a play. The lead characters were dressed in their costumes and bustling about outside. A young man dressed in flowing kurta and pyjama, his face painted blue, with a papier-mâché crown of snakes on his head, stood with his arms around a slim and lively girl, her long hair tied in a bun, and wearing dangling earrings and red lipstick. It was the lead couple of Krishna and Radha; since this is a monastery with only men, the beautiful Radha was being played by a boy. The pretty 'gopis' were also boys.

Androgyny is unremarkable in the Hindu tradition. There is fluidity of gender stereotypes. Krishna is often depicted as a beautiful man in a flowing dhoti, adorned with jewellery and wearing a crown of peacock feathers. He is the opposite of macho; yet, he is all powerful.

A lively performance followed, with the musicians who had opened the day's performance providing live music. The performance space was the middle of the hall, with audience on three sides peering in through the bars outside the hall. We saw young Krishna kill the great snake Kalia in the sequence known as 'Kalia daman'. We saw him grow into a beautiful youth with a golden crown adorned by a peacock feather that replaced his crown of snakes.

If this was religion, I could not tell where culture ended and religion began. Like braids of the river, they flowed into one another.

The Samaguri Satra, a few kilometres from Uttar Kamalabari, is the custodian of a tradition of mask-making that has been passed on from father to son, generation after generation, for the past 350 years. Mask-maker Khagen Goswami, who is part of this tradition, explained that they had started making the masks to solve practical problems. Bhaona, the folk theatre with its tales from Hindu mythology, was part of the religious tradition of the followers of Sankardev. They encountered difficulties in depicting certain important characters from the Ramayana. 'How to depict Ravana with only make-up?' asked Goswami. It could be done, but an easier way to do it in the world before special effects was via a mask with ten heads. Garuda, the giant eagle-man who is the steed of Lord Vishnu, presents a similar difficulty in representation. A mask again solved the problem. The monkey-god Hanuman and the monkey-kings Bali and Sugriva were similarly depicted through masks.

Goswami's family has been making masks for six generations. In the room we were in inside his modest house, masks of various sizes and hues looked down at us from all sides. Demon and monkey faces constituted the majority, but the show-stealer was a giant full-body mask, more like a sculpture, of a figure with four arms and the head of a rather emaciated lion. This was Narasimha, the half-man half-lion avatar of Vishnu.

There were also half-body masks and masks carved out of wood for temples. 'We work in all materials,' said Goswami. 'Clay, cement, wood.' We had first seen him, soon after arriving in Majuli, at work building a gateway out of cement adorned with a large lion mounting a rather small elephant from the rear. At the bottom, squashed under this duo, was a tortoise. This traditional motif can be seen all around Assam. It is called the 'Naamsingha'. The tortoise symbolizes the kuruma avatar of Vishnu; it is the tortoise on which the world-mountain rests. The elephant, poor fellow, symbolizes ego and sin. The lion on top is the symbol of spiritual power.

The traditional masks are built on frames of woven cane. Cloth forms the next layer, and then character is sculpted by plastering a layer of clay mixed with cow dung. After this there is another layer of cloth, and then the mask is finally painted.

The mask-makers get orders for the masks during Raas Lila, the dance of Krishna. They also make small ones for sale to visitors and tourists. Sometimes they get orders from museums as well. Goswami proudly said that their masks are displayed at the British Museum in London.

Across from his house, past a small courtyard surrounded by the houses of other members of the satra, was the namghar. Sounds of singing were coming from inside. We walked in to find the women of the satra singing a keertan while clapping along. It was a soulful song called '*Govinda murari bhagavata*'. On one side, a couple of men were washing, with meditative attention, the bananas that would be the 'prasad' or offerings at the evening worship.

The people from the satra are not cut off from the world. Many work at jobs outside. Goswami himself is an arts graduate. '*Hari kathar logot chawal kotha,*' he says. 'With talk of Hari (another name for Lord Krishna), talk of rice.' People have to make their livings.

The ways of the world outside are intruding into the secluded ways of the satras. Televisions and mobile phones bring news of the world. More worryingly, they also bring advertisements. The enticements of the latest phones and televisions and much else besides are there for all to see.

Something of the little intrigues and rivalries that undoubtedly spring from material rather than spiritual causes revealed itself to us even during our brief visit. Trying to find the Samaguri Satra, we had stopped at the first gate we encountered that bore the name. Inside was an artist workshop making masks. It turned out that this was not the satra we were looking for; there was another gate, a little further down the road, which was the one we had come to see. The reason for the two gates and the split in the satra was alleged greed. Some government funds had been sanctioned, and the money had not been shared with the satra as required by the rules of communal living. The satra had excommunicated the people who had not shared the money, and those people had set up their own branch of the satra.

The external form remains, but the vows of chastity and poverty that were important in the life of Madhavdev, the most celebrated disciple of Sankardev, are clearly no longer popular. The elephant of ego and sin rules the whole wide world, and everywhere, the lion of spirituality on top is often little more than a cloak.

37

A Dark Interlude

BENEATH MAJULI'S IDYLLIC EXTERIOR, intrigues lurk. The island was a hotbed of the ULFA militancy during the years when the insurgent group called the shots in the state. It was here that the NGO worker Sanjoy Ghose was kidnapped and killed by them in 1997. Ghose, then a young man of thirty-seven from a prominent Bengali family in Mumbai, had a history of taking the path less travelled. He had turned down offers from the Indian Institutes of Management to join the Indian Institute of Rural Management. After a subsequent degree from Oxford University, he chose to work in rural Rajasthan. He quit the successful NGO he founded there and moved on to Majuli, to work on preventing the river island's erosion decades before that cause, and Majuli, became fashionable.

Unfortunately for him, Ghose's work on erosion prevention using inexpensive local methods and voluntary labour by the local villagers was successful. Building embankments is an annual business of contractors in Assam. Some of the money went into the coffers of ULFA, whose business model, apart from outright extortion and robbery, included securing contracts for their favoured contractors by threats of violence, for a cut. By his voluntary work, Ghose disturbed the business of the contractors and of ULFA, a militant outfit of radical Assamese nationalists. They decided to get rid of him and his NGO. On 4 July 1997 he was lured away by one of his local acquaintances, who was, either from fear or choice, working for ULFA, to a remote part of Majuli. What exactly happened there is not clear, but he was killed either immediately or while trying to escape from his abductors later. His body, reportedly tossed into the Brahmaputra, was never found.[38]

ULFA's top leadership – some of whom had been in telephonic contact with Ghose's family to negotiate terms of release soon after his kidnapping – claimed the killing was carried out by the local unit without their knowledge. That remains their position to this day. They do not deny ULFA's role; in 2011, fourteen years after the murder, ULFA Chairman Arabinda Rajkhowa issued a public apology for the 'mistake'.[39]

Our host Beda, a history graduate whose family has been in Majuli for generations – they were among the original settlers on the island – remembers those years of insurgency well. 'There was nothing here,' he says. 'No electricity, no pucca roads, no piped water.' There was only the ULFA.

Boys growing up on the island during those days had no idea about the outside world and its possibilities, Beda said. Their role models were the older boys who went to the ULFA training camps in Bhutan and Myanmar and came back as militant commanders. Kidnappings, shootings and killings were common.

It was only around 2004–05 that the ULFA lost its grip and violence began to wind down. The return of peace saw the beginning of backpacker tourism. The cycle of violence gradually gave way to a positive cycle of peace and greater prosperity.

The first foreign travellers to visit Majuli were Europeans. A Frenchman had come and spent time on the island in 2004, Beda recalled. He stayed in the house of Beda's friend Danny Gam. When he was leaving, the Frenchman advised Danny to set up a resort and helped him with it. When Danny eventually got the place going he asked his French friend to name it.

A year later, a Danish traveller came and stayed with Beda. The hut we were staying in had come about as a result of that traveller's visit. It carried a Scandinavian name, Yggdrasil. It is the name of the Tree of Life in Norse mythology. Beda said, 'We cannot give them anything, so we ask them to give the name, to thank them.'

The violence of the past has mostly ended. Of the four ULFA men who kidnapped and killed Ghose, three died violent deaths. One, Mridul Hazarika, was shot dead by police in 2006. A second, Amrit Dutta, died in an encounter with CRPF and police in Majuli in 2008. The body of the gang leader, Rajib Das, was found in a forest in Majuli in 2013. Only one of the four men involved in Ghose's killing had the fortune to end up in jail, alive.

No harm came to the ULFA leadership who, after returning from Bangladesh where they were based during the years of insurgency, are now living comfortable lives with the assistance of the Indian government, in places like Delhi, Guwahati and Dibrugarh. Only Paresh Baruah, the group's military commander, did not return, and is now leading his own faction, the ULFA (Independent), reportedly from somewhere in Yunnan in China.

The concerns of locals now is turning more towards 'development', and all that it brings. The Assam Chief Minister Sarbananda Sonowal wants to link the island by rail. He also wants to make it Assam's first Wi-Fi district. A proposal to build a bridge to Majuli from Jorhat has been approved by the central and state governments.

The idea of busloads and trainloads of tourists descending on Majuli is one that Beda, despite being in the tourism business himself, shudders at. He prefers the backpackers from around the world who currently land up in Majuli. They are real travellers, he says, and they bring knowledge of the world to him.

With crowds, traffic jams and more office buildings and shops everywhere, the character of Majuli will be gone forever, Beda fears.

It is sad that the Chief Minister, who is from Majuli, is unable to discern what Beda does – that Majuli's soul, its uniqueness, is unlikely to survive the assaults of mass tourism. Profit and convenience are not what spiritual Majuli is about.

38

Onwards

NEXT MORNING, WE SET off from Majuli towards a smaller river island. Our boat was a wooden bhut-bhuti, its planks worn from years of battling the elements. The crew consisted of a trio of Mishing men: Asud, Manjit and Holiram. Out on the river, the water was the usual muddy brown, full of whorls and eddies. The sky above was grey, overcast.

An uneventful ride of around an hour on the river brought us to a small river island, with grassland that gave way to trees further inland. A short walk took us to a clearing where a couple of fishermen working a little wooden dugout canoe had set up their nets. Their boat was rented, they said, in Hindi. They were reticent about divulging where they had come from and where they were heading to. Shortly after we reached, they got into their boat and pushed off into the water. They seemed frightened by our presence.

We got back to looking for the man we had come to meet, Jadav Payeng. This chapori, called Aruna chapori, was where Payeng was from.

Payeng had come to international notice for having planted an entire forest on the chapori over four decades since April 1979. What was a sandbar forty years ago had been transformed to a 550 hectare forest called Molai Kathoni, visited by numerous bird species, elephants, tigers and rhinos.

We crossed a broken bamboo hut that Asud told us had been destroyed by elephants. Further along the track we came to a cluster of bamboo huts; this was the village Payeng was from. He was not in.

We found one of his brothers and sister-in-law on the river's edge, on a beach with the forest behind. A battered pot sat on a small firewood fire near their camp. A big herd of large buffaloes with huge sweeping horns stood about 50 m away.

The floods had just receded, Jadav's brother Malbuk said. The waters had been where we were now standing. Some of his buffaloes had been swept away. Elephants had come too. He had escaped from them by jumping into the water, he said.

We left them sitting by their fire in the solitude of the river island.

On the way back, Asud told us that although he was from Majuli, he would have preferred to live closer to Jorhat. He mentioned that the boat ride to the nearest town had some dangers. But he did not explain further. Shortly after this conversation, we ran aground. The engine was cut off and Asud poled us out using a bamboo pole.

We left Majuli the following morning. The ferry ghat from which we left Majuli, to the north of the island, was smaller than the one facing Jorhat on the south bank. When we reached it, there was only a single small ferry boat, built entirely of wood and metal in the shape of a large bhut-bhuti. People had started filling it already. There were cycles stacked on the tin roof near the prow. The deck was reserved for scooters and motorcycles which were driven onto the boat over thin wooden planks not much wider than a tyre's width. It was a severe test of riding ability. A shaky rider and his motorcycle could promptly land in the river. Seating was on benches made of wooden planks under the foredeck, atop whose tin roof a bunch of men sat playing a game of cards. No one spoke about what time the boat might leave. It was clearly the wrong question to ask here.

Commerce had not made much headway on the ghat. Unlike busier river ports where rows of shacks do business selling milky tea, rice and curry meals, and cigarettes, here there were only four small sheds. And not one of them sold tea. One was selling rice and curry meals, a couple sold cigarettes and bottled water. The last one had better fare. Akshay disappeared for a while as we were waiting for the ferry to fill up, and came back looking much more satisfied with life than he had a few minutes earlier. 'Apong?' I asked. 'Lao pani' was his laconic reply. Lao pani is the local rice beer.

Our co-passengers were a mix of rural and small-town folks, including many who by their appearance were from the Mishing tribe. The boat, which was like a local bus that went from village to village, set off and stopped a short while later at a chapori to pick up more passengers. People lined the river bank near their thatched huts waiting for it to halt. There were older women dressed in saris and men in plain and often frayed shirts and trousers. The younger ones were fashionably clad in churidar kurtas, skirts, jeans and tees.

The process of bringing the boat to a halt involved a bit of athletics. First, the ferry pulled near the bank. One man with a rope leapt across the gap between boat and land and raced to tie it to a tree. Another man leapt off from the other end of the boat and, in the absence of anywhere to tie his anchor rope to, simply kept hanging on to it for dear life. By this process, both ends of the boat were brought and held stationery at the river's edge against the current.

More passengers embarked and filled the benches around us. The boat started moving again, out over the fast, muddy waters. I heard some clucking noises from somewhere nearby, but could not see the source of the sounds. Eventually I realized that the bag the passenger in front of me, a woman with two small children, had deposited at my feet, was moving. It contained a live chicken, some grain and a motorcycle helmet. The chicken, not happy with this river journey, was announcing its displeasure between mouthfuls of grain.

In the distance, we could see lush green countryside, the occasional village and water. Lots of water. Waters of the Subansiri, a major tributary of the Brahmaputra – the two meet around Majuli. The topography was curious. One moment the river bank was close at hand, and the next a distant vision.

Floods had receded less than two weeks ago, the young man sitting next to me said, and the ferry service, which was suspended during the flooding, had resumed barely a week ago. His name was Ramayan, and he was from the Mishing tribe. He had come to Majuli to visit his sister who was married into a family there. Now he was on his way back home to Gohpur on the north bank. He was a college graduate, he said, but had no job; he worked as a trader, selling rice and other groceries. He had one brother who had found a lucrative job with the police and was posted in Guwahati. Another brother was in the army and was posted in Punjab, near India's border with Pakistan.

Ramayan looked out at the picturesque green landscape and rued the lack of development. There were no factories in these parts, he said. There were not even concrete buildings. He wished someone – perhaps the government – would build 'pucca' housing for people. He wanted factories that would provide jobs for people such as himself. He had no use for the idyllic scenery.

At the far bank where we disembarked at a ghat that was even smaller than the one we had started from – this one had no shacks at all, and no people waiting for boats – the sole Magic Van was full before we got to it. The driver tried valiantly to fit us in but even his heroic efforts were to no avail. There might have been room in that

vehicle for a chicken or two. We watched it depart and settled down
to wait at the empty riverbank for whatever might show up next.

We had barely finished a cigarette each when another Magic drove
up. The driver was a man not given to conversation; or perhaps he
could not understand my broken Assamese. He simply shook his
head when we asked whether he was going to Bihpuria, from where
we would find the connecting vehicle to our next stop. We could not
get out of him exactly where he was headed. So we waited silently
across the narrow road from him, while he sat in his empty van at
the empty ghat. After another smoke I gave it a second try. This
time he agreed to go to Bihpuria but asked for Rs 400 to reserve the
vehicle. I had no idea how far it was. We agreed on Rs 350 and got
in. We had driven barely a couple of hundred metres when a woman
with a baby hailed the vehicle. She was accompanied by a couple of
young men. The driver halted and, without bothering to check with
us, took on these passengers into the 'reserved' vehicle. We did not
protest; how could we leave this woman with her little baby on the
road in what seemed the middle of nowhere?

A little further down, an old woman hailed the vehicle and got
on. Then a young girl. Then a man. By the end we had nine people
in the vehicle, not counting the baby.

We got to Bihpuria and the driver asked us for our full Rs 350
… but he collected his tens and twenties from the other passengers
too. We found another Magic that got us to Narayanpur, from
where we found a bus that would take us to our next destination,
Biswanath Chariali.

39

Biswanath

BISWANATH CHARIALI TOWN HAS precious little going for it. It is a highway stop whose best landmark is a concrete 'ghanta ghar' or clock tower. For the rest, it is a collection of featureless shops and houses. The traffic is loony, with vehicles from rickshaws to buses jostling for space.

The town is a few kilometres from Biswanath Ghat on the north bank of the Brahmaputra which is an ancient Hindu temple town. According to myth, it was founded by Banasur, the king of Sonitpur, which is modern-day Tezpur. Banasur occurs as a character in the Mahabharata, an ancient text that grew by a gradual process of accretion over several centuries starting around 950 BC. He also appears in the Bhagavata Purana. He is described as a great asura devotee of Shiva who fought against Lord Krishna.

The oldest existing structure in Biswanath Ghat now is a Shiva temple from the Ahom era. Its date too is uncertain, but it is not less than 250 years old. The temple is said to have been built over an ancient Shiva Linga at the site.

There are scattered signs of far older structures from bygone eras. A major one among them is a 'yoni' around which are the remains of a Shiva temple that reappears each year during the winter months when the Brahmaputra's water levels fall. For the rest of the year, it is hidden under the water. This is described as 'pre-Ahom' by the Archaeological Survey of India. The Ahoms arrived in what is now called Assam in 1228, but came to have control of the north bank of the Brahmaputra only centuries later, after vanquishing the Chutiya kingdom. The Archaeological Survey does not say how long before the Ahom period the ruined temple was built. A legendary king named Arimatta is said to have ruled from Biswanath in the fourteenth century. Was this, perhaps, related to him?

The scenes around the ghat are picture postcards of timelessness. A few distant shapes of fishermen in dugout canoes. Silhouettes of hills on the horizon. Rippling waters reflecting watercolour skies. The ghat itself is sleepy, with the rhythms of life that seem unchanged for centuries.

It was overcast and started to rain as we reached there. Slippery old steps led down to the water where a few women were bathing, semi-clothed in saris, while others were washing their clothes. Not far off, a couple of men were repairing a small wooden canoe. We went walking up and down the length of the ghat to see if there was a slightly larger – and less leaky – boat to be found to take us to the island of Umatumoni across the narrow channel. There was none.

So we returned and asked the men if they would row us across. One of them agreed, and led us to a little wooden dugout canoe. The boat was barely three feet across at its widest and rode low in the water. When the two of us and the boatman embarked, the top was around six inches above the water line. It felt unstable, like riding a shaky bicycle, except that we were on water, and the water was deep and moving dangerously fast. There was, of course, no question of life jackets anywhere here.

After all the trips on ferries and motorized boats that effortlessly navigated the Brahmaputra, this was our first experience of watching a man wrestle with the mighty river.

The river looks different when you are so close to it. There are muscular ripples on its surface that speak of currents and eddies in its opaque depths. Our boatman was a good one, but the physical effort it took to row across the river was apparent. Akhsay and I barely stirred throughout the ride because it was clear that any sudden movement might cause the boat to tip over and send us to our deaths.

We got safely across and had just begun our walk on the island when it started to rain. The drizzle quickly turned into a downpour. We walked through the driving rain up the forested hill to a small temple built over an ancient rock that had at some time in the distant past been sacralized. This was the rock known as Sukreswar. It had ancient carvings of animals and bird forms on it. Over it, four walls and a tin roof had been erected.

The only visitors to this holy place apart from us was a group of goats trying to shelter from the rain. We joined them for a while before walking on down a path that had been cut into the hillside. It was slippery in the rain. The other side of the thin island lay before us, and then the main channel of the river. Across, visible in the distance as a line of green, was the Kaziranga forest. The Karbi hills loomed behind it.

We wandered on along the path and after some time found ourselves at the only human settlement on the island – a camp of forest guards. They welcomed us and brought us tea. We were chatting with them when a bhut-bhuti boat arrived. It was the forest ranger out on patrol from Kaziranga. All the guards except one picked up their ancient .303 rifles and rushed off into the rain.

The man who stayed back in camp with us was older than the rest. Upon hearing that we were visiting from Mumbai, he told us he had been there and seen the Elephanta Caves, the Taj Mahal Hotel and Shah Rukh Khan's house. He had even had a meal at the Hilton, he said – had we ever been there?

It transpired that his daughter, who grew up in his house in the small town of Pathshala in Barpeta district of Assam, had graduated in hotel management from an institute in Bengaluru and found a job at the Hilton. She was now on a cruise liner somewhere near the US, the proud father said. He pulled out a battered old Nokia phone and struggled with it, trying to show us photos of his daughter and himself.

There, that was him in Mumbai! And did we recognize the man next to him? No? It was none less than the general manager of the Hilton himself! And there, that was his daughter, with his son, who was younger.

The photo showed a smiling young woman with East Asian features standing next to a red hatchback car. The proud father on the little river island in the Brahamputra whose only habitation was the foresters' camp smiled at the photo.

40

What's in a Name?

THE NEXT DAY, WE left Biswanath Chariali by a local Magic minivan with a cracked windscreen for the next town down the highway towards Tezpur, a place called Jamuguri Hat. En route, the vehicle, a seven-seater carrying about twice that number, kept stopping to try and live up to its name by magically fitting in the entire travelling population of the district. 'You have to squeeze them in,' the driver berated the handyman when a couple of men refused to board the already overflowing minivan. His faith in the elasticity of human bodies was immense.

By and by, rattling and rolling, we reached a fork in the road that leads to the Nag Shankar temple. Here, we disembarked, and shouldering our luggage, started the walk of a kilometre or so to the temple. There was no transport available. The road was empty. It was a beautiful day, with light clouds, and the walk led past paddy fields an unreal shade of green. Old mango trees lined the road. At the end of the road was the temple, whose origins are lost in mythology. The present structure there is a relatively new one, an ordinary concrete temple. It is believed to be the reincarnation of older structures that have long since disappeared. The first temple at the spot is said to have been built by Nagasankara, a legendary king who was said to have been born of the Karatoya river – the great river of old, which is now reduced to a stream in Bangladesh – in the fourth century AD.

The present structure is of more recent vintage, but it houses weathered stone structures of indeterminate antiquity. There is also an old pond, its waters green with age, which houses a population of black soft shell turtles that are officially listed as extinct in the wild. Local legend has it that the creatures respond to the name 'Mohan'. I spotted one of the fellows swimming lazily at a distance and called out 'Mohan', upon which he – or perhaps she – immediately dove underwater. However, a few pieces of peanut sweets brought a Mohan back. The old turtle came right to the water's edge, where steps lead down to the pond, with a little Mohan riding on her back. A swarm of tiny fish followed the duo. She eyed me through beady eyes, waiting to catch the sweets as I tossed them into the water, before lazily swimming off.

The turtles share the pond with a gaggle of large geese who noisily walked about in a line around the water's edge squawking away at the few human visitors there. One of them had a red crown of sorts and looked quite unlike any goose I had seen until then. There were also a few goats and some overweight dogs who lolled around, eating biscuits from temple visitors and generally chilling out. The geese pushed and shoved with the dogs and goats for the biscuits but everyone gave the turtles, who have wicked teeth, a wide berth.

It was a placid, cheerful little menagerie.

We left this charming bubble to head to Tezpur, a city on the banks of the Brahmaputra, passing en route a little town with a nomenclature issue. It is called Sootea. The boards in Assamese spell it as 'Chutia,' with 'Ch' pronounced as 'S'. The bus conductor, who was calling out the names of stops, refrained from hollering the name of this particular one. Chutia is a popular cuss word in Hindi.

Tezpur claims origins that date back to the times before recorded history. Its origin myth is rooted in the Mahabharata, where it is known as Sonitpur, the city of blood. The story goes that Sonitpur was ruled by the great asura king named Banasura. This mighty asura was a devotee of Lord Shiva, and his penances to the God had been rewarded by a boon that made Shiva himself protector of Banasura. Accordingly, Banasura became invincible.

Unfortunately for him, his daughter Usha fell in love with Lord Krishna's grandson Aniruddha, after she saw him in a dream. The young lad was abducted and brought to Usha by use of magic. This, of course, brought Lord Krishna into the battle. He launched a rescue mission. At this, Lord Shiva, true to his role as Banasura's protector, arrived to battle Lord Krishna. The world would certainly have ended in this titanic struggle if Lord Krishna had not managed by some strategem to put Lord Shiva to sleep. After this feat, he began the war against Banasura. The battle raged and rivers of blood flowed. In the end, Lord Krishna lopped off 998 of the asura's 1,000 arms. At this, Banasura surrendered. The story had a happy ending – Usha and Aniruddha got married and so the asura became Aniruddha's 'sasura', meaning father-in-law.

Today's Tezpur is a bustling little city of over a lakh people. All its principal roads have names that are acronyms about whose full forms we could only speculate. We passed N.C. Road, N.B. Road, N.T. Road and J.B. Road. The only road whose full form we could confidently guess was M.G. Road. Every town and city in India has one and they all commemorate the Father of the Nation. However,

Tezpur's M.G. Road seemed unique in being the only road in the city that is *not* known by its abbreviated name. Locals refer to it simply as 'main road'.

There did not seem to be much to see on main road apart from Poki, the old home of Jyoti Prasad Agarwala, a pioneer of Assamese cinema. His ancestors had migrated to Assam from Rajasthan generations before his birth, and Jyoti Prasad grew up as a citizen of the state. He made the first Assamese film, *Joymoti*, shooting for which started in 1933 in a tea estate near Tezpur owned by the Agarwala family. The film, based on a play about an Ahom princess named Joymoti who was tortured to death as a result of internal machinations in the Ahom court, was written by one of the greats of Assamese literature: Lakshminath Bezbaroa. It was released in 1935. Unfortunately, Assam in those days did not have a single cinema hall. Assamese filmmaker and critic Utpal Borpujari, in an article on the history of cinema in Northeast India, mentioned that it had to be released at Raunak Cinema in Calcutta. 'The lack of screening space meant *Joymoti* was an unmitigated financial disaster,' wrote Borpujari.

Agarwala's contemporaries in the Tezpur art scene of the time included at least two other giants of Assamese culture, Bishnu Prasad Rabha and Phani Sarma. The 'Kala Guru' or culture guru of contemporary Assam, Rabha – a member of the Revolutionary Communist Party of India – was known for his work in music and theatre. One of his popular songs '*Joya nai*', also contains references to the princess Joymoti. Rabha and Agarwala worked with the younger Sarma, who rose from humble beginnings to become a star actor and playwright. Sarma's initiation into acting happened at the Baan Theatre in Tezpur, founded in 1906, where he was initially a gatekeeper. His early roles, including in *Joymati*, were mainly those of villains. By and by he became a hero.

The original theatre building is no longer around. A new building inaugurated in 1958 is the current structure. It remains in use as a place where plays are staged. It is located a couple of kilometres away from the river.

A walk or electric rickshaw ride from there leads to a hillock overlooking the Brahmaputra called Agnigarh, the fortress of fire. This is the location of the mythical fort of Banasur's daughter Usha. Today it hosts a modest park from the top of which there is a good view of the town and the river. Another walk or short ride that leads past two large ponds takes one to the Zahaz Ghat, meaning 'ship ghat', on the banks of the Brahmaputra. There were no ships on the ship ghat. A forlorn little rowboat stood tethered to a wooden post driven into the crumbling riverside earth. There were few people at the riverside to watch the spectacular sunset. The town carried on busily with its business; perhaps its inhabitants, long inured to the beauty of the daily sunsets, had no time to stand and stare.

41
Looking for the Xihu

NEXT MORNING WE SET off to go on a boat ride in search of a group of increasingly rare inhabitants who are truly indigenous to the Brahmaputra valley: river dolphins. The rivers around Tezpur are reputed to be home to many of them, and we wanted to glimpse the beautiful creatures that had eluded us so far on our journey. I had a number for a local boatman through my Shillong friend, the writer Ankush Saikia. When I called the boatman, he said he would meet us at his village under the Kalia Bhomora Bridge that spans the Brahmaputra on the outskirts of Tezpur.

Boatman Arfan Ali was very courteous, but demanded Rs 3,000 for a ride that Ankush had said should cost Rs 600. It was, Ankush had said, a short ride out to the spot where the dolphins were usually to be found. Even accounting for the usual difference in rates that tourists are subjected to, Ali's demand seemed like daylight robbery. However, while there were other boats at the spot, there were no other boatmen in sight whom we could approach for a better deal. We were forced to go with Ali.

He took us to a little sandbar in the middle of the river, hardly a kilometre upstream from the Kalia Bhomora Bridge. There he dropped anchor, and asked us to disembark and wait for the dolphins to make their appearance.

We waited. We tiptoed up and down the 100 m of fine white sand on the sandbar which was barely an inch or two higher than the surrounding waters. We scanned the surface of the muddy green-brown river in all directions, and spotted foam and branches of trees floating past. Ali suddenly shouted 'There!' and pointed at a spot somewhere between the sandbar and the bank on the Tezpur side. We looked but saw nothing.

Ali asked us to settle down for the watch. He had brought along two red plastic chairs. He now placed these on the sand. We sat there, literally in the middle of the river, and waited. After some time, there was what sounded like a splash somewhere in the river. We tried to follow the sound but saw nothing. A couple more splashes followed, with the same result. Then Akshay claimed he had spotted a dark shape in the water. I was looking blankly at the river, having given up hope of seeing anything, when I saw something flash out of the water. It was gone in a trice.

We waited on after that, but saw nothing more. Akshay, in exasperation, even turned to YouTube for help; amazingly enough, we had data signal on that sandbar. He found a soundtrack that he claimed was the mating call of the Amazon dolphin and played it from his phone, but the Assamese dolphins were immune to these fraudulent Brazilian charms and failed to put in an appearance. Akshay surmised that their languages were probably different.

A different question of languages had been bothering me since we met Ali. We had spoken to one another in Hindi and Assamese, but his Hindi was accented in an unusual way. Now, to fill the emptiness of what seemed a pointless wait, I tried to chat him up. 'Where are you from?' I asked. 'Tezpur,' he replied.

'Your family is originally from Tezpur?' I enquired.

'A little further down the river,' he replied, before exclaiming, 'There! Big one!'

I turned to look but saw nothing.

Anyway, after some more staring into the opaque waters of the Brahmaputra, even Ali felt the need to put in more of an effort. We got back in the boat and rode a little further upstream, to a larger sandbar close to the point where the Jia Bhoroli River – known as the Kameng in Arunachal Pradesh, from where it flows down into Assam – meets the Brahmaputra with a loud crash. It sounds like the sea, and there are waves that ripple down to the shore of the char a kilometre or so away on which we now dropped anchor.

We were rewarded almost immediately with the sight of a dolphin, sleek and black, flashing out of the water. Then another. And another; or perhaps it was the same one resurfacing in a different spot. There seemed to be at least two, one big and one small, and they were having a good time gambolling in the water. Gradually, their appearances grew more distant from us and after a while we lost sight of them. It had, however, been a satisfying sight. We had finally seen the Xihu.

The Xihu is the local name for the Ganges River Dolphin, or *Platanista gangetica*. The IUCN Red Data Book on Dolphins, Porpoises and Whales of the World lists it as a 'Vulnerable' species. 'Formerly apparently quite abundant, there is evidence that populations have declined more or less throughout the range,' the book says. 'The major problems are: extensive habitat damage, particularly through dam construction; indirect and incidental catching; pollution; and boat traffic'. The dolphin is found in the Ganges, Brahmaputra, Karnaphuli and Meghna river systems, from the foot of the Himalayas to the limits of the tidal zone in India, Bangladesh, Nepal and Bhutan, according to IUCN.

The female dolphin is bigger than the male. The average male gets to between 2.0 and 2.1 metres long, while the average female is 2.5 metres long.

The Brahmaputra, unlike the Ganges or Ganga, is a free flowing river. It is still possible for the dolphin to survive here. The two great rivers eventually merge into one another, and creatures big and small can move from one river to the other. If the Brahmaputra and its living creatures survive, they can flow back into the Ganga. The section of the Brahmaputra between Jorhat and Tezpur is one of the last remaining refuges of the Xihu. The IUCN Red Data Book recommends that this area should be declared a river dolphin sanctuary – a recommendation on which there has long been no progress.

We took the brief boat ride back and in a few minutes were at the riverside village below the bridge. Ali was most hospitable and insisted we join him for tea at the village tea shop, a ramshackle bamboo structure with a floor of beaten earth in which plastic tables and chairs had been placed. A group of men, most of them wearing lungis and sporting beards, sat inside engaged in a lively conversation. The language of conversation was one I instantly recognized. It was the language my maternal grandmother used to speak in, the Mymensingh dialect of Bengali, from what is now Bangladesh.

The village was one of the people known in Assam as Miyas, the Bengali Muslims, mostly of Mymensingh origin, whose ancestors had been lured to the state by the colonial administration as farmers to increase paddy and jute cultivation. At that time, in the late nineteenth and early twentieth century, there was no international boundary separating Assam from what is now Bangladesh. Indeed, there was not even a provincial or state boundary. From the time of the British annexation of the former Ahom kingdom's territories after the Anglo-Burmese war of 1826, until an administrative reorganization in 1874, Assam had been part of a Bengal that included today's West Bengal, Bangladesh, Bihar and Odisha. Between 1905 and 1911, when the Mymensinghia migration really peaked, East Bengal and Assam was a single province again. Driven by a desire to increase revenues, the East India Company and, after 1857, the British government of India, encouraged cultivation of 'wastelands' in Assam. The cultivation of rice and jute in these 'wastelands' in the Brahmaputra floodplains required human labour, for which the Bengali Muslim peasantry of neighbouring Mymensingh was encouraged, until about 1930, to migrate.

42

Rhino Country

THE NEPALI-SPEAKING DRIVER WHO drove us from Tezpur to Kaziranga pointed out several villages on the edges of the national park that he said had come up in the past seven or eight years. The people, according to him, were illegal Bangladeshi migrants who had been settled there by local politicians.

I had read something about this in the newspapers at various points. On checking, I found newspaper reports dated 3 September 2014 that said the Gauhati High Court had ordered the state government to clear encroachments in four 'additions' to the Kaziranga National Park and hand them over to park authorities. The state's Congress government headed by Tarun Gogoi had proposed paying compensation of Rs 10 lakh to each encroaching household and resettlement in model villages. The reports quoted state environment minister Rockybul Hussain as saying that there had been no encroachment in any of the Kaziranga National Park's notified areas, though he conceded that there may have been some encroachments in areas added later to the park.

There was also a report of the Comptroller and Auditor General of India from a year earlier that noted an increase in hotels, dhabas and resorts, including fancy ones, along the highway which were turning the agricultural lands into commercial use. The National Green Tribunal, too, had noted the existence of illegal structures near the park boundary and asked the Assam government to restrict such constructions.

At the charming place we were staying at in Kaziranga, called Wild Grass, the staff was local, a mix of people from the various communities that live in the neighbouring villages. The main population, since the days of the earliest tea estates, has been a mix of Assamese peoples of various castes and members of the plains tribes who were transported to Assam to work as tea-garden labour and came to be known as 'Baganiyas' or tea tribals. These people, from Adivasi groups such as the Santhal, Oraon, Munda and Telanga, gradually became one of the communities of Assam in the past 150 years. They all had different languages, but in time a new link language emerged. Its speakers often refer to it as Baganiya. It is a pidgin of Bengali, Bhojpuri, Assamese and the various tribal languages. There are differences between the Assam Baganiya, which has more Assamese words, and the Bengal Baganiya. Both of these are relatives of Sadri or Nagpuri, which has a greater Bhojpuri influence.

Gokul, our guide, was a Baganiya. A dark, wiry young man, he accompanied us in an open Maruti Gypsy on a drive around the edges of the national park. The season during which it is open to visitors had not yet begun when we visited. Entry into the park was not possible. This disadvantage was offset by one serious advantage: there were no tourists around.

The road was a mud track that runs on an embankment. On one side were the huts, mostly made of bamboo and mud, in which the local farmers stay, with their paddy fields stretching green around them. The floods had just receded; some fields still showed the signs. The dead brown paddy had not been replanted.

On the other side was the park itself – grassy plains and wetlands slowly giving way to taller elephant grass and then to a line of trees in the distance. The map showed that the Brahmaputra formed the boundary of the park on the far side. Entry from the river side was not permitted at any time.

Some trees in the fields near the road had branches festooned in long clumps of elephant grass that were slowly turning into hay. I wondered who had hung them up there, seven or eight feet above the ground, before realizing with a little shock that it was the flood waters.

The floods that year had been pretty bad, Gokul said. The waters had receded only about twenty days ago. Many of the small farmers had lost their crops and were now subsisting on fishing. The park animals too had been affected by the floods, as they are every year. Many of them had migrated out of the park towards the adjacent hills of Karbi Anglong that rise immediately after the narrow strip of flat land, with its highway and a smattering of tea estates and paddy farms, on which the human population of the area lives.

The main danger the animals encounter in their annual migration is the highway that runs between the park and the hills. For the park staff, ensuring that the animals are able to successfully cross that road without ending up as roadkill is a challenge. Once outside the park, the animals also face heightened risks from poachers. The forest department sends armed guards and police escorts to shadow the VIPs of Kaziranga, the rhinos, but that's not possible to do for all animals. Plenty of deer end up as bush meat.

Flood times are good times not only for hunters but also for fishermen. They put out lines with hooks on which they attach small fish as bait and leave them in the streams overnight. In the morning, they go to survey the catch and collect whatever they get.

Sometimes, when the flood waters are high, they also use traditional cane fish baskets to trap big fish. It is not uncommon for fish weighing a good 10 or 12 kg to end up on highways during floods, and I have seen mobile phone videos of people catching them with their bare hands, basically by jumping on them and grabbing them as they swim past.

By this time, more than two weeks after the floods, things were pretty much back to normal. We bumped along on the single lane mud track between the park and the paddy fields. In the distance, a dark shape was visible in the grasslands of the park, perhaps about 300 m away. At first I thought it was a buffalo. On closer inspection it turned out to be a rhino. Three small birds sat on its back and an egret stood at attention nearby. Gokul cut the engine off and we sat patiently like the birds, watching the ancient creature go about its daily routine.

Not far from the rhino – less than 100 m at the most – a villager on a makeshift raft continued with his daily routine. He was busy fishing. Women sat on the roadside chatting, their backs towards the animal. Little children ran along engrossed in their play. I enquired if the rhinos bothered the villagers. 'They go away if chased nicely,' Gokul replied. Politeness is grossly underrated.

The villagers seem to treat the rhinos much as they do buffalos. They coexist comfortably for the most part.

We drove along the road a little further to see if we could spot any more animals. Apart from mistaking a tree stump in the shadows for a rhino, we saw nothing. We were returning past the place where the rhino was still grazing when a bamboo raft emerged from the grassy wetlands. A little boy sat on it beating a drum. A man was propelling the raft with a bamboo pole.

From behind the raft, a second rhino emerged, moving at a fairly rapid clip. It was fairer than the first and carried an egret on its back.

It stopped its march not far from the first rhino and began grazing peacefully.

Leaving them to their meal, we headed off towards the park's main entrance, where a stream flows. A few fishermen were in the water, pulling in their lines. Across in the grasslands on the other side of the stream, close to the edge of the water, a herd of hog deer were busy grazing. Suddenly a warning cry went up in the gathering dusk. The deer stiffened, raised their heads. There were a few moments of tension; then, they put their heads back down and went on grazing.

That cry probably meant a predator, perhaps a tiger, was on the move somewhere not too far away, Gokul explained. We saw no sign of it. The only other creatures that came into view was a long line of elephants, all Kaziranga park employees (their job is to ferry visitors for safaris during the tourist season) many along with their babies in tow, arriving for dinner.

We woke up at 4 a.m. next morning to go for our own little elephant ride around the edges of the park. Gokul and the driver were there when we emerged from our room at 4.30 a.m. The sky was just lightening with the first rays of dawn. We drove down a narrow mud track to a culvert, where the mahout was supposed to meet us with the elephant. There was no sign of the mahout or the elephant.

After a while of waiting around, looking to see if the elephant was coming, Gokul and Akshay went in search of it. The driver drove off to turn the vehicle – the lane was too narrow to turn. I waited alone at the culvert, looking around at the first stirrings of daily life. Villagers in the remains of the washed out paddy fields around me were starting their day's work. A couple emerged from a hut and walked down to a little stream. There, they just stood, and then sat on their haunches, waiting. At another place, a man, barebodied and barefoot, clad only in the fine local towel of white with red borders known as gamosa, stood looking into a pond. Further away, two men stood staring into another pond.

There seemed to be an awful lot of staring into water bodies going on. What, I wondered, were they all looking for? Fish, naturally. They had come to check their nets that they had put out the previous night.

After a while, Gokul and Akshay returned. Then the car and driver. The elephant was on its way, apparently. We had enough time to nip back to the highway and have a cup of chai at a local dhaba before it made its stately way to the culvert where we were supposed to start our ride. Eventually, a big shape lumbered up. It was Lakshmi Prasad, thirty-five, a big male tusker.

The choice of the culvert for starting the ride immediately made sense when we saw him. Climbing on to an elephant's back can be a complicated affair. Real experts can run up an elephant trunk but novices attempting it risk frightening or annoying the elephant and ending up dead. The height makes climbing on a challenge even if the animal is seated. To climb on to an elephant, one has to get to an elevation from which one can drop on to its back.

Now the mahout took Lakshmi Prasad below the culvert and backed him up next to it. We stepped on board and commenced our much delayed ride.

Lakshmi Prasad had not had time for breakfast, and seemed to be determined to have it on the move. He walked along stopping, despite the mahouts goading him with an iron ankush, to tug at branches and break them off before stuffing them into his mouth. Once in a while, he snorted loudly. All the while, his great ears kept flapping.

Akshay and I looked at the scenery around us. 'I feel a little stupid riding an elephant past mobile towers,' Akshay said. I spotted one mobile tower near us as we made our majestic way past a village of mud and thatch homes. Akshay also wondered whether it is legal to use the mobile while driving your elephant, which our mahout was doing.

Our ruminations on these matters were interrupted by a low branch of a thorny tree. We had to duck to avoid getting swept off Lakshmi Prasad's back. We managed to push off the smaller branches but got a few scratches from the thorns. Elephant safaris even past mobile towers have their moments of adventure.

Up ahead, inside the park, we spotted a long line of elephants in the distance. There were no humans in sight. Were those wild elephants or park elephants? The mahout said there was no way to tell without getting closer, and we could not get closer. So we sat there watching the elephants while Lakshmi Prasad continued with his breakfast before beginning to amble back the way we had come. En route we crossed a rhino grazing in the grassland. All around, village life continued, seemingly unmindful of these creatures.

The peaceable nature of rural life, with wild animals and humans coexisting in close proximity, can be disturbed at times. At Wild Grass, there is a board with the names of Kaziranga Park staff who have died in the line of duty. The highest number of victims have been claimed by elephants and humans. Between 2000 and 2016, wild elephants had killed four, and the 'tame' park elephants had killed two people. In earlier years, between 1968 and 1985, it was poachers who had done most of the killing, murdering four forest and home guards. In 2000, two park employees were killed by a truck on the highway. That made it six kills each for elephants and humans. Rhinos had killed three and wild buffalos two, in all those years.

The casualties on the side of the animals is far higher. Elephants in particular have been at the receiving end of a lot of hostility from humans. They are forced to travel long distances in search of food, because they 'harvest' one area before moving on to another, and eventually circle back after the plants they feed on have had time to grow again. They naturally have elephantine appetites. As human populations have grown, their habitats have gradually shrunk. Even their corridors are now blocked in many places, for many reasons. They find foraging for food a problem; if they cannot move about freely, they starve. In Numaligarh, near Kaziranga, the Numaligarh Refinery built a golf course on an elephant corridor and erected a 2-km wall around it. Activists raised an outcry and eventually the National Green Tribunal ordered its demolition. By then, the wall had already caused an estimated twelve elephant deaths.

The annual floods, too, take a heavy toll, especially on the smaller animals, but experts view that very differently from the deaths due to artificial reasons. 'Kaziranga has been surviving floods for centuries,' Divisional Forest Officer Rohini Saikia explained. The floods, he said, are a 'necessary evil'. The unique park habitat exists because of the floods.

He viewed the death of animals due to floods as nature doing its work; merely the principle of 'survival of the fittest' in operation. However, his administration does lend a hand to the animals. They have constructed a few highlands inside the park and proposed to build thirty-three more so that mothers with babies have a place to take refuge when the waters rise.

The view that Kaziranga would not exist without floods is one that is echoed by wildlife veterinarian Dr Panjit Basumatary of the Centre for Wildlife Rehabilitation and Conservation. The CWRC hit global headlines when Prince William and his wife Kate Middleton visited the place in April 2016 during a visit to Kaziranga, and photos of them feeding baby elephants and rhinos were published around the world. This organization rescues animals, mostly babies, during floods, and brings them to the centre where they are looked after until they are old enough to look after themselves in the wild.

Kaziranga is around 70 per cent wetlands, and without the annual flooding this would gradually give way to forest, which is not a suitable habitat for rhinos, swamp deer, hog deer and other wetland species, Dr Basumatary explained. The Kaziranga wetlands are also the breeding place for a lot of fish species that disperse far and wide through the waters of the Brahmaputra, he said. The entire region's fish supply depends on this organic connection between the wetlands and the river – a connection largely snapped by human construction activities in case of unprotected wetlands.

Many fish species do not lay their eggs in the currents of the fast-moving river. They enter the wetlands called 'beel' with the rising waters of the rainy season, where their young hatch. The hatchlings swim out with the receding floodwaters. The process organically restores the fish population of both the wetlands and the river.

43

Wild Babies*

IT WAS THE START of a typical day at work for Tarun Gogoi. Pulling on his camouflage-patterned gumboots on a warm, humid morning, he took a large white canister in each hand and began to walk down a grassy path between the trees. His colleague Mahadeb, similarly attired and holding two canisters of his own, followed. Veterinarian Dr Basumatary brought up the rear. The trio carefully stepped over a low electric fence. Then Gogoi and Mahadeb walked into what looked like an unevenly shaped field, the perimeter of which was marked by bamboo sticks driven into the ground. There, Gogoi stopped.

He began to call out, a call that to my uninitiated ears sounded like he was trying to emulate a goose. Something quite different answered the call. From a corner of the field, where it had been hidden from view by trees and bushes, a baby rhinoceros emerged and began to walk towards Gogoi.

* This chapter first appeared in *The Hindu Sunday Magazine*

It was followed, in quick order, by three more – all of who marched briskly, in a polite line the likes of which any railway station in India would be proud to witness. There, without any pushing or shoving, they began to drink the lactogen milk from the canisters Gogoi and Mahadeb were holding. Barely a minute later, they were done. Morning feeding was over for the baby rhinos at CWRC.

The Centre was home to seven rhinos at the time I visited, all rescued orphans. They shared the grounds with four baby elephants, also orphans like the rhinos, and four leopards with similar personal histories who owing to their carnivorous, predatory dispositions, are kept in wire-mesh enclosures closed on all sides. Other creatures, big and small, keep passing through. There are various kinds of deer, from time to time, and birds and the odd tiger or snake. According to Rathin Barman, the head of CWRC, they had so far treated 5,262 cases.

The Brahmaputra's annual floods are the time when they get the most cases, as the rising waters engulf the wetlands that make up much of Kaziranga. Then they have to work practically around the clock, rescuing the bedraggled beasts and their offspring.

It was after one particularly bad flood, in 1998, that the Centre was born. 'The Kaziranga National Park lost many animals that year, including around a hundred rhinos. Many animals were rescued too, but no one knew what to do with them,' said Barman. 'There was no proper place or infrastructure. Then the thought of a rescue centre came to the minds of authorities.' They started with one rescue vehicle, one doctor and one animal keeper that year. By 2001, they had enough cases and expertise to justify a permanent centre.

On 28 August 2002, with the collaboration of the Assam government, the Wildlife Trust of India and International Fund for Animal Welfare, CWRC was inaugurated. Although there are other wildlife rescue centres in India, CWRC is the only one that takes in practically any wild creature, from tiger to eagle to snake. Its most unique residents, however, are the ones found only in Kaziranga, the rhinos.

The Centre got its first baby rhino in 2002. 'This building was still under construction. The baby was less than fifteen days old. We knew because the umbilical cord was still attached to it,' said Barman. They had only some small feeding bottles then, the kind used to feed human babies. 'We gave it lactogen. In hardly two seconds, it finished the milk and started asking for more ... again and again.' Exasperation drove Barman to experiment. 'I sent somebody to the market to buy a big, two-litre soft drink bottle. We emptied it, and used the bottle to feed the rhino,' he says. It worked, and that became the baby rhino's feeding bottle.

An elephant calf came soon after. Gogoi, who had joined the Forest Department as a mahout, was brought in to look after it. They discovered that caring for rhino and elephant calves was rather like caring for human babies. They had to be fed every few hours, day and night, and that meant some people had to stay up all night to look after them. There was also a bigger problem: the elephant calves cried if they were left alone. 'We installed bunks next to them for the keepers, who had to sleep where the elephant calves could touch them,' says Barman.

However, they had to learn not to give the animals too much love, said Gogoi. It becomes a problem if the animals get too attached to humans because then they can't handle the wild. Despite that, there are cases of animals, particularly elephants, who form deep and lasting attachments with people. 'So far, we have released around twenty elephants into the wild. But some just refuse to go. We have had three such cases,' said Barman. 'They kept coming back.'

Now those elephants are with the Forest Department, working in Kaziranga National Park. 'One of them came to us when he was around a month old, and the other two came when they were around six months old,' recalls Barman. He ascribes the return of these three elephants to their personalities. 'Every human being has his or her own personality. Similarly, most animals have their own personalities. Elephants, especially, are very intelligent animals. They have large brains. With them you can see personalities easily.'

He considered the three elephants who returned to be both gregarious and a tad lazy. 'These three love human company and the food they get ... they don't like the hardships of the wild,' he noted. Their character flaws may not be the only reasons for their return from freedom, however. Elephants, Barman pointed out, move in herds, unlike the solitary rhinos. When it is time to let them go, they are taken out for forest walks with their keepers. There, they come across herds of wild elephants. In time, they get adopted into one herd or another ... but the process is not easy. 'A wild herd will try to dominate the strangers. They will come and knock these elephants, push them around,' said Dr Basumatary, who is CWRC's lead veterinarian. The process of adoption into a herd is easier for the females, he added. The boys have a rougher time of it.

Life in the wild is hard for every creature, big or small. The relative safety of the Centre has made a great impression on at least one female barking deer. 'We hand-raised her,' said Barman, 'and eventually released her into the wild with an ear-tag (for identification). A year later, we found her back here. She had brought her baby! After three or four months, when the baby was relatively grown up, both of them disappeared. The following year, she was here again, with another baby. And this year again, with the latest baby!'

The smart deer had not been put off by the presence of the four leopards, one male and three females, who lived in two adjacent enclosures in the centre within what probably constitutes sniffing distance for both species. The male leopard was a big, sleek fellow, fully grown at five, and he was pacing up and down when I spotted him. 'He is very tame now,' Dr Basumatary informed me, although he didn't look anything like tame to me.

The enclosure next to his was much bigger, with thick undergrowth and many large trees. As I walked closer to it, I saw some dappled yellow and black in the green of the branches of a tree, a good twenty feet above the ground ... and then spotted the face of a snarling leopard baring its fangs. Looking around, I saw two more in the branches of nearby trees, eyeing me warily. These three female leopards, now two-and-a-half years old, were hardly three or four days old when they first came to the centre, Dr Basumatary told us. They had been found in a hole in the ground in a nearby tea estate; their mother had been killed by humans.

The most dangerous animal in the forest or outside it, even for animal rescuers who have to quite literally wrestle the beasts on occasion, is man. There is unanimity on this among the animal-keeper Gogoi, the vet Dr Basumatary and the Centre's head, Barman. 'There is only one problem during rescues. That is managing crowds,' said Barman. Around Kaziranga, people see wild animals all the time, he says, but even then, a sight as ordinary as an injured deer is enough for a crowd to gather.

The size of the crowd grows with the place of the animal in the food chain hierarchy. A tiger is sure to draw an entire village or two. 'Once a tiger strayed out from the park. It was hiding in a small bush, probably confused. Hundreds of people came out and surrounded it. The villagers wanted to see the animal,' says Barman. CWRC was called, and a vet went to tranquilize the tiger. By then, a crowd of around a hundred, including security guards armed with guns, had gathered. Suddenly, the cornered tiger burst out of the bush and charged. The guards let loose a volley of shots ... and managed to hit the vet. He was fortunate to survive but has since quit the job and now teaches in a college.

Almost everyone on the staff has their own tale of close calls and misadventures. The portly, genial Gogoi had his moment of reckoning during a leopard rescue. A sub-adult leopard – the

equivalent of a human teenager – had come out of the forest and
attacked villagers near Kaziranga. When CWRC got a call, Gogoi
went to check on it. By the time he reached the spot, a mob had
gathered, armed with sticks, and people were baying for blood; they
wanted to beat the animal to death. Gogoi spotted the leopard and
was forced to act immediately; he had to either catch the animal or
get out of the mob's way. 'So, I went and caught the animal with
my bare hands,' he said. 'It bit me here,' he pointed to his arm, 'and
scratched me.' Gogoi was able to wrestle the leopard into submission.
Apart from being one tough nut, Gogoi was also fortunate; a sub-
adult leopard is big enough to do serious damage.

Dr Basumatary had his lucky escape when he went to rescue a
grown elephant that had fallen upside down into a trench near a tea
estate. It would have taken at least three to four hours for a tame
elephant from the park to arrive to tug the trapped jumbo upright,
and he reckoned the animal might not survive that long. So, he
simply went close to the animal, ran a rope under it, and told the
crowd to pull. It worked, but of course, the wild elephant charged
right at them the moment it was upright. They had only a small lead
and were fortunate to outrun it on the wet, slippery ground.

Sometimes, luck runs out. One animal keeper who answered a
call to catch a snake did so with ease but was bitten while trying
to release it back into the forest. 'I would say it was because of
overconfidence,' said Barman. It was a black krait, one of the
deadliest and most poisonous snakes in the Indian jungle. 'Doctors
said, he's gone … within a few minutes he will be gone. For three
days, they kept saying that. He survived though.'

The animal keepers are the most important people for the
Centre, Barman said. 'They are our backbone in the field.' He rates
them, and the people from the surrounding villages – despite their
habit of gathering into crowds, which he does not like – as the
biggest supporters of Kaziranga. 'The animals from Kaziranga come

out and destroy their paddies and their houses, kill their animals and sometimes even attack them,' he says. 'With city people, for instance, if a monkey steals something from them, they say, remove all the monkeys from here.'

He is non-committal, like the rest of the staff, about the famous visit of Britain's Prince William and Kate Middleton. The stars of the tales told with relish here are those for whom the place was built: the rhinos, elephants, leopards, tigers and other animals that make CWRC their temporary home.

44

Wild Grass

A GROUP OF PEOPLE descended on Wild Grass, where we were
staying, that evening. It was the crew of an Assamese TV sitcom.
A man with a long flowing beard in a style somewhere between Karl
Marx and Rabindranath Tagore was at the head of what was clearly
the power table. Two hours later, all the other tables had emptied
out, but this one was still going strong. The man with the Marx-
Tagore beard asked us to join him. I had taken him to be the director
of the serial. It turned out that he was Manju Baruah, co-owner of
Wild Grass, and the man about whom I had read in the account
of my sole predecessor, Mark Shand, who had written a charming
travelogue called *River Dog* on his journey down the Brahmaputra.
Shand had also stayed at Wild Grass, and found Baruah's beard to
be like Fidel Castro's.

Mr Baruah, upon hearing about the object of my visit,
immediately launched into what he called a brief lecture on
Kaziranga. He repeated the by now familiar tale of the annual floods

being essential to Kaziranga's survival, but he had a few other things to add.

The rivers in Assam change course every few decades or centuries, Mr Baruah said, and this ceaseless process renews the soil. Now, notions of preventing erosion and floods had curbed that natural process. In the natural course of events, the Brahmaputra would wash the earth away from one place and deposit it, renewed, as topsoil in another. Grass would gradually take root there. Then the animals would come. 'The cow is the JCB,' he explained, referring to road construction equipment. The hooves of the cow tamped down the soft earth, hardening it for plants to grow.

In Wild Grass, he always had a few cows roaming around. They ate the lawn grass, keeping it nicely mowed, and of course they tamped down the soil with their walking about. They also contributed manure, which improved the fertility of the soil, though it didn't add to the immediate beauty of the lawn.

Manju Baruah's views on the human geography were in line with his views on natural geography. Yes, he said, there were a lot of migrants coming up the river and many of them might be Bangladeshis – there was no way to tell, because similar populations had long existed on both sides of the border. 'They are river people,' he said. 'They can live on boats and cultivate chars and chaporis.' He praised them fulsomely for being hardy and hard-working. 'The vegetables they grow are being sold by people who are not Bangladeshis, and are being eaten by everyone … without them the cost of vegetables would rise,' he said.

The caste Assamese do not generally live near the river, and certainly not on the river, Mr Baruah pointed out. Nor do the indigenous tribes. The Mishings in the upper reaches of the river are an exception, but now with jobs under the tribal quota, even there the local youths were running off to join the modern economy. 'There is a growing vacuum. Who will fill that vacuum?' he asked.

The answer, of course, was the hard-working Miyas, who might or might not be Bangladeshis. 'Kids these days around Kaziranga don't even know how to cut a big stick of bamboo. If the job has to be done, they go and call someone else, who is always a man in his forties or fifties,' he said. The simple knowledge of cutting bamboo, to which there is a technique, had been lost to the new generation, Mr Baruah complained. The more advanced knowledge involved in cutting the bamboo into strips that can then be woven was obviously beyond the feckless modern Kaziranga kids.

Alongside his logical, if unusual, perspectives on Bangladeshis in his home state – Assam politics for decades has revolved around agitations against the alleged migrants that eventually led to a contentious National Register of Citizens – were some more eccentric ones on other matters. He had a firm belief that establishments named after rivers do not succeed in business, and challenged Akshay and me to name one successful example. We racked our brains, in vain. I named Volga, the restaurant and bar in Connaught Place in Delhi, but apparently even that had shut down.

Volga restaurant was doubly damned according to Baruah's laws of misfortune. He had formulated that selling alcohol brings unhappiness in some form or the other, and therefore had no alcohol on the menu at Wild Grass – though visitors were free to bring in their own sinful supplies, and thus pay for their own sins. He gave numerous examples of people who had made money from alcohol only to have a near and dear one develop some rare and incurable disease. There was also the poor rich man, seller of alcohol, who sadly ended up living with his wife, his mother-in-law and two elder unmarried sisters in the same house. And there was Vijay Mallya, the business baron whose businesses had failed, who now had the Central Bureau of Investigation on his tail and had been forced to escape from the country … to a mansion in England.

I nodded my agreement to Mr Baruah's hypothesis, and contributed one more case study to his cause. There was the case of liquor baron Ponty Chadha, the multimillionaire who had ended up being shot dead by his own brother.

It was past 11.30 p.m. when we finally wound up our chat, a very late hour in the night out there near the forest. We had begun talking at 5.30 p.m. or so. Our conversation had lasted six hours without the aid of a drop of the fluid that Mr Baruah held in deep suspicion, alcohol. Nor was there any wild grass to be had.

SECTION III
Lower Assam and Bangladesh

45

Saraighat

NO ONE CAN TRAVEL in the Brahmaputra Valley without hearing the terms 'Upper Assam' and 'Lower Assam'. These are the basic units of the valley's geography, with Upper Assam denoting places along the upper course of the Brahmaputra and Lower Assam referring to places further downriver. The fluidity and vagueness of a riverine geography has impressed itself upon the mental maps that come with river terms – everyone in Assam speaks of 'Upper Assam' and 'Lower Assam' but it would take a scholar or administrator to delineate exactly where one ends and the other begins, not least because the border between the two keeps shifting like an unruly braid of the river.

The government of Assam now lists areas from Kamrup district down as Lower Assam. The term itself originates from the British administrative division of Assam when it was created as a Chief Commissioner's province in 1874. At that time a Lower Assam Division was made, which included all the territories west of the

Dhansiri river near the eastern end of the Kaziranga National Park. All of Kaziranga would have been in Lower Assam by that definition, but the sense of space associated with the term 'Lower Assam' has changed over time. The border of Lower Assam has shifted steadily westwards and the territories included in it have gradually shrunk, along with Kamrup district, even as the importance of the district and its biggest city, Guwahati, has grown.

Guwahati today is a bustle of people and vehicles – around a million of each. The city's population according to the Census of 2011 was close to one million, but Guwahati sprawls beyond its official boundaries. In a part of the world where other state capitals have populations around half of that number, the de facto capital of Assam – the official capital is Dispur, which in practical terms is a part of Guwahati – is a giant.

The core of the city, the old areas, are laid out in a line along the south bank of the Brahmaputra which flows past the city. The river here is at its narrowest. At the point where it was first bridged in 1962, near the Kamakhya temple on what used to be the city's outskirts forty or fifty years ago, it is only a little over a kilometre wide.

The bridge is called the Saraighat bridge. It connects the old river port of Pandu on the river's south bank with a ghat or riverside stop on the north bank called Saraighat. These are names with a storied place in Assam's history. The Battle of Saraighat, fought between the Ahoms and the Mughals in 1671, was a crucial one that is remembered to this day. As is often the case with history, the reason for its particular salience in contemporary popular memory has a lot to do with today's politics rather than the seventeenth century's. The Bharatiya Janata Party has made inroads into the Northeast and the Battle of Saraighat, along with its heroic general Lachit Borphukan, have been appropriated for advancing its agenda.

Oddly enough, the battle finds no mention by name in the otherwise comprehensive history of Assam by Sir Edward Gait. There is, instead, a long chapter on 'The Period of the Muhammedan Wars', but it is clear from the outset that the Muhammedans and Ahoms were not the only forces on the battlefield. Gait opens his chapter at the beginning of the seventeenth century with a description of the Jaintia King Jasa Manik, who was on bad terms with his neighbour the Kachari King Pratap Narayan, enticing the Ahom King Pratap Singha by offering him his daughter in marriage. The first conflict described, in 1606, is between the Kacharis and the Ahoms, sparked off by the aging Pratap Singha's efforts to collect the new bride he had been gifted, because his route lay through Kachari territory. The neighbouring Koch kingdom, which was the successor to the most ancient known kingdom in what is now Assam – the Kamrup kingdom – had by then split into two, in a tale as old as the Mahabharata: a power struggle between cousins vying for the throne. The eastern Koch kingdom known as Koch Hajo stretched from Dhubri to Mangaldoi; the town of Mangaldoi is named after a Koch princess who was given in marriage to the much-married Pratap Singha. The king of the western Koch kingdom, Koch Behar, which covered North Bengal and part of what is now Bangladesh, had meanwhile given his daughter in marriage to the Rajput king Raja Man Singh, who was the Mughal governor of Bengal.

'The friction between the cousins continued to increase and at last, in 1612, Lakshmi Narayan (the king of Koch Behar) went in person to Dacca and begged the Nawab to intervene,' writes Gait. The Nawab at the time was Islam Khan, foster brother of the Emperor Jehangir. In response to Lakshmi Narayan's entreaties, the Mughals invaded Koch Hajo, whose ruler Parikshit sought assistance from the Ahoms. They agreed upon the condition that he place all his forces under the command of the Ahom army, which he refused to do, and so ended up facing the Mughals and his estranged cousin on his own. He was defeated, captured and sent to Delhi to Emperor Jehangir's court. His dominions were annexed to the Mughal Empire. His brother Bali Narayan managed to flee to the Ahom court where he was given shelter. Bali Narayan then became king of Darrang under the title Dharma Narayan and gave his daughter Mangaldahi or Mangaldoi in marriage to Pratap Singha.

In 1617, Pratap Singha and his new father-in-law advanced towards Hajo. They captured Pandu. The war between the two rival Koch armies and their powerful allies began. Gait narrates a long list of battles that stretch on till 1637, when the Mughals finally killed Dharma Narayan and his two sons, and consolidated their rule over Kamrup. With that, the eastern Koch kingdom came to an end. A series of other conflicts involving the Jaintia, Kachari and Ahom kings ran on, but the next highlight in the war with the Mughals came after Shah Jahan fell ill in 1658, and a war of succession broke out in the Mughal empire. Taking advantage of this, the remaining Koch king, of Koch Behar, attacked and took Goalpara, before being driven out of there by the Ahoms, who thus became rulers of the entire Brahmaputra valley.

When the war of succession ended with Aurangzeb emerging victorious, the Mughals set about recovering their lost territories. Mir Jumla, the Persian general who had been made Mughal governor of Bengal, moved first against Koch Behar and captured it, with the king being forced to flee to Bhutan. The Mughals then advanced into the former eastern Koch territories and rapidly retook Guwahati but Mir Jumla did not stop there; he advanced to capture the Ahom capital, Garhgaon, near Sivasagar. He managed it successfully and with fairly little resistance from the Ahoms, whose king, Jayadhwaj Singha, fled along with his nobles. The troubles for the Mughals began after this victory; the rains began, and with it, floods and diseases. Communication became difficult.

The Ahoms started a guerrilla campaign to recover their capital. They were unsuccessful, and things might have gone badly for the Ahom king after the rainy season ended and troop movements became easier, but they were in luck: Mir Jumla fell seriously ill and decided to leave Assam. A treaty was concluded by which the Ahom king would send a daughter to the Mughal harem, and pay a heavy tribute in gold, silver and elephants to Aurangzeb, and Guwahati and the former Koch king's lands further west would remain with the Mughals. Mir Jumla, having secured these favourable terms, began his journey back to Dhaka by boat. He died of illness on the way somewhere near where the Brahmaputra curves around the Garo Hills before entering what is now Bangladesh, and is believed to be buried in what is today part of Meghalaya; in those days, the river flowed closer to the Garo Hills than it does now. Mir Jumla's opponent, Jayadhwaj Singha, did not long survive him, passing away in the same year, 1663.

The next round of fighting started when the following Ahom king, Chakradhwaj Singha, refused to pay the war indemnity his predecessor had promised, and moved to recover Guwahati from the Mughals.

The task was given to Lachit Borphukan, who proved to be a very capable general. The Ahoms successfully re-captured Guwahati. News of this reached Aurangzeb, who despatched an army under the Rajput king Raja Ram Singh of Amber, in today's Jaipur in Rajasthan, to recover the territories. The Battle of Saraighat, fought in 1671, was the final battle in a series of battles between the Mughals under Ram Singh and the Ahoms. It was a battle fought on water, in the Brahmaputra near Saraighat where the Mughals were trying to land their forces. On land, in open battle, they had the advantage, especially on account of their cavalry. Ram Singh, a man from the western desert used to fighting cavalry wars, was out of his element in water. It was, therefore, a clever strategic move on the part of the Ahoms to engage them in a decisive naval encounter. Nonetheless, the battle between Ahom and Mughal warboats armed with cannons was evenly poised until the Mughal navy's commander Munawwar Khan died when a musket shot hit him as he was filling his hookah. Meanwhile, Lachit Borphukan, who was severely ill, rallied the Ahom forces and entered the battle himself. His valiant efforts carried the day. The Mughals were forced to retreat, and left the Brahmaputra Valley in defeat.

Today, much of this long and complicated history is forgotten. What is remembered by some chauvinists is a battle between the Ahom forces, characterized as a Hindu army, and the Mughal forces, seen as a Muslim force. This is a vast oversimplification; it was a battle between two empires, not a riot between two religious communities. Not only was the Mughal general a Hindu Rajput, there were also Muslim commanders in the Ahom army at key positions. One of them, Bagh Hazarika alias Ismail Siddique, is remembered for having slipped into the Mughal camps and disabled their cannons before the Battle of Saraighat. His name, Bagh Hazarika, is really a title. He was called 'Bagh', meaning tiger, because legend has it that he fought and killed one with his bare hands. The Hazarika title was given by the Ahom king who put him in charge of 1,000 foot soldiers.

Assamese 'jatiyobadi' chauvinists tend to remember it in different ethnic terms. For them, it was a battle between Ahoms and Bongals. In their language, the world consists of Axomiyas, meaning Assamese, who are true sons of the Assam soil, and Bongals, who are not. Technically even a Portuguese mercenary – some of whom fought in the Mughal navy – would thus be a Bongal, though here skin colour begins to play a role; the white outsiders used to be called Boga Bongals, meanings white Bongals, by the Ahom kingdom's peasantry. Local hill tribes, though, were and are recognized as having distinct 'insider' identities; thus the Jaintia, Bodo, Kachari,

Naga, Adi and other tribes from the neighbourhood, while not Axomiyas, were also not Bongals. The Rajput Ram Singh from Jaipur, who led the Mughal invasion of Assam on Aurangzeb's command, and the Persian from Isfahan, Mir Jumla, were both Bongals by this definition. Their identities are largely forgotten; in popular lore, only Lachit's name remains and the memory that he inflicted a crushing defeat on the Bongals. The term came gradually to be identified with speakers of the Bengali language and, after the birth of Bangladesh in 1971, with Bangladeshis. Following the advent of British colonial rule in Assam and the standardization of languages that accompanied the spread of the printing press, linguistic identities came to be fixed, and what had previously been a political conflict between neighbouring kingdoms now became an ethnic conflict between neighbouring ethnicities. Even the Battle of Saraighat became, in this imagination, a conflict between Assamese and Bengali forces, or Hindus and Muslims.

46

Guwahati

GUWAHATI, WHICH LIES ACROSS the river from Saraighat, was a relatively sleepy riverside town with charming Assam-type houses even until the 1980s. The balmy mornings in the residential neighbourhoods would begin with the cries of a series of vendors as they passed by. There would be the vegetable seller with his handcart, the fruit seller, the egg seller with his cane baskets full of eggs and the busy fish seller. In winter, there would sometimes be the strange, almost musical, twang of the quilt and pillow maker, who would make you a fresh cotton quilt at home. The screech and sparks of the knife sharpener at work was one that inevitably drew a small crowd. There was also the 'Sil-pata dhaar wala' who would resharpen the stone grinding slabs on which masalas were ground.

The cool, hip places, then as now, were close to the river. The artificial lake of Dighili Pukhri, with the Handique Girls' College and Cotton College nearby, was a popular hangout with young people. I didn't know then that the lake had once been a boatyard of the Ahom navy, and connected to the Brahmaputra which flows nearby. There were no cool cafés then and no coffee chain shops. The neighbourhood extending up to the Uzan Bazar riverfront now has a whole host of cafes and restaurants. In the evenings, couples and families drive down there to eat out and chill out. The riverside itself has a series of parks, which charge entry tickets that only couples in search of places to canoodle find a worthwhile investment. Come sunset, every bench in those riverside parks is occupied by a different couple in some state of romance. You can see a large part of the life cycle of love, from the first hesitant date to a break-up, played out in those parks.

Closer to the water, down past the parks, there's still the odd temporary settlement of fisherfolk. The mosquitoes are pestilential, but for sheer location, it's hard to beat the riverside near Uzan Bazar. Beyond these ephemeral distractions and concerns of puny humans is the river itself. It flows past, as the bard of the Brahmaputra Bhupen Hazarika sang in a celebrated composition called '*Bistirno parore*', silently, unmindful of the chaos of countless human lives on its shores.

Today there is not much long-distance traffic on it. A steady stream of boats and ferries plies between a couple of the ghats on the Guwahati side and the river island of Umananda, touted to be the smallest continuously inhabited island in the world, a short hop away. I took one of those ferries. The island itself is small, steep and rocky. It would be little more than a very large rock in the middle of the river, which at this point is narrow – barely a couple of kilometres across – if it had not been thickly forested. There are tall old tropical trees inhabited by a population of rare golden langurs. At the top of the island, to which a series of steps lead, is an old Shiva temple dating back to Ahom times built towards the end of Gadadhar Singha's reign in AD 1694. It is among the earliest surviving Ahom structures around Guwahati; the older inscriptions speak of other kings and dynasties. This temple was built on the site of an older temple to the same deity that is said to have been destroyed during the long years of war that began with the Mughal invasion following the civil war between the two Koch kingdoms in the early part of the same century. Before its destruction, its head priest had received land, according to historians, from an unlikely source: the Mughal emperor Aurangzeb, who according to an inscription gifted him two plots in Hajo in AD 1667.

It was early evening, with the sun on its way down and the waters shimmering golden, when my ferry pulled in to the rocky shore of Umananda. A steep cemented path led up away from the water and everyone took this. The more devout Hindus seemed to be in a rush to get as quickly as possible to the temple; they darted up at top speed. A few stragglers, of whom I was one, made a more leisurely way uphill. We were the ones rewarded with a sighting that would have been interpreted as a good omen by our racing brethren: a large golden langur that came leaping and swinging, from tree to tree, until it sat almost directly over our heads, its long bushy tail dangling behind. There it paused for a few moments before carrying on along its journey.

At the temple was the usual long line of devotees. The reason people had been racing up the hill became clear; if you were not well ahead in the queue, you risked missing either the 'darshan' or the last ferry back. I satisfied myself with a good look at the facade of the gateway, which was freshly painted in white and red, and looked almost new. Behind the facade I could see, from the sides, the straggly edges of broken bricks. The gateway was at least five feet thick and of considerable age. Whatever had shattered the rest of it had to have been a considerable power – perhaps the great earthquake of 1897, which had an estimated magnitude of 8.0 on the Richter scale and, according to a paper published in the journal *Nature* in 2001, 'reduced to rubble all masonry buildings within a region of northeastern India roughly the size of England', or the earthquake of 1950, which was even stronger.

Umananda is a word made of two others joined together: Uma and ananda. Uma is Parvati, wife of Shiva. Ananda means bliss. This is said to be the place where Shiva and Uma would make love. It is also called Bhasmachal, because according to myth, it is the same place where Shiva went into a deep meditative trance only to be woken by Kamadeva, the god of love, who paid the price for this disturbance – Shiva's third eye opened and reduced the hapless Kamadeva to 'bhasma', meaning ashes. Eventually, at the pleadings of Rati, the wife of Kama, Shiva relented, and Kama was restored his life and form. The lands where he regained his 'rupa' or form were henceforth known as 'Kama-rupa'. According to tradition, devotees would first pray here at Umananda before proceeding to the temple complex of Kamakhya on the Nilachal Hill along the riverbank a few kilometres away.

The stretch of the south bank facing Umananda is the core of the old British city of Guwahati. Here is where a key institution of government power in district towns – the 'kutcherry', from where the European magistrate would administer the law – was located. The ghat was called the Kutcherry Ghat, a name it still retains, though the spelling and pronunciation have changed now to Kachari, after the tribes, which is a word more familiar to locals. The seat of the district and sessions judge has now grown to become the Gauhati High Court. The post office, now the General Post Office (GPO), the main post office for the city, is also nearby. The district collector's office is there right up on the riverbank, at a safe elevation. There are also a couple of massive old colonial bungalows with sprawling, manicured grounds overlooking the river, gracious remnants from the days of the Raj. These are now occupied by the chief justice of the Gauhati High Court and a senior judge.

Everywhere around the British town are symbols of much older rulers.

A short distance from the DC's office a cemented footpath lined with disinterested beggars leads to the Sukreswar Temple, a structure built by the Ahom king Pramatta Singha in the eighteenth century. I reached this place on a slow temple day; the usual long temple queue was absent. Instead of the crush of devotees, there was only the quiet of the empty temple complex. I walked into what seemed to be the main temple, a concrete structure that appears to be no more than a few decades old. The idol in the sanctum, though, looked much older. It was made of black stone and depicted a deity whose face was so worn that there was barely a nose and the eyes and mouth were faint smudges. The figure was seated in padmasana pose, meditating. There was a topknot on the head. It could have been the Buddha, but the throne on which the figure sat had carved images of a discus and mace – the symbols of Vishnu.

It was a statue of Vishnu Janardan, a replica of a large sculpture cut in a rock face overlooking the river, which is the oldest known thing in this temple complex. To get to that sculpture you have to go past all the temples and down a steep but short flight of concrete stairs that lead to the Sukreswar Ghat. The sculpture sits now under a canopy of concrete that serves as an observation deck of sorts, with a grand view of the river below. There's Vishnu in his Janardan form, as the helper of people, and Ganesha with his elephant head, Goddess Durga and Surya, the sun god. Their unknown sculptor had probably carved them on this rocky hillside around 800 years ago, in the dying days of the ancient Kamrup kingdom whose memory still lives in the name of the district, Kamrup Metropolitan, in which Guwahati is located.

At its height, the Kamrup kingdom stretched from the now much-reduced Karatoya river, which flows in the district of Rangpur in northern Bangladesh, in the west, to the Dikkorbasini river in the east. The Dikkorbasini was a fourteen-day journey upriver by country boat from Jorhat. It entered the Brahmaputra 'a little to the east of the eastern Kamakhya' (distinct from the temple in Guwahati), according to the 1838 account of historian Robert Montgomery Martin. The *Assam Buranji* of Harakanta Sarma-Barua seems to identify it with the Kechai-Khaiti temple of Sadiya. The Dikkorbasini has lost its old name over the centuries; its present location is uncertain, but it probably lay at the foothills of what is now Arunachal Pradesh, somewhere near Sadiya. The southern boundary of the kingdom was a distributary of the Brahmaputra called the Lakhya, which still exists as the Shitalakhya in the Narayanganj district adjacent to Dhaka in Bangladesh. Beyond this lay Bonggo, or Bengal. The kingdom of Bhutan bounded Kamrup on the north. The northern extremity of Kamrup was at a mountain called Kongjogiri whose present name is again uncertain; it may have been Kanchenjunga in the Himalayas.

47

The Kamakhya Temple

THE TEMPLE OF KAMAKHYA, according to the Kalika Purana, was at the geographical centre of Kamrup. North Bengal, the Brahmaputra valley and parts of northern Bangladesh were part of its undivided territories.

It had ceased to be the centre of even Guwahati, but the city has grown around it; today it is back to a more or less central location. I took a city bus to the foot of the Nilachal Hill from where an astonishingly overcrowded little van ferried me and my fellow pilgrims up the hill at good speed. There was one brief stretch along the way where the van slowed down. A saree-clad woman was crawling her way up the hill. Or rather, she was prostrating repeatedly on the road, before rising to join her hands in prayer, and taking a step, only to repeat the process. When we passed her she seemed to have fainted. Her family was sitting around with water bottles and towels. Someone was fanning her as she lay motionless. She was only halfway up the hill.

The vicinity of the temple complex near the top of the hill was crowded with vehicles and people. Temple priests in red dhotis wandered about or waited for devotees to approach them with requests to perform puja, meaning worship rituals. Steps wound up past little shops selling the puja paraphernalia – coconuts, marigold garlands, vermillion – and mementos of Kamakhya. The first, small temples along the route had few visitors. Everyone headed past them with barely a glance. Their singular focus was on reaching the main temple, the one that gives Kamakhya its name. It is a structure raised over a natural hollow in the hillside.

The present temple, according to an inscription there, was built by the Koch King Naranarayan and his brother Chilarai. It was completed in 1565 using material from the ruins of an older structure that had been destroyed by an invading general, said by tradition to be the Brahmin convert to Islam, Kalapahar, from the adjacent Sultanate of Bengal, sometime in the 1500s. That older structure had been built shortly after 1515 by the first Koch king, Biswasingha, who is said to have discovered the ruins of an even older structure while out on a hunt. The origins of those ruins are uncertain. There are, however, stone sculptures and figurines in Kamakhya that resemble those of Khajuraho and, closer home, the temple complex of Madan Kamdev near Guwahati. The Madan Kamdev temple complex was built by the Pala kings of Kamrup who ruled the area between 900 and 1100. It is possible that they may have built one or more temples on Nilachal Hill.

But those would not have been the first; there were definitely temples on Nilachal Hills even before the Palas got there. The oldest epigraphic evidence to have been found till date within the current boundaries of Assam is the Umachal inscription, which was found on Nilachal Hill. It is in Sanskrit, and says, 'This cave-temple of the illustrious Lord Balabhadra was constructed by Maharaja Sri Surendravarman'. It is usually dated to the fifth century and Surendravarman is thought to be the same person as Mahendravarman of the Varman dynasty, who was king of Kamrup from AD 470 to 494. The curious thing is that the temple was of Balabhadra, the brother of Lord Jagannath of Puri, a Vaishnav deity more popular in Odisha. Close connections between what are now Odisha, Bengal and Assam seem to have existed in those times.

The Chinese pilgrim Hiuen Tsang, who visited the court of King Bhaskar Varman around AD 643 and left a detailed account, made no mention of any Kamakhya temple; he only wrote that there were abundant Deva temples of myriad sects. Was there no Devi worship in Kamrup, home of the Shakta tradition of Hinduism, at the time, or did the visitor from China not bother with making a distinction?

The Shakta tradition probably existed in the land that is now Assam and was then Kamrup before Hiuen Tsang's time, although whether it was a part of polite Hindu faith is uncertain. It influenced the Vajrayana tradition of tantric Buddhism popular in Tibet. Kamakhya is *the* centre of tantric worship. Among all the fifty-one places of Devi worship across Bharat, an ancient territorial concept that marked the shifting sociocultural – but not political – geography of Hindu India, it is the most important for tantrics because it is said to be the place where the yoni, or vagina, of the Goddess Shakti fell after being dismembered by the discus of Lord Vishnu, who had to cut her up to prevent Lord Shiva's 'tandav' dance from destroying all creation.

There is a legend among the matrilineal Khasi tribal people of neighbouring Meghalaya, the oldest inhabitants of the area and speakers of the only Austroasiatic language endemic to this part of the country, who now occupy the hills that begin at the edges of modern Guwahati, that Kamakhya was originally their place of worship. The name, they say, is 'Ka mei-kha', which in Khasi is still the term used for the paternal grandmother, but in this case would suggest the progenitor of the tribe. The rituals of worship in today's Kamakhya and in a temple in Nartiang in the Jaintia Hills of Meghalaya were and still are similar, and the priests in Nartiang claim that blood from the sacrifices they make there reaches Kamakhya through a natural tunnel. There is also mention of other temples called Kamakhya, such as the one east of Jorhat in Montgomery Martin's account. A smaller temple called Kamakhya, at least 250 years old, exists even today in the riverside town of Silghat, east of Guwahati.

A lot of things in Kamakhya carry the symbolism of blood. The colour red is all around, in the uniforms of the temple priests, in the clothes of devotees, on the foreheads of women and men as vermillion marks, on ancient stone sculptures of gods and goddesses painted red, on ancient Shiva lingas smeared with vermillion. It is there in the red pieces of cloth, rather like bandannas with glittery golden edges and 'Jai Kamakhya Devi,' meaning 'Victory to Kamakhya Devi,' written nowadays in Hindi, that devotees wrap their offerings in. It is there, alternating with saffron, in the potentially sacred threads that the little shops near the temple sell. It is also there in the blood that spills from the severed bodies of goats, ducks and pigeons that are sacrificed at the temple.

The replacement of human sacrifice with goat sacrifice is of relatively recent origin. The historical record mentions that the rebuilt temple was consecrated in 1565 by King Naranarayan with the sacrifice of 140 men. The Devi has a gender preference; she prefers male heads. Such heads were definitely offered to her in 1615, when the son of Satrajit, the Hindu commander of an invading Mughal army, was sacrificed at the temple after defeat in battle. The practice continued without eliciting remark, presumably because it was not news, until the advent of British rule. Since then the human sacrifices have been replaced with a mix of goat sacrifices and a curious practice of ritually 'sacrificing' a human form made of flour. Even the goats that go to the ritual slaughter are unfortunate males.

The atmosphere at the temple on the day I visited, a regular day rather than a big festival day, was one of bustle and general good cheer. People milled about taking photos or paying obeisance to some statue or idol around the main temple. Among the plethora of sculptures on the building's exterior some had been recognized as those of particular superstar gods and drew crowds. There was a Ganesha form in a nook that had been painted red and was especially popular; it had coins stuck in the wall at its feet, and people milled about trying to add their coins to the lot. A near-naked female form, its face worn off with time or perhaps chipped away by some invader, similarly drew homages. It was recognized as Kali, the dread goddess of 'kaal', meaning time.

A serpentine queue, contained by a metal cage, wound around the temple. It was the line for entry into the sanctum sanctorum. The layers of the temple are evident in its very structure; a passage inside and downwards through a tunnel towards the sanctum is a passage back in time. The exterior and its signs of the contemporary give way to the sixteenth century and then, finally, to the dark moistness of a natural underground cave in which a little stream flows through a rock cleft shaped like a yoni. It is said to be connected to the Brahmaputra that flows just below the hill. This is the object of worship, symbol of the mythical yoni of Shakti that fell on this spot on earth during Shiva's cosmic tandav. It is the original and oldest part of the temple, created by nature or heavenly design rather than any human hand.

Surrounding the main temple and scattered around Nilachal Hill there are temples to the ten Mahavidyas, goddesses who are revered in both Tantric Hinduism and Tantric Buddhism. There is, for instance, Tara, a form of the Hindu Goddess Durga and of the Buddha Avalokitesvara, and Kali, who is also sometimes known as Maa Tara. The Chinese Goddess Guanyin and the Japanese Goddess Kannon may be related to her. There are similarly other divinities each with their own temples. They are generally locally popular in different parts of the subcontinent, except one, Dhumavati, goddess of the cremation ground and the void, who represents death and is feared.

Hardly anyone visits the Mahavidyas, the great goddesses of wisdom, any more; everyone follows each other to join the queue in the cage that leads to the sanctum sanctorum. The walk around Nilachal, with the ancient temples and views of the Brahmaputra, is thus uncrowded and pleasant. It took me through a little village where the temple priests have their homes. The character of the place is very Assamese, though its origins are syncretic. The temple's head priest was a Brahmin named Krishnaram Bhattacharjee originally brought in from Nadia in Bengal by the Ahom King Rudra Singha in the early 1700s. The houses are concrete, untidily modern, and the ubiquitous television makes its occasional presence felt. Vehicles cannot reach homes here, and getting gas cylinders in is a bit of a job. I saw a small, wiry man carrying two of those slung on either end of a bamboo stick down a steep, narrow alleyway.

The old tantrics have largely disappeared from view, even at Kamakhya. Hinduism alone among the great world religions openly preserves within itself the ancient pagan past, but it has undergone a process of gentrifiction going back centuries. The old gods of Greece and Rome, Egypt and Persia and Arabia, Mexico and Scandinavia ... they are all long dead. Hinduism retains its ancient polytheistic traditions and flows in multiple braids, but under the influence of a political Hinduism with a distinct Brahmin–Baniya flavour, the faith is, for better and for worse, becoming homogenized and getting 'cleaned up' to be more vegetarian, more abstemious and less Shakta.

The road below Nilachal hill bustles with traffic and activity. On one side, it runs parallel to the river past the adjacent cemetery of Bhootnath – where once ghastly tantric rituals were said to have been held on moonless nights – back towards the old city centre of Fancy Bazar, Pan Bazar and Paltan Bazar, the locations of shops selling every conceivable kind of ware. The journalist Anil Yadav, who travelled around parts of Northeast India in 2000 and wrote a memorable travelogue in Hindi called *Woh Bhi Koi Des Hai, Maharaj!*, which was later translated into English, had described these areas of the city pithily. 'A small, prosperous Rajasthan thrives in the heart of Fancy Bazaar and Pan Bazaar, the commercial centres of the city; its religious icons are Vitthalji and Rani Sati who are duly covered in gauzy fabric and installed in small marble temples. Marwari hotels which serve onion- and garlic-less food, jalebis, phuchkas and vehicles of the latest models stuffed into the narrow lanes proclaim other glories.'

Yadav's account also left a reminder of the situation in Assam in late 2000, when he had arrived there. 'On reading the newspapers, it became clear that things were much worse than we had anticipated on the train,' he wrote. The situation, he said, perhaps with some exaggeration, was 'much more complicated and fearsome than even in Kashmir.' His anxiety, however, was understandable. 'In Duliajan and Kakojan, on 22 October, sixteen Hindi-speakers had been murdered; in Nalbari, on 27 October, ten; in Barpeta, on 8 November, ten; in Betawar, on 16 November, eight; in Nalbari, on 25 November, four; and in Bongaigaon, ten Hindi-speakers had been killed on 30 November. Apart from these, at least seven murders had happened in remote areas which had not been reported,' he wrote.[40]

The killings were part of an ongoing blood feud. Family members of ULFA militants, and their friends and sympathizers, were then being dragged out of their homes and shot by masked gunmen in a series of murders remembered in Assam as 'secret killings'. The hand of Indian security agencies and the surrendered ULFA elements was suspected. The ULFA was hitting back by randomly killing Hindi-speakers.[41]

Today's Assam shows no traces of that bloody past. Guwahati itself has left behind its days of militancy, as it has the tantriks of Bhootnath and even the leisurely ways of lahe lahe. The city bristles with new developments. Fancy malls and brand stores have come up inland, away from the river, on both sides of the Guwahati–Shillong road. Every brand wants a piece of the action in Guwahati, it seems. From the Jockey innerwear store to the Harley Davidson motorcycle one, they're all in the city, though the latter has gone to an even newer area of development, along a national highway that also runs towards Shillong. That highway is a part of Asian Highway 1, an international highway that connects Northeast India to Myanmar on one side and Bangladesh on the other. That's also where one of the new five-star hotels now in the city has opened. Until 2013, there was no five-star hotel in Guwahati, or in all of Northeast India, and no Mercedes, BMW or Harley showroom. The first five-star opened in 2014. Three others followed in quick succession. By 2018, Guwahati had changed. Its days of lahe lahe and insurgency were over; it had become a city where it was possible to buy most of the goodies that money can buy.

48

Development?

THE INFLUX OF 'NEW money' has changed the pace and orientation of life in Northeast India. In Assam, it has started changing people's relationship with the river too. There is now a premium on riverfront locations and properties. A whole neighbourhood of Guwahati overlooking the river, Kharghuli Hills, has become the site of new developments, with posh apartment complexes and luxurious bungalows cropping up. Some of it is a peace dividend; former ULFA underground members too have invested in property there.

There are luxury cruises on the river now. The first of these started in 2003. Prices are high, and advertised in dollars; cabins start at USD 195 a night, and can go up to USD 425, and most cruises are for seven or ten nights. They sell out months in advance. Indians from India are not the usual customers.

Our countrymen and women mostly make do with the lunch, tea or dinner cruise on the Alfresco Grand, a large cruise boat that was launched in 1998. From its berthing place near Pan Bazar, it takes passengers on a ride along Guwahati's waterfront. There's food and drink on the deck, and pretty scenes, and live music. It's pleasant and affordable.

The Northeast is newly popular with tourists from everywhere in mainland India, and Guwahati is the hub through which most of them transit. It was always the gateway to the region, and its importance is only increasing now. The Government of India's 'Act East' foreign policy initiative has to go through Guwahati. Connecting India by land to Southeast Asia is only possibly through Northeast India. There is widespread recognition of this in the government. The airport is getting a much-needed facelift. Highways are snaking through the region connecting it to neighbouring countries. Bridges are being commissioned and rail links are expanding.

All this is bringing in people from everywhere in Northeast India to Guwahati. After Assam's capital moved here from Shillong in 1972–73, the city gradually became the unrivalled melting pot of the region. Nagas, Khasis, Manipuris, Garos, Marwaris, Bengalis, Biharis, Punjabis and people from every community of the wider region are in Guwahati, working and living there as many of their ancestors did, often becoming culturally Assamese in the process.

There are plans afoot to make Guwahati a 'smart city'. One of the proposals is to redevelop the waterfront and introduce speedboat rides. There is also a Rs 40,000 crore plan to dredge the river along its entire length in Assam to enable its use as a navigation corridor – a project of questionable merit, since the Brahmaputra has one of the highest sediment loads of any river in the world – and to build two highways along it. A lavishly funded Namami Brahmaputra Festival was also held for the first time in 2017.

Crossing the river at Guwahati now is no trouble at all. The river is at its narrowest here, and the first bridge across it, the Saraighat Bridge that connected the south bank where the modern city of Guwahati is located to the site of the historic battle on the north bank, has since 2017 been upstaged by a swanky new concrete structure. It is the second Saraighat Bridge. Vehicles race across it; the presence of the river below might register if the passenger lifts his or her head from the phone screen.

Until 1962, shortly before the China war, when the first Saraighat Bridge was inaugurated, there was no bridge over the Brahmaputra. Travelling to Calcutta, the nearest metropolis, involved a multitude of transports, as rail routes were disrupted by Partition. One started from Gauhati, as it was then called. The bus deposited the traveller a short distance away on the south bank near Pandu ghat. From there, it was a ferry ride across the river to Amingaon on the north bank.

It was a slow process, made pleasant for the passengers by the meals that were served on the boats as people waited to make the crossing. Then the travellers would need to shift their luggage, no doubt aided by coolies – that was the time before luggage had wheels, when people travelled with bedrolls called 'holdalls' – to a metre-gauge train that ran from Amingaon to Kishanganj in Bihar. This was later replaced by a metre-gauge line from Guwahati to New Jalpaiguri in north Bengal, from where the broad-gauge line began. So, you would scramble to get bag and baggage out at New Jalpaiguri, and rush, again aided by coolies, to find your seat on the connecting train. From there it was finally a usually speedier run to Calcutta. The train was not merely a train. Even until the 1980s, it was a veritable travelling 'mela' or fair. There would be a procession of hawkers selling jhal muri (puffed rice with diced green chillies), chana jor garam (spicy Bengal gram), chai, cheap electronics, coconut water and much else. The wandering Baul minstrels would come by, and you would know they were there from the sudden sound of ghungroos (anklets) and the twang of an ektara (a one-stringed musical instrument) before a raw voice rose from some end of the compartment and people craned their necks to see who the singer was.

The journey across the river is now seamless. Pandu port has fallen off the map and the consciousness of most Guwahati residents; it is only now finding mention again in news reports because of efforts to revive it as a container terminal on National Waterway 2, meaning the Brahmaputra from Dhubri to Sadiya. The first shipment of 400 tonnes of cement went downriver from Pandu to Dhubri by barge in 2017. It would have cost far more to transport by road; the river is a cheap means of transport.

Across on the north bank, there is now an Indian Institute of Technology. Its sprawling modern campus sits close to the river. There's also an export promotion park and an oil installation. The new developments in north Guwahati are a kind of rebirth of Durjaya, which was the ancient capital of Kamrup under the Pala dynasty between 900 and 1100. It was located somewhere in the vicinity of the new north Guwahati. The name Durjaya itself is interesting. In the Mahabharata, Durjaya was the name of Duryodhan's son; the Kaurav king was married to Bhanumati, daughter of Bhagadatta, the mighty Asura king of Pragjyotishpur or 'City of Eastern Astrology' believed to have been located at the site of today's Guwahati. His father Naraksura is said in myth to have been the first Asura king of the kingdom, a terrible and powerful ruler who was eventually killed by Lord Krishna. There is till today a hill in Guwahati named after Narakasura, and bits and pieces of ancient artefacts are occasionally found there. Myths speak of even older rulers, called Kiratas, led by a great king named Ghatak, from whom the Asuras won the kingdom.

Around 15 km downriver from the IIT there's a village called Sualkuchi which is the traditional centre of Assam's indigenous silk industry. A ferry used to ply there from Guwahati but I was told that it had been discontinued. Buses and the ubiquitous shared, overcrowded tempos ply to the town and it is an easy ride on a road that runs parallel to the river, albeit at a safe distance from it. The village itself is a quiet one, with a narrow main street lined with shops selling garments made from Assam silk. The silk comes in three principal variants: the golden-yellow muga, the coarse white eri and the shimmery white paat. Sarees, mekhela chadors and gamosas seem to be the most popular products.

There are signs of relative prosperity. The HDFC and ICICI banks have found it worthwhile to open local branches here. There's even a college and an institute of fashion technology. There are also old Vaishnav satras housed in graceful little buildings with sloping tin roofs and carved, colourfully painted wooden doors.

Down by the riverside, it was deserted except for one lone man standing under a tree having a smoke. His 100cc motorcycle stood parked nearby. He worked in the silk business. The silk factories, little units that operate from people's homes where the silk is woven on hand looms, were shut for the festival of Bihu, he said. The workers had gone home for the holiday. He began to complain, between long drags, about how difficult it had become to find skilled silk weavers. Most of the weavers used to come from the adjacent Bodo areas, he said, but now that the militancy there had wound down and the former militant chiefs had become ministers in the Assam government or the new Bodoland Territorial Council, a lot of families and friends of former militants had suddenly found jobs and business opportunities. They had become rich, he said, with a seeming mix of admiration and annoyance. They no longer wanted to work in weaving.

Profits were low and uncertain in the Sualkuchi silk business, he said, and he himself was considering exiting. Even a Class-3 government job was more stable, and the avenues for making 'extra' money were plentiful. It was unnecessary to delve into the details of how the extra money was made; everyone in the country knows it is made from bribes.

I asked him about the giant statue of Gandhiji sitting under a fake plastic-thatch roof a few metres from us. The statue sat inside a complex that was visibly empty. Perhaps once or twice a year, on his birth and death anniversaries, a politician would come with his convoy of SUVs and armed guards and his retinue of hangers-ons, to place a garland on the statue and extol virtues that the politician – to have gotten so far in life – had probably not had the opportunity or the desire to practise.

'Gandhiji gave us silk when he came here before Independence,' the man said. 'We owe our identity to Gandhiji for the silk and Sankaradev for the religion.'

He was being far too generous in crediting the silk to the Father of the Nation. There is evidence of silk weaving in Kamrup going back many centuries. There is, for instance, the written record of Bana from the seventh century, which lists silk fabrics and musk in silken bags among the gifts sent by the Kamrup King Kumar Bhaskar Varman to the Thansesar King Harsha. It would seem that Kamrup silk was a gift fit for kings 1,300 years before Gandhiji set foot in Sualkuchi.

49

Pilgrimage of Three Faiths

BARELY 10 KM INLAND from Sualkuchi lies the old town of Hajo, formerly the capital of the kingdom of Koch Hajo. Although it is not, strictly speaking, on the river, I decided to pay it a visit. There are many ways of following a river, and of telling its tales. If it is navigable, and the writer is a skilled sailor, the story may be told as a river voyage. If not, a sufficiently wealthy writer may be able to afford hiring boats and boatmen for the entire journey. That form of travelling and mode of transport has its merits; but in the case of a river such as the Brahmaputra, it also has its demerits. It so happens that, for centuries, wariness of the river's destructive propensities has driven people to build whatever might be considered permanent at a safe distance from the river or atop rocky hills and mountains that can withstand its might. To journey on the river, or stick pedantically to its shores, is to miss almost the entire human history of the Brahmaputra Valley along its entire length, because most of that history – from the old Ahom capitals around Sivasagar, down to Hajo and beyond – is situated a few kilometres inland.

The first major historical landmark we came across on our way to Hajo after a short drive through the green countryside was the dargah called Poa Mecca, or 'Quarter Mecca', located atop a high hill named after Vishnu's vahana Garuda that rises sudden and sheer from the plains around it. A narrow road lined with groves of sal trees winds up to it. It was a lazy morning during the Muslim fasting period of Ramzan when I got there with my friends Nishat and Mary. The place was empty but for the shopkeepers selling the religious paraphernalia that exists at every major temple, dargah and church in India. Even they looked bored and listless. At the dargah itself, a small group of men sat on the floor, chatting. They rose when we walked up the steps into the building. One of them came up to us and motioned for us to sit on the carpets placed before the central object in the shrine, the tomb of the Sufi pir Ghiyasuddin Auliya who is said to have come to this place from what is now Iraq with soil from Mecca in the fourteenth century.

The man who had asked us to sit, a priest of the dargah, then proceeded to chant some prayers for our Amar-Akbar-Antony troika, which ended with a secular prayer for donations. He had barely finished with us when two young women walked in. He moved on to reciting prayers for them.

We walked around the structure, which seems relatively new, and found embedded in one of its walls an old stone plaque with carvings in Arabic and Persian. A translation of this in English had been stuck into another adjacent wall. The first two lines, the ones in Arabic, consisted of praises of Allah and His Holy Prophet. The subsequent lines, in Persian, went thus:

During the reign of the just, the emperor of the world, the centre of bounties and religions, and time of governorship

of Muhammad Shuja, may the king and prince be blessed
(by Allah), the holy masjid was built by Lutfullah Shirazai.

Shujabad, a land noted for peace in the entire world, may
Allah protect it from all calamities, was built at a time when
the royal banner was on march towards Bengal with glory
and dignity. May this religious centre flourish and survive
with all its glory and dignity forever.

The original structure, of which the plaque had been a part, had
been built during the reign of Shah Jahan in 1657, when his son
Shah Muhammad Shuja was the Mughal governor of Bengal and
Bihar. It seemed likely that the structure still survives under layers of
what the Archaeological Survey of India's plaque at the site described
as 'renovations'. These renovations had basically encased the whole
thing in a coat of plaster, marble and coatings of white, green and
gilt paint.

We left after making obeisances and paying our dues to the saint
and his present-day priests.

Next stop was a temple. A long flight of old stone steps lead up
to it. The structure itself in this case is visibly old; it was built in the
sixteenth century by the Koch Rajbongshi King Raghudeva, son of
Chilarai and nephew of Naranarayan.

This temple had sculpted on its outer walls figures of the ten
avatars of Vishnu, with the Buddha as the ninth avatar. The place
is also holy to Buddhists, particularly those from Bhutan and
Tibet, and the controversial imperialist of fascist leanings Laurence
Waddell, who was there in the late 1800s, left an intriguing account
of how this came to be so.

Waddell wrote in his book, *Tibetan Buddhism*, published in 1895:

No description of this Buddhist site seems to be on record,
except a very brief note by Col Dalton on the modern

Hindu temple of Hajo, which shrines a Buddhist image. So as I have had an opportunity of visiting the site, and enjoyed the rare advantage of being conducted over it by a Lama of eastern Tibet who chanced to be on the spot, and who had previously visited the site several times, and possessed the traditional stories regarding it. I give the following brief description of it in illustration of how the Lamas, originally misled by an identity of name, have subsequently clothed the neighbourhood with a legendary dress in keeping with the story of Buddha, and how this place, with its various associated holy spots, is now implicitly believed by the pilgrims to be the site of Buddha's pari-nirvana. And in this belief, undeterred by the intemperate heat of the plains, Buddhist pilgrims from all parts of Bhotan, Tibet, and even from Ladak and south-western China visit these spots and carry off scrapings of the rock and soil in the neighbourhood, measuring up this precious dust in amulets, and for placing beside their dead body, as saving from dire calamities during life, and from transmigration into lower animals hereafter.

The present temple is not the first at the site. The Assam Tourism plaque at the base of Manikut Hill on which the temple stands announces that there was an earlier temple at the site built in the seventh century. The dating is interesting; the seventh century was when the Chinese pilgrim Hiuen Tsang visited Kamrup. His account makes no mention of any great Buddhist site. In fact, he lamented their absence. Waddell pointed out that Hiuen Tsang had written in his account, 'The people have no faith in Buddha, hence from the time Buddha appeared in the world, even down to the present time there never as yet has been built one Sangharama as a place for the priests to assemble.'

Waddell suspected that the Buddhist saint associated with Hajo was probably not the Buddha himself but Guru Padmasambhava, the great Guru Rimpoche revered in Tibet and Bhutan as the master who spread dharma, meaning Tantric Buddhism in this context, in the lands of snows. Guru Padmasambhava is believed to have reached Tibet around AD 750 – after Hiuen Tsang's time – and spent half a century there. Where he left from is unclear; however, it is quite possible that he was from Kamrup. The place has, from ancient times till date, been known as the greatest centre of Tantra. Waddell quoted H.H. Wilson's preface to the Vishnu Purana where the latter noted that: 'Asam, or at least the north-east of Bengal (i.e. Kamrup), seems to have been in a great degree the source from which the Tantrica and Sakta corruptions of the religion of the Vedas and Puranas proceeded.'

It is known that followers of the religion of the Vedas and Puranas came in conflict with the kings of Kamrup in times that precede history; evidence of it is there in names of asura kings that survive till today in the geography of Guwahati, where a hill named Narakasura after a great asura king of legend still exists, and in the tales of battles between Lord Krishna and Banasur in Tezpur. The Kamakhya temple even now is the centre of Tantric Hinduism, a Hinduism very different from the Hinduism of casteist vegetarianism, obsession with ritual purity and disgust for menstruating women.

The connections between Tantric Hinduism and Tantric Buddhism are far too many to ignore. They extend from shared deities and iconographic congruences to living traditions.

The temple of Hayagriva Madhava was bustling with devotees when we arrived. People ascended the steps holding steel plates with offerings of marigold garlands, earthen lamps, lotus blooms and incense. The temple priests clothed in yellow kurtas and dhotis chanted mantras as the devotees were led to a long table at the end of a hall before the sanctum sanctorum where they lit the lamps and incense sticks. The hall doubled as a dining hall during lunch time, with free vegetarian food served to all.

Worship inside the temple had been suspended till evening for lunch, first for the deities, and then for the worshippers. Instead, a priest, who had latched on to us, chanted the relevant mantras for us as we placed our diyas and lit our incense sticks. Mary had smartly marched off to take photos by the time he asked our gotras but the priest was not the least bit surprised to find Nishat was a Muslim, and therefore did not have a gotra. He simply carried on with his prayers before guiding us to an old statue of Narasimha with face obscured, it seemed deliberately, by marigold garlands. Is it because, as the name of the temple suggests, it is a Hayagriva Narasimha – Narasimha with a horse's head? En route we spotted the two girls who had arrived in the Poa Mecca dargah just after us. Clearly, we were not the only ones doing a temple and dargah run. Nor could any of us tell, from looking at one another, whether we were Hindus, Muslims, Christians or Buddhists.

The high priests of the temple here are called 'doloi', which is the same word as Dalai, as in Dalai Lama. In several temples of Kamrup, this tradition of high priests called dalais still exists. It is likely that the connections between Kamrup and the kingdoms of Bhutan, Tibet and China in ancient times were closer than they are at present.

Beyond Hajo, further downriver on the north bank of the Brahmaputra, is Barpeta. It is one of the heart-centres of the old satras of Vaishnavite Assam – the place where Srimanta Sankardev's foremost disciple Madhavdev's established the Barpeta satra in 1583. According to the writer and scholar Birinchi Kumar Barua:

Madhavadeva outlived Sankardeva by twenty-eight years and during this period he mostly stayed at Ganakkuchi

and Sunaridiya satras close to the principal satra, Barpeta,
which remains to the present day the source of attraction
and inspiration to the Vaishnavas. Here, Madhavadeva came
into conflict with Raghudeva, king of the Eastern Koch
Kingdom. It was reported to the king that the saint was
preaching against the worship of Kamakhya, the guardian
deity of the Koch kings. So Raghudeva had him brought
to his court at Vijaynagara, Kamrup, as a prisoner. The
allegations, however, proved false, and the preceptor was
released with due respect. Madahavadeva thereafter stayed
for sometime at Hajo, near the present Hayagriva Madhava
temple. But there also he could not live in peace owing to the
hostile activities of both the king and the Brahmanas, and
therefore left for Cooch Behar, the capital of the Western
Koch Kingdom ruled at the time by Lakshminarayan, son
of Naranarayan.

Barua goes on to write that the king received him with honour
and gave him and his disciples land for a satra at a village called
Bheladuar near Cooch Behar in today's West Bengal. He completed
his masterwork, the *Namaghosa*, there, and eventually passed away
at the Bheladuar satra in 1596.

50

Language and Identity

THE BEKI RIVER, WHICH flows past Barpeta, and the Manas
river further west, join the Brahmaputra west of Hajo. Across
on the opposite bank a short distance downriver from the confluence
of these rivers with the Brahmaputra is the town of Goalpara, once a
part of the kingdom of Koch Hajo.

In *A Tea-Planter's Life in Assam*, George Barker described
Goalpara as being 'beautifully situated on the side of a low hill
facing the Himalayas'. It was the last major stop on the river route
before entering Assam. 'At a point between Goalpara and Gowhatty,
the traditional boundary of Assam used to be marked in the river by
two rocky islands suddenly rising in mid-stream,' he wrote, echoing
the earlier account of James Rennell.

Today Goalpara is a town of uncertain charm, reached almost
exclusively by a road that runs between the Garo Hills and the
Brahmaputra. The hills are visible in the distance. The river remains
an invisible presence, though during floods the waters often spill

over onto the highway, from wetlands and mountain streams that are everywhere, and people even catch fish on the highway. The lands nearest to the river were traditionally left uninhabited and largely uncultivated before British colonial times, when the East India Company's goal of increasing revenues drove many lasting changes in the landscape and demography. The population along this belt is a mix of Assamese castes, Bengali Hindus and Muslims, Rajbongshis, and tribal communities such as the Garo, Hajong, Koch and Rabha. Each of these groups has its own language, but there is a language that is particular to the place itself: Goalpariya, a form of Kamrupi.

It is a confusing language, an in-between language of an in-between space. Hearing a popular folk song called '*Hostir kanya*', meaning daughter of the elephant, Bengalis unfamiliar with Goalpariya tend to think it is a song in a dialect of Bengali. Assamese speakers think it is a dialect of Assamese. The Koch Rajbongshis say it is their song in their own language … but it is not the same as the tribal Koch language. Goalpariyas assert it is their language, the language of Goalpara, the 'desi bhasha', which it is, but it gets more specific than that. It is the song of the mahouts of the erstwhile zamindari of Gauripur. It reached a wider audience in the voice of Pratima Barua Pandey from the Gauripur zamindar, or landowning, family. Her soulful rendition was described as 'Goalpariya lokgeet', Goalpariya folk song.

The linguistic identity of the Baruas of Gauripur is, like their language, interstitial. Pramathesh Chandra Barua, singer Pratima's uncle, was a famous filmmaker who made the first version of the celebrated film *Devdas*, based on the Bengali novel by Sarat Chandra Chattopadhyay. The film was in Bengali and starred Barua himself in the title role of the lovelorn drunkard zamindar Devdas. It was a hit, and Barua followed up with a Hindi and then an Assamese version. His father Prabhat Chandra Barua, founder president of the

Assam Association, along with the Goalpara zamindars' association, campaigned in favour of the return of Goalpara to Bengal when the Government of India Act of 1919 was bringing reforms in administration to the country. It was still possible then to straddle both Bengali and Assamese identities, but the line between the two identities was deepening. It would eventually spill over into rioting, and remain an issue in the state's politics for decades. Even the National Register of Citizens in Assam and the related matter of the Citizenship Amendment Act, which became national issues, have their background and origins in the history of these two clashing linguistic identities in Assam.

Bengali and Assamese are close relatives. Both languages trace their origins to an older language called Magadhi Apabhramsa that was spoken over a wide area of eastern India a thousand years ago. According to linguist Suniti Kumar Chatterji in his masterwork *The Origin and Development of the Bengali Language*, Bengali, Assamese and Odia all derive from eastern Magadhan. The dialect of eastern Magadhan spoken in Kamrup came to be known as Kamrupi.

This Kamrupi language had a place of importance in the history of Assam. It was Kamrup – meaning Lower Assam and north Bengal – where the early stalwarts of Assamese culture did their life's work. Assam from ancient times till the end of Koch rule in the seventeenthth century was known as Kamrupa, according to the renowned Assamese linguist Upendranath Goswami. In his research paper (later published as a book) *A Study On Kamrupi: A Dialect of Assamese,* published in 1958, Goswami wrote that ' ... the Aryan language spoken first in Assam was the Kamrupi language spoken in Rangpur, Cooch Behar, Goalpara, Kamrup district and some parts of Nowgong and Darrang districts.'

He further wrote, 'It is in this Kamrupi language that the early Assamese literature was mainly written. Up to the seventeenth century, as the centres of art, literature and culture were confined within western Assam and the poets and writers hailed from this part, the language of this part also acquired prestige.' The most considerable Assamese poet of the pre-Vaishnavite period in Goswami's estimation was Madhava Kandali, who belonged to the present district of Nagaon in central Assam and rendered the entire Ramayana into Assamese verse under the patronage of King Mahamanikya, a Kachari king.

'The golden age of Assamese literature opened with the reign of Naranarayan, the Koch king. He gathered around him at his court at Cooch Behar a galaxy of learned men. Sankardev, the real founder of Assamese literature, and his follower Madhavdev worked under his patronage,' wrote Goswami. Sankardev and Madhavdev's Vaishnava devotional songs are still performed to this day. They are in a literary language called Brajabuli, first popularized by Maithili poet Vidyapati in the fourteenth century.

It was only after the decline of Koch power by the seventeenth century that the centre of literary importance shifted from western Assam to the Ahom court in eastern Assam. Colonialism and the advent of a new technology played a significant part in cementing the shift.

'In 1836, two remarkable members of the American Baptist Mission, the Rev. N. Brown and O.T. Cutter, with their families, first set foot on Assamese soil. Among other things a printing press was part of their missionary equipment. The missionaries made Sivasagar the centre of their activities and used the dialect of Sivasagar for their literary purposes,' wrote Goswami.

These missionaries published, from their press, the first Assamese grammar and the first Assamese-English dictionary. According to Goswami, 'Under the influence of the missionaries, a set of native writers grew up, and books and periodicals in the language of eastern Assam multiplied. Thus the traditions of the Ahom court supported by the mission press established the language of eastern Assam as the literary language of the entire province.' The eastern Assam dialect became the language of newspapers, education, courts and government, and was established as the standard Assamese. 'The differences between the standard and Kamrupi dialect are not insignificant. They range over the whole field of phonology, morphology and vocabulary,' Goswami wrote.[42]

Under colonial influence, the ancient Kamrupi language of Lower Assam shrank into a dialect of yokels and its speakers came to be derisively called 'dhekeris'.

Dhekeri was originally a territory of the kingdom of Koch Hajo, which, following the civil war between the Koch and the defeat of King Parikshit Narayan to Mughal forces, fell into Mughal hands in the early 1600s. The Mughals brought in their systems of administration that divided the kingdom into four sarkars or regions, which were further divided into parganas. Sarkar Dhekeri, which was the area around Mangaldoi, was one of those, the others being Sarkar Kamrup, Sarkar Dakhinkul and Sarkar Bangalbhum.

The term 'dhekeri' is used even today as a pejorative term reserved for speakers of the dialects of Lower Assam.

51

Culture Wars to NRC and CAA

THE CULTURE OF THE rulers has long been seen as the superior one, the one to aspire to and become a part of. The global success of the British Empire and its successor, the American Empire, has ensured that today's elite class among Indians are broadly drawn from those who speak, read and write in English, and often, those who have been to British or American universities. The recent rise to power of the BJP with its partiality for a Hindi–Hindu–Hindustan has to some extent seen a toppling of that elite by the even older Brahmin-Bania Hindu elites of the Hindi-speaking heartland of north and west India, who are keen that their language and culture should be the one with most prestige.

Before British colonial times, in Mughal India it was the Persian language and culture that enjoyed an exalted status. In Ahom territories, over a period of centuries, the original Tai Ahom language and religion of the kings, nobles and priestly classes gradually gave way by the seventeenth century to Hinduism and the Assamese language of Upper Assam, where they ruled. With the end of the Ahom rule and the advent of the British Raj, the language of power changed. At the start of their rule in 1826, the British East India Company Raj only annexed the old Koch kingdom's territories in Lower Assam to their adjacent territory, the Bengal Presidency, which they ruled from their capital in Calcutta. Between 1838–42, Upper Assam corresponding to the Ahom and Motok kingdoms was also annexed.

During this period a vigorous debate was raging on the question of which language was to be used as the language of administration of British India. The British had initially continued with the Mughal court language, Persian, as their official language, and up until 1837 this was the language of government of the new rulers. In January 1838, the Judicial and Revenue Department of the British Company Raj ordered that 'in the districts comprised in the Bengal division of the presidency of Fort William, the vernacular language of those provinces shall be substituted for the Persian in judicial proceedings, and in the proceedings relating to the revenue, and the period of twelve months from the first instant shall be allowed for effecting the substitution.'[43]

The Bengal Presidency then stretched from the North-West Frontier Province to Burma. Until 1874, the Lieutenant-Governor of Bengal administered five provinces: 'Bengal Proper, Behar, Odisha, Chota Nagpore and Assam'. Henry Beverley, the author of 'The Census of Bengal' published in 1874, provided a brief description of each of these territories and their inhabitants: 'Assam is the valley of the upper Brahmapootra, with such of the hill territory on either side as lies within the British frontier. It is inhabited, though sparsely, by a variety of races. The Assamese language appears to be merely a dialect of Bengali.'[44]

The combination of changing language policies, substituting vernaculars for Persian, and the British administration's notion that Assamese was a dialect of Bengali, which persisted until many decades after 1838, led to Bengali becoming the language of lower courts and bureaucracy in Assam. This is the source of the Assamese–Bengali linguistic clash. It is remembered with anger to this day in Assam, as an imposition of Bengali crafted by the Bengali clerks, rather than the British rulers. For this reason, Bengali-speakers alive today are viewed by many staunch Assamese nationalists in much the same way that Muslims are viewed by Hindu nationalists.

There are no records of major protests immediately after the imposition of Bengali in Assam. That was to happen only later, through the efforts of the two American Baptist missionaries, Nathan Brown and O.T. Cutter, who had arrived in 1836. They had brought with them the first printing press and had set about preaching the Bible, initially among the Singphos and Khamptis, who chased them and the British rulers out of Sadiya. Brown and Cutter then turned their attention to the Brahmaputra Valley and began their missionary task by publishing literature in the local dialect of their new base, Sivasagar, not far from the Naga Hills. Here they began to have greater success, with the Sivasagar tank next to the Siva Dol temples being used for baptisms. From 1846, they also began to publish *Orunodoi*, the first newspaper in Assamese, to propagate the news and views of their choice. The writers who wrote for *Orunodoi* under Brown's editorial leadership were people like Anandaram Dhekial Phukan, Hemchandra Barua and Gunabhiram Barua, remembered now as the founders of modern Assamese literature and vocabulary.

The Baptist Missionaries, who had already translated the Bible into what they considered pure Assamese (there was an older translation into Assamese which they rejected), led the campaign against the imposition of Bengali on Assam. The mission press published the first Assamese grammar, compiled by Reverend Nathan Brown, and the first dictionary, put together by the Reverend Miles Bronson.

The missionaries also petitioned the British government on behalf of the Assamese language. When A.J. Moffat Mills, a judge, arrived in Assam in 1853 to prepare a report on the revenue administration, the missionaries presented him with a petition on the issue of language. Mills was greatly impressed. 'Assamese is described by Mr. Brown, the best scholar in the province, differing in more respects than agreeing with the Bengalee, and I think we made a great mistake in directing that all business must be transacted in Bengalee, and the Assamese must acquire it,' he wrote.

However, government policy has always been slow to change, and nothing came of Mills' observations. Nonetheless, Bronson kept up the efforts after Brown's departure from Assam. In 1872, he submitted a memorandum titled 'Humble memorial of the Assamese Community of Nowgong, Assam,' signed by 216 persons of whom he was the leader.

By this time, a reorganization of the Bengal Presidency was already on. It was a vast and unwieldy territory, and a gradual process of reorganizing it had been on since 1836 when the North-Western Provinces bordering Afghanistan were separated and placed under a lieutenant governor. A spate of Lushai raids on Cachar, which was then in Dhaka Division, prompted a relook at the North Eastern end of the British Indian Empire as well. In 1874, the British administration finally decided to reorganize Bengal by creating a chief commissionerate for the North East Frontier. In the ensuing redrawing of maps, Goalpara, Cachar and Sylhet, the Garo, Khasi and Jaintia Hills, the Naga, and subsequently also the Lushai Hills, were merged with Kamrup and the erstwhile Ahom and Motok territories to create the province of Assam. The logic broadly followed was dictated by commercial interests – as the Viceroy Lord Mayo had declared it would be unwise to split the tea-growing country, this led to the inclusion of Sylhet and Cachar, which were then part of Bengal.[45] Goalpara, which had been part of Bengal since Mughal times, was also transferred to Assam.

The inclusion of these predominantly Bengali-speaking areas brought a large Bengali population into Assam. The area of the newly created Chief Commissionership of Assam was 41,798 square miles and its total population was 41,32,019, out of which the three districts of Sylhet, Cachar and Goalpara, which were transferred from Bengal to the new province, accounted for 13,623 square miles and a population of 27,02,327, as per the census of 1872.[46]

This sharpened the divide between the Bengali and other identities; literacy was then not widespread, and the relatively more literate Bengalis, mainly caste Hindus from Sylhet, came to dominate jobs in the new administration, to the chagrin of the caste Assamese, who were their rivals for the same jobs. Moves to get rid of them manifested in identity politics. The competition for dominance sharpened once electoral politics entered the picture when elections with limited franchise were introduced after the Assam assembly was established, before Partition and independence, in 1937.

The insecurities of competition for jobs, land and resources have fuelled different waves of identity politics in Assam from its formation till date. The first separation, that of Assam from Bengal, was followed by multiple separations of smaller territories and identities from Assam. After the overbearing presence of Bengalis had been whittled down to size, the tribal groups rebelled next against Assamese domination. The Naga Hills became Nagaland in 1963. The Garo, Khasi and Jaintia Hills broke away and became the state of Meghalaya in 1971–72. The Lushai Hills became the union territory of Mizoram in 1972 and was upgraded to a state in 1987. Arunachal Pradesh, earlier known as North East Frontier Agency, followed a similar trajectory. That's not all. There are long-running movements for a separate Bodoland state, a Dimarji of the Dimasa Cacharis, and a Karbi state. The Koch Rajbongshis have a demand for a state that would include parts of Assam and West Bengal. There have also been occasional murmurs from the

Bengali-speaking Barak Valley areas of Assam in favour of becoming a separate state.

The issue of who belongs in Assam is still not settled. It is a question that has led over the years to many massacres. After Independence, starting 1960, there were riots against the Bengali-speaking populations, mainly directed against the Hindu Bengalis who had come as Partition refugees fleeing riots in East Pakistan. The slogan of the rioters then was '*Bongal kheda*', meaning 'drive out the Bongals', a term which originally meant outsiders but by then had come to mean Bengalis. The Assamese fears of Bengali domination led in 1979 to a movement called the Assam Agitation, aimed at evicting 'foreigners' with the slogan of '*bidekhi kheda*', meaning 'drive out the foreigners'. The foreigners targeted were once again Bengalis, Hindu as well as Muslim, who were seen as illegal immigrants from Bangladesh. In 1983, in a place called Nellie upriver from Guwahati, mobs armed with bows and arrows, machetes, sticks, and other such weapons surrounded and massacred at least 2,191 Bengali Muslim men, women and children overnight. Not a single person was ever charged with any crime for the thousands of murders.

In 1985, an accord was signed by the Government of India with the All Assam Students Union and the All Assam Gana Sangram Parishad which had led the Assam Agitation. A key clause of the accord related to the detection, deletion from electoral rolls, and deportation, of foreigners who had entered Assam on or after 25 March 1971 – the day that Operation Searchlight in neighbouring East Pakistan kicked off a genocide, one of the worst in world history, in which somewhere between one and three million Bengali civilians were massacred by the Pakistan military. The Assam Accord's cut-off date was thus selected so as to exclude those who fled the Bangladesh genocide that began from 25th March.

Unfulfilled promises of implementation of the Assam Accord by governments since 1985 led, more than thirty years later, to the legal activism that kicked off the attempt to draw up a National Register of Citizens specifically for Assam.

The massive NRC exercise was on in the state when I reached Goalpara. A total of four million people, mostly Bengali speakers, both Hindu and Muslim, had been excluded from the first list that had then been published. There were reports of all kinds of people being excluded. Even the name of a former chief minister of Assam, a Muslim woman named Syeda Anwara Taimur, was not in the list. Mohammad Sanaullah, a former soldier of the Indian Army who had participated in the Kargil War, was not in the list. Pinaki Bhattacharjee, a descendant of the high priest of the Kamakhya temple whose ancestors had come there from Bengal centuries ago, was also among those excluded.

Eventually, after a process of corrections, a final NRC list with 1.9 million people left out was published. It pleased no one. The Assam government and the Assam unit of the Bharatiya Janata Party rejected it, with minister Himanta Biswa Sarma saying it had 'failed to fulfil the aspirations of the people of Assam' and demanding that the list be scrapped.[47] The All Assam Students' Union also rejected the list, with its advisor Samujjal Bhattacharya saying the figure of 1.9 million excluded was too low. Efforts began in earnest to push up the numbers by pushing back the cut-off year from 1971 to 1951.

The NRC process had been carried out under the direct supervision of Ranjan Gogoi, the Assamese Chief Justice of the Supreme Court of India, who months after retirement became a nominated Member of Parliament with the support of the BJP government of Prime Minister Narendra Modi. It had cost Rs 1,600 crore and taken over 50,000 Assam state government employees five years. It failed to satisfy those who wanted a few million more Bengali speakers of East Bengal origin, who are often labelled Bangladeshis, to be evicted. The ethnic composition of those excluded presented a problem for the BJP; media reports suggested that a very large number of Bengali Hindus had been left out, followed by Bengali Muslims, Nepali speakers, and tribals such as Bodos and Hajongs. Sarma, the BJP leader, held out a 'safety net' for the excluded Hindus: they would be saved from internment in detention camps by the Citizenship Amendment Bill (CAB), to be passed in Parliament by the BJP. This Bill reduced the period of mandatory residency required to acquire Indian citizenship by naturalization to six years from eleven years for Hindus, Buddhists, Sikhs, Jains, Parsis, and Christians who had migrated from Afghanistan, Pakistan and Bangladesh before 31 December 2014.

This idea spread and caught on. Speaking at a press conference in neighbouring West Bengal in April 2019, Amit Shah, the then BJP president, dropped a line that would subsequently become famous: *'Aap chronology samajh lijiye'* (You understand the chronology). The chronology he explained was as follows: first, CAB would come, then NRC would come, for the whole country. CAB would give citizenship to all refugees, he said, therefore they had nothing to worry about. Only infiltrators need worry.

Implicit in this plan of a national NRC and an amendment to the country's citizenship laws was the fact that while all communities might be equally affected by the vagaries of the NRC, those professing faiths other than Islam woud be rescued by the CAB. The amendment was pushed through Parliament in December 2019. The first place to erupt in protest against it was Guwahati, where protestors tore down a hoarding of Prime Minister Narendra Modi and his Japanese counterpart Shinzo Abe. The PMs were scheduled to meet in Assam for a summit, which had to be cancelled as protests escalated across Assam and then spread out to the whole country, leading eventually to riots in Delhi.

The combination of NRC and Citizenship Amendment Act reopened old wounds across the country. It brought back to the fore divides between Assamese and Bengalis in Assam, tribals and non-tribals in the hills of Northeast India, and Hindus and Muslims everywhere. It did this without serving a single useful purpose for anyone. More than a year after the Bill was rushed through Parliament, the rules for implementation of the new law had not been notified, meaning that exactly zero persons had got citizenship under the Citizenship Amendment Act which, it had been advertised, would give instant citizenship to millions of Hindus waiting for citizenship.

Goalpara is one of the key sites of the project to evict 'Bangladeshis' from Assam. A brand new detention centre, India's largest, with a capacity to hold 3,000 inmates, is being built there, a few kilometres upriver from the town.

At a ramshackle, cheap, busy tea shop, near the centre of the town, I ordered my tea in broken Assamese. The waiter replied in the same language. While paying at the counter, I again spoke in Assamese. The next day, with the comfort of greater familiarity, I tried Bengali. The waiter replied in the same language. So did the man at the counter. I did not discover whether they were Bengalis who spoke Assamese, or Assamese who spoke Bengalis, or, more likely, Goalpariyas who spoke both. Perhaps the question itself was unnatural, a product of colonial politics and an imagination that boxed people in neat categories, like animal species, and ordered the world into neat coloured maps of ethnic territories, ethnically pure homelands whose ultimate expression was the Nazi German dream and the Jews in concentration camps.

I took a big autorickshaw down to the river, a drive of some fifteen minutes away on bumpy roads little better than a dirt track. The town itself is at a slight elevation. Below this, the land falls away sharply to the riverbed. It was winter and the river had receded. A thick fog shrouded visibility. It was nine in the morning, late for these parts, but it was still dark, and cold in the open autorickshaw. The road followed the curve of a hill along the riverside. I could vaguely see colours on the riverbed at times through the fog; a patch of blue on the sand, where a net was drying. The green of a paddy field. On closer inspection, the paddy turned out to be nurseries for saplings, walled off by low walls of cloth and bamboo. The main channel of the river was out there somewhere in the fog. Small streams flowed down into the channel near the road, and lone fishermen in little canoes sat fishing at the mouths of these streams.

I met a group of five fishermen huddled outside a fire of twigs on the roadside near the river at a place called Panchratna, meaning 'five jewels', a little outside Goalpara. They were from the nearby village. Two were dark, bearded men with weatherbeaten faces wearing checked lungis and shawls – the stereotypical Bengali Muslim fisherman or farmer. Two others, both younger, wore trousers, shirts and jackets. I started speaking to one of them. His name was Nazrul. Like his father, he was a fisherman. The family owned a twenty-feet long country boat without an engine, he said. He was not sure he wanted to continue in the family trade. He was studying to clear his Higher Secondary, meaning Class Twelve, exams. If he managed to pass the exams, he would try and find some other work. Fishing, he said, was hard work, and the rewards were insufficient for his liking. Nazrul didn't like the uncertainties. 'There is no surety in this profession. Some days you earn, some days you don't,' he said. The other young man, Gautam Malo, a Hindu Bengali, however liked his work. 'It is my own business, I am the owner. I am not serving under anyone,' he said. He liked being his own boss. His father had gone out fishing in their family boat, and he would go after his father returned. Between the two of them they managed to make enough, he said.

There was no particular time to their fishing, but usually most of them went out around two or three in the morning, in complete darkness, and returned around six. There by the riverside, they

would auction their catches to agents who would buy whole lots
and distribute them to retailers in the Goalpara bazaar. The auction,
like any auction, was a matter of calling out bids, with the catch
going to the highest bidder.

There were many kinds and sizes of fish in the river, the
fishermen said. The biggest was one they call the 'baghair', a fish
listed as critically endangered by IUCN. It could weigh as much
as 120 or 130 kg, and fetch over Rs 1 lakh. I asked if any of them
had ever caught one of those. 'I caught a 120 kg baghair myself
last season,' Nazrul claimed. To pull it in required more than just
a net; it required a hook as well, he said. This year, though, no
one had caught any baghair so far. 'Why?' I asked, and one of the
old bearded men started to reply but was cut off by Nazrul. 'It is a
seasonal thing,' he said. There was a pause. Then another of the old
men, silent so far, spoke. 'The dirty water has reduced the catch.'
Then, in bits, the story emerged. The waters had been unusually
muddy this season. They had heard and seen on TV that China was
damming the waters upriver in Tibet. Perhaps that was the reason.
The fish catch had been bad for around forty-five days. Now it was
starting to get back to normal, but in a good year fishermen from
Goalpara would have caught two or three baghairs by this date, they
said. This year they had caught none.

Species of catfish and carp, mainly rohu, are the common catches.
However, catches in general had been falling, they said.

I left them sitting huddled around their little fire in the dense
river fog. As the day progressed, sunlight managed to push weakly
through the greyness, to reveal a ridiculously pastoral landscape.
Women dressed in saris or tribal wraps worked in the green fields
of freshly planted paddy. Fields of lotus bloomed wild on wetlands.
Mustard fields of golden yellow alternated with fields of pink.
Little wooden canoes floated on rivulets. Somewhere, an occasional
fishing net dangled from bamboo supports. The river itself was

quiet, its waters still. A great stillness hung over it as it lay under its blanket of fog. Huge sandbars were everywhere. Near the bridge, only two channels remained, separated by a massive sandbar as big as an island.

Goalpara and the places around it bear traces of ancient Buddhist and Hindu sites dating back to before the birth of Jesus Christ 2,000 years ago, from which point the Gregorian calendar now used around the world begins. There is, for instance, a stupa cut into a single large rock. There is also a sacred hill called Dadan Hill, and the Surya Pahar, a green hillside strewn with rocks, on many of which Shiva lingas, in their hundreds, are carved. Surya Pahar also has ancient Buddhist stupas, and it is possible that the site was a Buddhist place of worship before it became a Hindu place of worship. Hindus today have forgotten that temples and idol worship did not exist in the Vedic faith – there were only yagnas and mantras. Idol worship in Hinduism dates to the days of the Mauryan empire, coincidentally also the time when Buddhism was on the rise.

It wasn't only the ideas of Buddhism that flowed into Hinduism. Ancient tribal folk practices also entered the Hindu faith. Many still exist, although they have long been undergoing a process of Sanskritization and gentrification, becoming more sanitized over time. In the district of Goalpara, there was a practice called the Hudum puja, worship of the Hudu god who appears in the shape of a barn owl. There is a short story about it in a book called *Hudumdeo Aru Annnanya Golpo* by the Assamese writer Imran Hussain.[48] It is a folk rite associated with fertility, and with rain; the worship is believed to bring about the onset of rains. In the original form, it involved a song and dance around a 'hudum pole' of plantain or bamboo ... in deserted forest clearings, by married and widowed women, in the middle of the night, dancing naked.

51

Vapour and Vigour

DOWNRIVER FROM GOALPARA IS the last riverside town of note on the Indian side of the border, Dhubri. Beyond this, the river flows into Bangladesh. Back when there were no international borders here and the river was the main highway of travel into Assam, Dhubri was an important river port.

Travel on the river, especially before the advent of steamers, was an experience so distant from ours as to be unimaginable. Writing in the closing years of the 1800s, Alfred Brame, historian of the India General Steam Navigation Company Ltd which ran steamer services from Calcutta to Dibrugarh and Allahabad, wrote, 'The India of the early years of the present century (1800s) is so far removed from the India of today as to make one marvel how our predecessors of but a generation or two back managed to make life worth living.'

'The Ganges,' wrote Brame, 'was then the great highway from Calcutta into the interior; for although the Grand Trunk Road was in existence, it was used in cases of great emergency only and involved the utmost discomfort. The civilian, the soldier, the planter and trader all journeyed to Patna, Allahabad, or Delhi by water, in pinnaces, bauliahs, or budgerows, according to their means and station in life.' These different kinds of wooden boats, all powered by oars and sails, differed from one another in size. The budgerow was the big boat, one with a cabin and a roof, both vital necessities for long journeys on the river where the sun beats down mercilessly and the rain comes lashing. It was the boat the wealthy took.

'The boats were generally tracked along the bank by ropes when ascending the river, unless the wind was favourable, when sail was set and the weary crew had a welcome rest,' wrote Brame. 'Government servants had a fixed allowance for boat-hire when moved from station to station; so much per month according to the rank of the traveller.'

There was also a scale of time allowed between different points. 'Calcutta to Monghyr (Munger) 1 month 8 days, Calcutta to Buxar 2 months, Calcutta to Allahabad 3 months ... Calcutta to Dacca took 1 month in those days, and such far-away places as Assam or Sylhet were beyond the range of any fixed timing.' Basically, until the early 1800s, if you were going to Assam or Sylhet from Calcutta, or vice versa, you set sail hoping you would eventually reach someday, months hence. For example, when the first American Baptists made the journey from Calcutta to Sadiya, the journey took them four months from December 1835 to March 1836.

The advent of steamers changed that. It revolutionized travel. 'It was only in 1828 that it took 3 months to make a journey that is now traversed in 18 hours,' wrote Brame in 1899. The specific route he was referring to was the journey from Calcutta to Allahabad. It had taken seventy years, and the Industrial Revolution, for the distance between these hitherto remote lands to shrink to practically nothing.

The first steamer to reach India was called the *Enterprise*. It was a steamer of the East India Company built in England that reached

Calcutta in 1825, after a sea journey of 113 days. It ran between Calcutta, Rangoon, Penang and Singapore, which by Brame's time were known as the Straits Settlements, and were parts of the British empire. The first inland steamer, named the *Lord William Bentinck* after the Governor General who had proposed introduction of such services, was launched in 1834. By 1836, there were four government steamers in India, all plying on the Ganges. Those early steamers were large paddleboats with a chimney stack rising into the air at one end, and masts and sails at the other. They carried cargo only and provided quarters for the ship's officers, wrote Brame, while a separate 'accommodation boat' that was tugged along by the steamer 'conveyed passengers who occupied cabins of various classes, but messed at the captain's table on the steamer, the communication between the two vessels being provided by a gangway'. Travel from Calcutta to Allahabad in those early steamers took between twenty-two to twenty-eight days. It also cost what was then a minor fortune; a first-class passage including meals was worth around Rs 400, and Brame lamented that this did not even include wines.

The growth of steamer travel in India took off in earnest after the India General Steam Navigation Company, with the motto of 'vapor et vigor' was formed in 1844 due to the efforts of Carr, Tagore & Co., a large partnership firm set up by William Carr and Dwarkanath Tagore, grandfather of poet Rabindranath Tagore. The same year, it purchased a steamer and a flat (a boat with a flat deck rather like a barge) called the *Assam* and *Naga* respectively, from the Assam Company, the first commercial tea company in the world, of which Dwarkanath Tagore was also a founder. The two companies shared close links and had a common chairman in John Storm.

The steamer business soon faced competition from another new technology. By the 1860s, the railways had begun to expand in Gangetic India. Steamer traffic was affected. 'About the same time that trade on the Ganges was declining, the tea industry of

Assam was beginning to show signs of development, and India General, slowly driven from the Ganges, held council whether the Brahmaputra might not find employment for some of their vessels,' wrote Brame. 'Assam at this time was a most forsaken province. The only means of communication was by a government steamer which left Calcutta once in six weeks.' This government steamer service had been launched in 1847, and ran from Calcutta to Guwahati, covering the distance in roughly sixteen days. The India General steamer company worked out a deal with the government by which the government steamer service was withdrawn and the company was given the monopoly, on an experimental basis for six months, to run a steamer and flat from Calcutta to Dibrugarh once every six weeks.

It was with much trepidation that the company's directors launched the service. 'Unlike the Ganges, which flowed through thickly populated districts, and had an enormous volume of trade ready to hand, the Brahmaputra passed through a practically unknown country; there were no towns of any note on its banks, the districts on either side were sparsely peopled with inhabitants, whose wants were small; and leaving out the item of tea, the exports were practically nil,' Brame observed. The Assam line, as it was called, however, proved a commercial success. By 1862, the service was increased to monthly instead of six-weekly. In 1864, Brame reported a 'great rush of capital into the tea industry, and the best steamers of the company were placed on this service.'

This created new business opportunities for the steamer company. It also changed the design of the steamers, which until then had been fitted with cabins – typically four first class, four second class, and six third class. 'Assam itself supplies no labour, and every coolie employed on a tea garden has to be imported, as is also every maund of food stuff on which he is fed,' Brame wrote. 'The vessels of the company had at this date very little accommodation for passengers of this class, and there was a rapid rush towards fitting upper decks to both steamers and flats, to accommodate the crowds of labourers proceeding to the newly opened tea gardens of the province.'

The original route for boats from Calcutta to Assam was down the Hooghly, across the Sundarbans delta and then up the Meghna, Jamuna and Brahmaputra. The route and mode of transport by which tea garden labourers and planters reached Assam changed when the East Bengal Railway reached a place called Goalando in 1873. This was a ghat located at the junction of what Brame called 'the three great waterways of Bengal, the Ganges, Brahmaputra and Pudda'. This became the 'natural point of embarkation for passengers to Assam and Cachar'. The steamer service for Calcutta to Assam via Goalando became a weekly one by 1875. By then, the India General steamers were facing stiff competition from a rival, the River Steam Navigation Company.

It was a competition whose fruits passengers travelling on the route enjoyed. Barker, in his *A Tea-Planter's Life in Assam*, wrote, 'This rivalry is very necessary and of great convenience to the planters, ensuring as it does regularity – so far as the river itself allows – speedier transit, and a fixed price for cargo, the rates being much lower now than in the former days of monopoly.' Writing in 1881 – the book was published in 1884 – he wrote that 'Dhubri is now regarded as the boundary point to the province of Assam. The station is one of rapidly-increasing importance, that will every day be augmented by the new railway route opened between Calcutta and Dhubri.'

He found life on the river steamer to be monotonous. He was not much impressed by the scenery, and finding nothing 'attractively striking' to look at went back to 'a never-failing source of interest and amusement–viz. studying the manners and customs of the natives'.

In December 1935, a native travelling on a steamer through the same places – a Bengali lawyer from Calcutta named Atulchandra

Gupta who left an account of his journey in the Bangla language – had kinder words for the surrounding country. He was travelling upriver, like Barker fifty-four years before him, and wrote:

> Since leaving Dhubri we have come along seeing ranges of hills. From a gigantic river like the Brahmaputra, such a scene of hills on both banks is perhaps seen in very few places on earth. The hills are green, covered with trees. When during the Non-Cooperation time, Mahatma Gandhi came to Assam, during a reception he said to the residents of Assam – 'your bewitchingly beautiful country'. Looking at the Brahmaputra and the ranges of green-blue hills on both banks, that description can be understood exactly.

Both Barker and Gupta noted the character of the river in winter, which I too had witnessed. 'During the cold season dense fogs hang close down over the surface of the river, thereby adding greatly to the trouble of the already difficult navigation. Sometimes these fogs are so heavy that the steamer cannot proceed on her way until twelve or one o'clock, by which time the sun has generally asserted his supremacy and dispersed the enemy,' wrote Barker. Gupta on his part noted, 'The winter Brahmaputra is smooth, it seems still. Only the small and large clumps of water hyacinth rapidly heading down towards the fields of East Bengal indicate the speed of its interior.'

52

Guru Tegh Bahadur and the Sorceress

I ENQUIRED ABOUT FERRIES down to Dhubri from Goalpara. There were none. I would have to hire a small boat – an expensive and risky proposition – or take the road. The condition of my wallet, and a meeting in Goalpara with a friend of a friend who had been kidnapped for ransom and held captive somewhere in the neighbouring Garo Hills decided the issue. I took the road.

The bus from Goalpara was playing Bollywood music when it started out. By the time it reached Abhayapuri, 34 km away, the music had changed to a Bengali pop number I had never heard, whose refrain, in tune with the times, was 'confusion, confusion'. This was followed by a song about the sad travails of someone who was not getting any calls on his new mobile or any likes on Facebook. These new troubles had perhaps been added to the lives of my fellow passengers, several of whom reminded me of the fishermen I had met in Panchratna.

I had heard so much about illegal Bangladeshi immigrants swamping the far ends of Lower Assam that I expected to find a crowded town filled with poor Bengali Muslims. Dhubri surprised me from the start. It has an old-world pace and charm to it, a grace of times gone by, that revealed itself from the moment I reached the town. It was night. I had not booked a hotel but had googled the name of one on the bus. I asked the bus conductor, while disembarking, for directions. The man not only helped me with my luggage but also walked me down to the nearest rickshaw and explained the directions to the hotel to the rickshaw-wallah. 'How much will you take?' he asked. The rickshaw-wallah answered, 'The fare is Rs 20, naturally I will take Rs 20.' I cannot recall ever hearing this simple and dignified answer from any rickshaw-wallah anywhere, before or since. The next surprise came at the hotel. It was a simple and neat property near the riverfront ... and it was full. No rooms. I had walked in thinking, who goes to Dhubri nowadays? Well, evidently a lot of people still do. I asked the rickshaw-wallah if he knew of other places nearby. He did. We set off again into the night.

The town, its streets poorly and intermittently lit, was alive, in a laid-back sort of way. People, men and women, hung about eating food at roadside stalls along the town's main thoroughfare, the Guru Tegh Bahadur Road. There was a modest traffic on the narrow road lined with little shops. I soon found a Hotel Brahmaputra. It was spotlessly clean, simply but comfortably furnished, and a double room cost a very modest Rs 800 a night. It was too early to sleep, only about 8.30 p.m., so I went out for a walk after checking in. Luckily, there was a good tea stall just down the road. The chai-wallah, again a surprisingly polite and dignified man, pointed me towards a new establishment when I asked him where I could eat dinner. Perhaps he wanted to direct the tourist to the touristy place, or what he may consider the posh new place. It was a place with the beginnings of commerce-trapped pretensions. There was a printed paper menu instead of the usual painted board, a flat-screen TV and a couch in one corner. It listed the usual Indian Chinese dishes that have no existence outside India, culinary nonsense such as Gobi Manchurian and Chicken Manchurian, and for a place where a decent hotel room cost Rs 800, the prices were steep. The local fish curry is famous, but this fashionable place did not serve it. They did, however, have a chicken curry, and I ordered that.

My fellow diners were two groups of the town's stylish youth. The couch had been occupied by a bunch of teenage boys in jeans and tees with stylish haircuts. The table next to them was occupied by a group of girls of similar age, also similarly dressed, except that they wore heels rather than sneakers and flaunted knee-length coats and fancy handbags. Both groups had their mobiles out and took endless selfies while surreptitiously eyeing one another. No one said anything; not even a smile was exchanged. They ate their Indian Chinese meals in near-silence and left. I ploughed through my overpriced chicken curry, spiced like something I might have bought in a cheap Delhi establishment, with fork and knife because there was no washbasin to wash my hands, and cursed this daft notion of progress that forced me to eat rubbish food at marked up prices and wipe my hands with paper napkins afterwards. The honest to goodness Dhubri of which I had caught early glimpses will probably disappear soon. The only concepts of progress and development we have are of malls and paper napkins and imitation Chinese food and pizzas. It will be a while before the myriad local cultures, in the plural, begin to live again in an unselfconscious and unaggressive way. Now, they battle their own internal insecurities either by imitation or by attack.

The town itself has been around a while, and it will endure. It is old, perhaps ancient. In India, and around, forms change but the essence remains. Dhubri today has no ancient archaeological remains, but its medieval past is very much around. It is there in the name of the town's main arterial road which leads to a large gurdwara built on an elevation overlooking the Brahmaputra. Both

the road and the gurdwara are named after Guru Tegh Bahadur, the
ninth Guru of Sikhism who had set up camp at this site in 1669. A
pamphlet published by the Sri Guru Tegh Bahadur Sahib Gurdwara
authorities explains the circumstances leading to his arrival:

> While morning prayer was being enchanted as per daily
> routine, an envoy from Raja Ram Singh, son of Mirza Raja
> Jai Singh of Ambar (Jaipur) arrived and later made offerings
> to Gurujee. The envoy narrated the object: the Emperor
> Aurangzeb has ordered my master to invade Kamrup
> (Assam). Kindly extend your protection as the area is full
> of *jadumantar* black magic which plays disasterous role for
> human being. My master will soon arrive in person to offer
> homage at your lotus feet and solicit your mercy.

Aurangzeb's brave Rajput General had developed cold feet at the
prospect of invading Kamrup because of its reputation as a land of
black magic and sorcery. Perhaps the contemporaneous account of
Shihabuddin Talish, the writer who had accompanied Mir Jumla
during his invasion only seven years earlier, frightened Ram Singh.
Shihabuddin wrote:

> Assam is a wild and dreadful country, abounding in danger
> ... at a distance from the river, though the climate agrees
> with the natives, it is rank poison to foreigners ... In short,
> every army that entered this country made its exit from
> the realm of life, every caravan that set foot on this land
> deposited its baggage of residence in the halting place of
> death ... And as no one who entered this country ever
> returned, and the manners of its natives were never made
> known to any outsiders, the people of Hindustan used to
> call the inhabitants of Assam sorcerers and magicians and

consider them as standing outside the human species. They say whoever enters this country is overcome by charms and never comes out of it.

All this would not be very encouraging to the potential invader, and considering Mir Jumla died of dysentery on his way back from Assam, Ram Singh may have considered it prudent to seek armour against the 'jadumantar' black magic that he probably blamed for his predecessor's fate. He was greatly relieved when Guru Tegh Bahadur agreed to proceed to Assam to deal with the black magic. The gurdwara's pamphlet says, 'On hearing that his prayer was accepted, Raja Ram Singh, commander of Emperor Aurangzeb's army, felt inspired that at the mercy of Sri Guru Tegh Bahadur his victory is sure and started preparations to march ahead on expedition to Assam.' The Guru, who was then in Patna and on a tour eastwards, went to Malda in Bengal and then to Dhaka, where he blessed Ram Singh and 'assured all protection against evil action of black magic *jadumantar* … the Guru then set out for Assam and after crossing River Brahmaputra reached Dam Dama Sahib (visiting place of Guru Nanak) on the river bank, which was named as Dhubri by the Guru Tegh Bahadur.'

The story goes that this was the same spot where Guru Nanak had met Srimanta Sankardev around 1505. The first Sikh Guru is said to have arrived there via Dhanpur near Dhaka, where he had also had to battle '*jadumantar*', or black magic. The gurdwara pamphlet also says, 'At Dhanpur his companion Mardana felt hungry and went to the village in search of food but was enchanted and fell victim to witchcraft enacted by notorious women of that village. Guru could visualise with his divine power and dispelled the enchantment.' The details of this enchantment dispel the mystery about the origins of a story that is whispered to this day. S.K. Bhuyan writes in his *Background of Assamese Culture* that:

Rang Ghar, an Ahom
monument near Sibsagar.
Among its relatively recent
claims to fame is the fact
that insurgent group ULFA
was founded here in 1979.
Photo: Akshay Mahajan

Rhino orphans at CWRC Kaziranga.
Photo: Subhamoy Bhattacharjee/IFAW-WTI

Elephants employed
by the Kaziranga National
Park with a mahout.
Photo: Subhamoy
Bhattacharjee

Sacrificial lambs await slaughter, Kamakhya.
Photo: Samrat Choudhury

Young leopard at CWRC.
Photo: Subhamoy Bhattacharjee/
IFAW-WTI

Feeding time for the rhino babies at CWRC.
Photo: Subhamoy Bhattacharjee/IFAW-WTI

Waiting for river
dolphins on a
sandbar near Tezpur.
Photo: Akshay Mahajan

Memorial to Lachit Borphukan being erected in the
Brahmaputra near Guwahati.
Photo: Akshay Mahajan

A sacrificial altar at
Kamakhya.
Photo: Samrat Choudhury

Shiva lingam, Kamakhya.
Photo: Samrat Choudhury

Umananda river island.
Photo: Samrat Choudhury

Water level meter.
Photo: Akshay Mahajan

The clayey riverside
near Goalpara.
Photo: Akshay Mahajan

Under the Goalpara bridge.
Photo: Akshay Mahajan

Goalpara riverside.
Photo: Akshay Mahajan

Abu Said, Bangladeshi riverboat pilot and champion of Chinese-English.
Photo: Samrat Choudhury

The Sajib at anchor
on a char upriver from
Sirajganj in Bangladesh.
Photo: Samrat Choudhury

The Jamuna rail and road bridge in Bangladesh. The Brahmaputra, on entering that
country, changes name and gender.
Photo: Samrat Choudhury

Riverside embankment near Sirajganj.
Photo: Samrat Choudhury

Public transport on the river in Bangladesh, ferrying people and produce between riverbanks and the numerous river islands.

Photo: Samrat Choudhury

Crocodile amid the mangroves, Sundarbans. Green marks the high tide line; everything below is the colour of mud.

Photo: Samrat Choudhury

... so late as 1500 AD Guru Nanak, the first Guru and founder of the valiant Sikh Nation, while reaching Dhanpur, on his world wide tour, near Dacca, had a bitter anguish of finding his brave companion Mardana, a Punjabi musician accompanying him on his tour, converted into a lamb before his very eyes, by a woman of this country, who could reconvert the young man to his natural anatomical shape according to her personal and private needs of worldly desires.

The Guru is said to have rescued his companion from his sheepish fate. The story of his success in rescuing Bhai Mardana, along with Shihabuddin's account of the many horrors that lay in this area, probably drove Ram Singh to seek Guru Tegh Bahadur's protection and blessings. Which invading general would feel secure knowing his army might be transformed by the local women into a flock of lambs reconvertible into anatomical men only for their 'personal and private needs of worldly desires'?

His precautions came in handy, according to the Dhubri gurdwara pamphlet:

When Raja Chakradhar of Kamrup heard of Raja Ram Singh's arrival to attack him he vowed to destroy him and his army. He ordered all women who were famous for their magical skills. One such woman was Netai Dhoban by name. On the other side Sri Guru Tegh Bahadur jee alerted Raja Ram Singh to shift his army, camped alongside river bank, to higher place, as a created flood is likely at night. Thus the flood created at night with the power of black art had washed away those did not shift to higher altitude and those shifted were saved ... when the magical attempt could not do much harm due to the presence of Guru Tegh Bahadur, she (Netai) became furious and hurled a 'judge' stone (several metres long) at Gurujee but with the spiritual power of Guru, the stone fell aside with such force that more than half of it was penetrated into the ground. Failing in her effort she uprooted a Pipal tree and riding on it, made another attack on Guru. The Pipal tree stopped in the air before it reached him. When Netai felt powerless and grew weary of her efforts, she was convinced of the divine power of Guru Tegh Bahadur and begged to be pardoned.

The name 'Chakradhar' in the account is probably a reference to king Chakradhwaj Singha, the Ahom monarch at the time.

Having vanquished the sorceress, the Guru then brokered a peace deal between Ram Singh and the Kamrup king (meaning the Ahom king, who had recaptured Guwahati and the lands west of it two years earlier from the Mughals) according to the gurdwara account.

There are, however, other versions of the story and of the curious persona of Netai Dhobani, after whom Dhubri is named. In the writings of historian and civil servant Robert Montgomery Martin, in the third volume of his book on *The History, Antiquities, Topography and Statistics of Eastern India* first published in 1838, there is mention of another origin story for the name of Dhubri:

Dhubri has become celebrated in Hindu legend by the writings of Khyamanondo, a learned Sudro of Bordhoman (near Kolkata), who was dedicated to the service (Das) of god, and composed the Monsargit, which is sung by a very numerous class of musicians in honour of Monsa or Bishohori, the goddess of serpents and poisons. The name of the place, according to this authority, is derived from it having been the residence of Netaidhobani, washerwoman to Indro chief of the gods. Now it so happened that there was a very great merchant, Chand Sodagor of Champanogor in Bordhoman, who was very religious but would not offer sacrifices to Monsa. At this neglect, the goddess was enraged, destroyed his seven richest vessels, killed his six eldest sons, and threatened to kill the only remaining youth on the day of his marriage.

Chand Sodagor refused to relent, and the Goddess carried out her threat, upon which the new bride, Behula, was inconsolable and, placing the dead body on a raft of plantain stems, committed herself to the river. Instead of being washed out to sea her raft ascended to Dhubri where Netai Dhobani, who was at work, took pity on Behula. Montgomery wrote:

> The young woman being very handsome, was introduced by the washerwoman to her master Indro, who was so pleased with her dancing and singing, that he desired Sib to order Monsa to restore the life of the young man. This was accordingly done, and the merchant no longer continuing obstinate, Monsa not only restored his six elder sons but all the wealth of which he had been deprived. The natives are very much delighted with the poem, in which this is related, and the circumstances are not ill suited for the flowery art. How far the composition would suit European taste, I cannot pretend to judge, for want of sufficient skill in the language, which is the polite dialect of Bengal.

In today's Dhubri too, the lingua franca remains the polite dialect of Bengal. There is often consternation in Guwahati and the former Ahom territories of Upper Assam at this, and it is commonly assumed that this is the result of en masse migration of millions of 'Bangladeshis' from the neighbouring country. It is a curious inversion of history: Dhubri and the lands around it became part of

Assam only under British rule in 1874, having been part of Bengal, the Koch kingdom, and the Kamrup kingdom for most of the 1,500 years before that. While all Bengalis are considered suspect, the Bengali Muslim peasant is the one who typically faces the maximum suspicion. However, the bulk of the Muslim peasant migration from Mymensingh district of today's Bangladesh into these areas occurred at a large scale in the early 1900s, before the Partition of India, because of colonial policies of land use. The British rulers of Assam viewed the flood plains of the Brahmaputra, which were typically left uncultivated, as wastelands that could be put to good use growing crops of rice and jute. While tribals from Central India were brought in as plantation labour for tea, the growing of rice and jute required other skills. The peasants of Bengal, mainly Muslim, were encouraged to migrate to the floodplains of Lower Assam for cultivating those crops.

Politics produced a three-way conflict in subsequent years. The Partition of 1947 occurred on religious lines, and in the east it pitted the Bengali Hindu against the Bengali Muslim. In Assam, the Bengali Hindus found themselves more unwelcome than the Bengali Muslims – differences in class composition of the groups meant the latter were necessary labour, while the former were competitors for jobs and social authority. Sylheti Hindus became the worst victims of this constellation of events; the Muslim-majority district, which had also been appended to Assam in 1874 in the same administrative reorganization that brought Dhubri and Goalpara, went to East Pakistan in a contentious referendum in which a large population of tea tribals was famously denied the vote. The Sylheti Hindus, who were forced to leave their ancestral homeland due to communal tensions, became unwanted refugees in Northeast India.

The political faultlines in the aftermath of Partition in Assam saw another turn in the history of communal politics. In the 1951 Census, the Bengali Muslims of Lower Assam, who had reason to fear their dispossessed Bengali Hindu brethren from across the new border, were persuaded to declare themselves 'Na Asamiya' or New Assamese en masse. As a result of this Goalpara district including Dhubri was retained in Assam during the subsequent reorganization of states on linguistic lines – otherwise it might have gone to West Bengal. These Bengal-origin Muslims, who are known as 'Miyas' in Assam to distinguish them from the Assamese Muslims known as Goriyas and Moriyas who are descendants of earlier arrivals, were never quite accepted as fully Assamese, and as their numbers and political power has grown, they have now come to be seen as a threat. They face condemnation and police cases even for so much as writing poetry in their own ancestral tongues. From being New Assamese they are largely back to being old Bongals, and suspected Bangladeshis. They are now the targets of exclusion of both the NRC, which aims to evict all 'Bangladeshis' irrespective of religion, and of the Citizenship Amendment Act, which leaves Muslims out of its list of those who may apply for citizenship under its provisions.

53

Citizenship Tensions

MY AUTO DRIVER IN Dhubri that foggy winter's morning was a dark, lean, bearded Bengali Muslim named Nazrul. His family had lived in a village on the outskirts of the town for more than three generations, he said, even before his grandfather's time. I asked him about the ongoing National Register of Citizenship exercise. He was hesitant; his name had not made it to the list of the NRC that had just been released earlier in the month. Most people he knew were not on the list. Their local leaders had advised them to be patient and wait for the final list to be published later in the year. Even the local MLA's name was not on the list. They were all hoping that their names would be in that final list.

Only 39 per cent of people from Dhubri made it to the first NRC list. The corresponding figure for Sivasagar, the former Ahom capital, was over 90 per cent. Arunabh Saikia, a reporter for Scroll.in, asked the NRC state coordinator Prateek Hajela about the disparity in enrolment between Upper Assam districts and places with large

Bengali Muslim populations in an interview. Mr Hajela replied as follows:[49]

> In Upper Assam, a large number would be coming through the original inhabitant category, whose citizenship we have established beyond reasonable doubt through field verifications.
>
> If you read the final Supreme Court order on the original inhabitant issue, it says that Clause 3 (3), which governs inclusion through the original inhabitants' category, 'provides for identification of persons entitled to be included in the National Register of Citizens (NRC) by a process different from what is enumerated in Clause 3 (2). Clause 3 (3) contemplates a less strict and vigorous process for deciding claims for inclusion in the NRC insofar as persons who are originally inhabitants of the State of Assam are concerned.'
>
> Now, those people, I collected their documents. I saw prima facie they seemed to be okay. They did not have to go through such a vigorous process of matching like others as their citizenship is proven beyond doubt through local inquiry. So that is why you find the time taken for this is less.

How anyone might be 'prima facie okay' and someone else not remained unexplained. There was also, till that time, no definition of either original inhabitant or Assamese, a problem that later caused the home ministry to set up a committee among whose tasks was defining the latter term. According to several people I spoke to, 'prima facie okay' or not was determined by the ground-level state government staff conducting the exercise primarily on the basis of people's names and linguistic as well as religious backgrounds, with local hearsay being the 'local inquiry' mentioned, and ample room for prejudice and extortion of bribes in the exercise.

The Supreme Court judgment Mr Hajela referred to was one in which the bench of Justices Ranjan Gogoi and R.F. Nariman had struck down a bunch of petitions seeking clarification of the term 'original inhabitants of the state of Assam'. The learned justices had found apprehensions of differential treatment resulting from the categorization of some communities as 'original inhabitants' to be 'wholly unfounded'.

Gogoi, who was Chief Justice of India when the NRC list was published, is from Assam himself, and undoubtedly has close familiarity with the state and its politics. His father was briefly chief minister of Assam. He himself spent much of his professional life there. His address listed on the Rajya Sabha website is of Guwahati, and as a resident of Assam his own name would have to be in the NRC – unless he had not applied for inclusion, in which case his citizenship might come into question like those of others whose names are not in the list.

Nazrul was oblivious to all these distant facts. I asked him if there was migration from Bangladesh, if people did indeed come to settle even now. 'Not in our village ... or in the town ... but I can't say if anyone comes in the remote areas,' he said. The older residents did not want illegal migration, according to him, because it put them in danger. They would face harassment from the police if there were any suspicious characters about.

The truth of the matter is hard to discern. The Assam government's attempts, spurred by agitations in Assamese society to detect illegal immigrants from Bangladesh, are older than that country, which only came into existence in 1971. A white paper on the issue published by the Assam government's Home and Political Department stated that various Tribunals had since 1985 declared 61,774 persons as foreigners, after going through cases going back to 1966. The majority of these were people who had arrived before 25 March 1971, and therefore were eligible for citizenship under the terms of the Assam Accord. The ordinary rules of citizenship by naturalization in India, without any Citizenship Amendment Act, normally provided for conferring citizenship to eligible foreigners in twelve years. However, this had clearly not happened in thousands of cases; otherwise, people who arrived before 1971 should have become legal citizens by 1985.

There is undoubtedly some illegal movement of people across the long and porous border between the two countries, in both directions. Sanjoy Hazarika had reported in detail his meeting with several Bangladeshi men who freely admitted to having lived and worked in Assam, in his book *Rites of Passage*. Hazarika was in Chilmari, the first ghat of note on the Bangladesh side of the border, when he was surprised to meet a man who spoke to him in Assamese. Keramat Bhai had lived and worked in Assam, fishing and building boats, on and off for thirty-five years. 'It was an Assamese contractor from Neamati Ghat (near Jorhat) who hired me for all those years,' Hazarika had quoted him as saying. He had been up and down the Brahmaputra Valley, including places such as Jorhat, Sivasagar and Majuli, usually staying for the fishing season from September to December, but sometimes longer.[50]

It is practically impossible to tell people such as Keramat Bhai apart from their brethren on this side of the border. This leads to an unfortunate tendency on the part of many to label all Muslims in Assam of Bengali origin – and many in West Bengal, which had a substantial Muslim minority even immediately after Partition in 1947 – as Bangladeshis. In fact, a very old Muslim population exists in the neighbourhood of Dhubri. The oldest mosque in Northeast India, the 500-year old Panbari mosque on Rangamati Hill, is a little more than 20 km from the town. The road to Rangamati Hill is straight upriver past the little town of Gauripur where the zamindar of Rangamati, Pratap Chandra Barua, had shifted around 1860. He died without leaving any children and his wife adopted a son. This was Prabhat Chandra Barua, a man of energy and vision who left a legacy of works, including the Kamarupa Anusandhan Samiti's research, and an illustrious lineage. The director P.C. Barua, singer Pratima Barua Pandey and the elephant-tamer Parbati Barua were among his descendants. Among the family's properties was one noted for its architectural beauty, a large and gracious bungalow called Matiabag Palace, built by Chinese artisans, which Prabhat Chandra had commissioned as a guest house for eminent guests.

Around 10 km beyond Gauripur is the Rangamati Hill. The Rangamati or Panbari Masjid that stands atop it was built, according to the Archaeological Survey of India, by Husain Shah, the Nawab of Gaur in Bengal, who reigned from 1494 to 1519. Husain Shah's army under his General Shah Ismail Ghazi conquered and annexed the territory up to Hajo between 1499 and 1502. The mosque, a three-domed structure, itself probably dates to that time.

Apart from emperors, one empress has left her mark around these parts. Back in Dhubri, we reached a forlorn, empty and overgrown park not far from the Guru Tegh Bahadur Gurdwara. In the middle of it, on a tall pedestal several metres high, stood a white statue of a woman in a gown with a crown on her head. I disembarked for a closer look. It was a statue of Queen Victoria that had been shipped all the way from England and installed in 1905, the year of the first Partition of Bengal. There was a relatively fresh marigold garland around her neck. How the garland had got there was a mystery; it would have taken a ladder to reach its height of around twenty feet. The only other statue in the park, even larger than the British Queen's, but standing without a pedestal, was of a cement dinosaur, painted green. I marvelled at the perspicacity of the artist who had put together this curious collection.

The river was nearby. It was thinly peopled in the winter morning. Thick fog covered everything. It rolled in from the river, cold and clammy, driving the few people who were about to seek shelter and comfort near small fires of twigs or wood on which the riverside shacks make their simple tea and food. Only a couple of these were open at eight in the morning. The bare bamboo frames of the rest stood empty and silent.

There was only one small ferry on the river, heading towards South Salmara on the opposite bank, just beyond which the Garo Hills start. It was filling up. It looked like a ghost ship, with ghostly figures standing on it. An unusual silence accentuated the eerie air.

'How will the ferry pilot navigate?' I wondered aloud. Visibility was down to no more than twenty or thirty feet. Clear visibility was less than that. The river in these parts, slower than it is in its upper reaches, deposits a lot of its load of silt and sand. There are many chars, and chances of running aground.

'They go very slowly,' Nazrul replied, by way of explanation.

They basically feel their way across, to the other side of the river, where it curves around the Garo Hills before entering Bangladesh.

Their days, like that of ferries and ghats everywhere, are numbered. India's longest river bridge, of over 19 km, is planned here. It will run between Dhubri and Phulbari in Meghalaya on the opposite bank.

There is a second ghat a short distance from the ferry ghat. It had no ferries at that time, only a few government boats parked there by various government departments such as the police, whose jobs might involve forays on the river. The rest of the boats were small fishing boats. A small dugout canoe with a crew of two came in from the fog. I asked an old man wrapped in a shawl who sat at the prow how they found their way in that fog. '*Idea hain* (we have an idea),' he replied laconically. And that was it.

They have an idea of the lay of the land and the river. For communication between boats in the fog, they holler. It's a system that has worked for a few thousand years, so I guess it does the job.

I heard some voices coming through the fog and vaguely saw some women in colourful sarees with pots. They were speaking a dialect that sounded like Maithili or Bhojpuri. I was curious to know whether they were travellers or locals, but speaking to women in such settings can be a risky venture if one is not a white foreigner. It may be mistaken for an attempt at flirtation. Especially when different communities are involved, as was the case here, prudence demands silence. Nazrul cautiously walked off from the place and I followed his lead.

It was only when I was leaving the ghat that I realized this was the Netai Dhobani ghat, the ghat where the legendary washerwoman of Indra had rescued Behula and – time being malleable and fluid – had also, perhaps ages later, or centuries earlier, done magical battle with Guru Tegh Bahadur.

54

Into Bangladesh

THERE WAS A LEGENDARY folk singer in Bangladesh named Abbasuddin Ahmed, born in Cooch Behar in undivided India in 1901, who was known for his 'bhawaiya' songs. These were songs of emotion, often of sweet melancholy. Rivers and river metaphors were a common theme in his songs, and in many of the folk songs of the river-laced region of Bengal called Bhati, from which comes the word 'bhatiyali' for songs of boatmen and fisherfolk. There is a Coke Studio Pakistan performance of one that became widely popular; it is called '*Aamay bhashaili rey*' and was performed by the Pakistani singer of Bangladeshi origin, Alamgir, and the Pakistani singer of Indian origin, Fariha Pervez. The song was written by poet and lyricist Jasimuddin, a contemporary of Abbasuddin's. Both these greats of Bengali folk music were born as Indians in British India and became Pakistanis after the Partition when the new borders came up. Jasimuddin lived long enough to see the birth of

Bangladesh. He died a Bangladeshi. *Aamay bhashaili rey ...* means 'you sweep me away... '

Abbasuddin's most celebrated song during his lifetime, though, would arguably be one called '*O ki gariyal bhai*' which urges the 'gariyal' or bullock cart driver to drive his cart quickly towards the port of Chilmari, across the river from a ghat called Rowmari at the edge of the Garo Hills. During Abbasuddin's youth this was an important river port on the Brahmaputra, near its confluence with the Teesta, and the teenage Abbasuddin had spent a year there. The land where the port once stood is now under the river. The water has been eating away the land. The river is growing wider.

Over the centuries, the wayward river has cut itself new paths again and again, sweeping away anything that stands in its way. Until the late 1700s, it followed an easterly course through Mymensingh that is now reduced to a relative trickle; this is called the Old Brahmaputra in Bangladesh. It is the course of the river marked on the earliest maps, such as the Bengal Atlas of Major James Rennell published in 1781. The river shifted west between 1782, when there was a strong earthquake, and 1787, to follow a new course through the channel of what used to be a small river, the Jamuna. The old name stuck, however, and the Brahmaputra now undergoes a sex change upon entering Bangladesh. The 'male' son of Brahma becomes the 'female' Jamuna, without changing any aspect of its appearance or character.

Flooding is particularly severe in Chilmari and the broader Kurigram area in which it is located. Yet, the long-suffering people of Chilmari have their hopes pinned on the river; they want their old river port back. Their wish might just be granted. India and Bangladesh signed a protocol on inland water transit in 2015 by which Indian cargo boats will pass through the old routes, up and down the riverine systems now in Bangladesh. Chilmari has been identified as the port of entry to and exit from Bangladesh on the northern side. There is no move yet to revive passenger traffic on the route; that would probably lead to hostile reactions in Assam.

Yet this riverine route was one by which travellers for centuries went to and from Assam. The first view of the land was usually from a boat sailing up the Brahmaputra.

The river as a highway developed under the organizing acumen of the British. The old eastern ways did not give importance to printed maps; there are no Indian maps of India from before the colonial period – the oldest maps are foreign ones. The Europeans had their own new ways of organizing things, people, space and time. They classified the lands with neat maps and the people, like the rest of the animal kingdom, with censuses. Mechanical clocks and watches came, and clock-time with its neat temporal divisions and the notion of punctuality with it.

Such were the necessities of commerce. It is fitting that the first steamer in India at a time when the country was run by a company, The East India Company, was called the *Enterprise*. Company Raj facilitated the development of rail infrastructure along with waterways to allow for the smooth movement of goods and passengers. It encouraged the mapping of the country and its rivers, as James Rennell had observed – although the celebrated geographer took it to be motivated by an interest in the development of science, rather than the development of commerce.

A century after the publication of Rennell's Bengal Atlas in 1779, both science and commerce had developed enough to invent a whole new world. It was the world we recognize as modern, and the lived reality of it was being experienced then in places such as Dhubri and Goalando as the coming of fast new steamers and the railways that cut journey times from months to days. There was a movement and a ferment.

It was still a time when long-distance travel was undertaken, whether by planters, plantation labourers or pilgrims, out of necessity. It would be a rare traveller indeed who travelled for the mere joy of it. As for tourists, there were none, until the rail and steamer companies began to popularize travel for purposes other than the materially or socially utilitarian.

A book published in 1913, *From the Hooghly to the Himalayas*, 'Being an Illustrated Handbook to the chief places of interest reached by the Eastern Bengal State Railways' did its bit to sell the journey out to destinations in Assam, such as its then capital of Shillong. Getting there, though, could not be accomplished without crossing the Brahmaputra or travelling on it. The anonymous author of *From the Hooghly to Himalayas* made a virtue of this necessity:

> To visit Bengal without travelling on the great rivers which intersect that province would be almost as bad as going to Agra without seeing the Taj Mahal, and one may see something of the rivers and appreciate their importance as highways of commerce without making the long journey to Dibrugarh. For example, if one goes from Calcutta to Dacca the rail journey is broken at Goalando and from there to Narayangunj (near Dhaka) is continued by steamer.

Goalando, the terminus of one section of the Eastern Bengal State Railway, was then a village of thatched huts whose appearance was 'a poor index to the transhipment trade of this busy mart,' says the book. 'It is situated at the junction of the Padma, or Ganges, and the Brahmaputra, and daily services of steamers connect it with the railway systems at Narayanganj and Chandpur, and with the steamer services to Madaripur, Barisal, Sylhet, and Cachar. There are also daily services of steamers up the Padma to Digha Ghat in the dry season, and Buxar in the rains, and up the Brahmaputra to Dibrugarh.'

This made it the hub of transport for East Bengal and Assam. The India General Steam Navigation Company, realizing it couldn't beat the railways, had by then undergone a change of name and was called the India General Navigation and Railway Company. Along with its rival the Rivers Steam Navigation Company the combined fleet of the two companies then stood at 208 steamers, 252 running flats and a host of other craft altogether totalling 800.

It was a fleet that formed the arteries of commerce, administration and communications in the form of mail for all of eastern India at the beginning of World War I. According to *From the Hooghly to Himalayas*, 'The despatch service lines are from Calcutta to Assam, terminating at Dibrugarh (1,108 miles); Calcutta to Cachar terminating at Silchar (771 miles); and Calcutta to Dinajpore (936 miles); whence feeder lines branch off and terminate at Buxar on the Ganges (1,018 miles) and Ajodhya (Faizabad) on the Gogra, 1,229 miles from Calcutta.'

Goalando was the junction where, after 1865 when trains on newly laid lines began to ply, the river traffic met the rail traffic from Calcutta and beyond. On the river, there were the steamers and the smaller country boats of many types and sizes. Every steamer was accompanied by one or two flats that carried cargo. The journey itself was one that not everyone took to. 'Between Goalando and Dhubri the scenery is terribly monotonous,' the grouchy tea planter Barker complained in his 1884 book. He wrote:

Nothing breaks the line of the long low-lying banks of sand that confine the Brahmapootra, only here and there an occasional patch of vegetation crops up, a beauty spot on the interminable flatness of the landscape, and around these oases are collected a few wooden huts, occupied by fishermen. This portion of the journey takes between four and five days, and for intense monotony could only be equalled by a trip into the great Sahara.

Once again, a less sanguine description of the same landscape occurs in the 1935 account of the Calcutta lawyer Atulchandra Gupta in his Bengali-language book *Nodi Path*, meaning river path.

> High banks with cracked earth, villages of thatched huts surrounded by banana and mango trees; low chars of white sand glistening in the sun; boats sailing with white and the occasional coloured sail; sometimes a fisherman's dinghy. Towards Goalando, small and big steamers are plying, with flats and without.

Food was cooked and served to passengers. The ghat is located where the Ganga, in its Bangladeshi avatar of Padma, meets the Brahmaputra in its avatar of Jamuna. The river that flows past Goalando after this union is called the Padma. It so happens that the hilsa of the Padma river is the stuff of Bengali legends; the hilsa is the fish most beloved to Bengalis, and of all the hilsas in the world, it is said, none is more tasty than the hilsa of the Padma. However, on the steamers' menu, a different dish was legendary: the meat curry. Long after the steamers to Assam are gone, stories about Goalando chicken curry survive in the collective Bengali memory. An article in *The Times of India* in 2014 by Pritha Sen recalled the nostalgia of the Goalando steamer chicken curry through references from the writings of the celebrated author, journalist and academic from Karimganj in Assam's Barak Valley, Syed Mujtaba Ali. 'For 30 years I have travelled on the Goalondo steamer. A few things have changed here and there but not the smell. It's a little damp, a little musty but the overriding smell is that of the "murgir jhol" being cooked by the khalasis. I have often imagined the entire steamer itself to be a giant chicken being cooked inside out, the aroma permeating the entire route from Chandpur to Narayanganj to Goalondo,' Sen quoted Ali as writing.

There are no steamers plying the long route from Goalando to Dibrugarh via Dhubri and Guwahati any more, and no steamer chicken curry. The old River Steam Navigation Company shut down in 1967; it was a casualty of war. The 1965 war between India and Pakistan had done what even Partition had been unable to. It had finally cut off the ancient river links between what had become separate, hostile countries.

The end of regular steamer services didn't mean the route was forgotten. In 1971, the Pakistan Army under military dictator Yahya Khan began a genocide, in which – according to official Bangladesh government figures which are contested by Pakistan – an estimated three million people, mostly Bengali Hindus, were killed in one of the worst mass murders in world history. The river again provided an escape route to people fleeing for their lives.

55

River Pilot

I MET SAGAR 'POLTU' Choudhury, a dark, swarthy, moustachioed former river ferry pilot, in the courtyard of his home near the Sirjganj ghat downriver from Chilmari. Sirajganj today is a nondescript old district town in Bangladesh, but in the 1870s and for decades after, it was a key river port. 'The busy emporium of Sirajganj, on the western bank of the Brahmaputra, collects the produce of the districts for transmission to Calcutta. Fifty thousand native craft, beside steamers, passed Sirajganj in 1876,' a book titled *The Indian Empire: It's People, History and Products* by W.W. Hunter, published in 1886, noted.

By 1971, when the genocide began the town had shrunk from its erstwhile glory, and steamers had stopped plying the river route, but the river itself was still its open, vast and unstoppable self. Poltu, then a young man, along with his father Surja Choudhury who was also a riverboat captain, or serang in the riverboat lingo, took a sail boat and sailed it up the river to Dhubri in Assam with their family to escape the Pakistan Army. They stayed there for six months with relatives; the family was originally from Dhubri, and Poltu's grandfather, also a river man, had sailed downriver and settled in Sirajganj before Partition. He stayed on after, and when new borders came up Poltu's father and then Poltu became East Pakistanis. Six months after making the journey upriver to the land of their ancestors, when the Indian Army and Mukti Bahini guerillas had defeated West Pakistan forces paving the way for the birth of Bangladesh, Poltu's father took the family back home to Sirajganj. The old man, like many others of his place and time, had been born an Indian, lived as a Pakistani, and died a Bangladeshi.

The war itself lasted only thirteen days, but it was three more months before the chaos of the war finally ended, and ferry services resumed. Poltu remembers this because his father had been without a salary for nine months.

He himself started work as a river pilot in 1981, and retired in 2012. 'I was pilot of the Suhrawardy. It was a ship gifted by the Japan government to Sheikh Mujib's government,' he recalls. 'I used to take it from Siraj ghat to Jagannathganj ghat on the other bank. It used to take three-and-a-half hours going upriver and two-and-a-half coming back.' There was no bridge across the Brahmaputra – or the Jamuna as it is called in Bangladesh – and the ferry was the only way across. The distance, even allowing for meandering river routes, would not be more than 50 km at most. The vessel itself was a big one. 'It was 280 feet long, with a capacity of 300 passengers, but during Eid the numbers would rise to as many as 1100,' Poltu said with evident pride. Hugely overloaded ferries are common enough on the river.

The ship had a staff of twenty-three with designations such as 'Tandel' and 'Khalasi', apart from the more English ones such as 'Master'. The generic term for sailors on sea and river was 'Laskar', also spelled as Lascar.

The coming of the Jamuna bridge, the first one across the river in Bangladesh, spelt an end for the glory days of the river ferries. It opened only in 1998; before that people from everywhere used to come to the ghat by train and then take the ferry across. Now, trains, cars, buses, trucks, people, all use the bridge. The staff that was employed on the Sirajganj ferries have been shifted to places such as the Bahadurabad ghat where ferry services still operate, but increasingly, they are used only for goods, not passengers, Poltu says. At Bahadurabad, a major crossing point on the eastern bank, rail freight wagons are still ferried across the river, as they used to be back when the British ruled undivided India. The stretch of river up from Bahadurabad where it bends around the Garo Hills used to be known for its deadly river pirates; even during the 1971 war, these pirates carried on their business. The ghat itself is less than 20 km from the town of Mahendraganj in the Garo Hills of Meghalaya, but the two are now separated by an international border.

'The river that was there is not there any more,' Poltu laments. 'The water, the current ... all have shrunk. It was a river like an ocean! Now there are so many chars.' He blames erosion for the many chars. 'Whole hills come down from Assam because of erosion,' he says.

There used to be hundreds of turtles and tortoises in the river. Now they are mostly gone. The big fish are gone too. 'We used to get pangas fish ten feet long, weighing at least 50–60 kg. Now it's gone. Even the ilish (hilsa) is gone. Only a few have been visible this year. The sisu (river dolphin) has become rare. There used to be giant baghair fish going up to 70–80 kg each. Now we hardly see them,' he says. The declining fish catch has affected the livelihoods of families that survived by fishing. 'They used to be prosperous, comfortable. Now if there is no fish in the river how will they be comfortable?'

The kids these days from families of traditional river people such as his are now studying in colleges to compete for jobs, but getting a job is an uphill task. There are few avenues in places such as Sirajganj. The only jobs are in government service, and the police department is especially popular, but almost impossible to get into. 'You have to pay Rs 12–14 lakh for a constable job,' he says. 'For inspector, it is more than double. Those who pay and get in become dacoits immediately after getting the job. What else will they do?'

His elder son Raju is studying for a bachelor's degree in the local college. The boy likes his town much better than the chaos of Dhaka, the capital, but he does not know what he will do after graduation.

Poltu called in a couple of local youths, Salim and Kalam, and with these two, Raju and his younger brother Sourav and I walked down in a little entourage to the riverfront ghat. It is a 'busy emporium' even now, but much of the products being shipped and traded are items of small value, useful to the rural residents of the many river islands nearby. Bales of jute are still shipped, as in the old days, along with bundles of hay, twigs, bamboo and firewood. Old wooden boats of various sizes with blackened hulls ferry these and passengers across in a scene that appears to have changed little from a hundred years ago.

One boat stood out from the rest. It had the approximate design of a budgerow and the appearance of a pleasure boat, painted blue and decorated all over with colourful illustrations of flowers, fruits, and a house with a distinctly European look to it. Curtains fluttered from its windows. Inside, one end was taken up by a 20-hp diesel engine of Chinese make. The living section – a space of about fifteen feet in length – consisted of wooden planks overlaid on the boat's metal body, capped by a linoleum covering. There was nothing else inside, not even a light.

Our little crew boarded. The boatman, a dark, smiling man in his early thirties named Abu Said clad, unlike most of his counterparts on the Sirajganj riverfront, in a T-shirt and trousers rather than the customary check-patterned lungi, piloted the craft upriver. The green-brown waters of the river, busy at the ghat with its traffic of boats ferrying passengers and their humble goods, gradually gave way to more open vistas of water and bare sandy land topped with grass. After some time we reached what looked like a relatively new cement embankment of considerable height, near which there was a field of sugarcane. Little Saurav, who is ten years old, set the agenda here: He wanted to eat sugarcane. The others seemed to approve of this idea and so we proceeded to head ashore and made a quick foray into the sugarcane field, armed with a knife. Fortunately, our raid was quick and silent, and a stick of sugarcane was safely stolen, after which we returned to the boat and sailed off, now happily chewing on pieces of excellent and literally farm-fresh sugarcane.

My peaceful sugarcane-sweet reverie was suddenly broken by a sight that I had never expected to see in my life – a man walking through the waters of the Brahmaputra. His dark shape in the water became visible from a distance. At first I was unsure of what it was, but as our boat got closer, I saw him quite clearly. He was upto his chest in water, a lean, dark man holding high a black jerry can, with a small fishing net slung on one shoulder, and he was calmly strolling across to shore from a tiny sandbar some 100 m away. He seemed to be coming from a river island further away, around half a kilometre from shore. His shape became gradually indistinct in the distance.

We came on the other side to what looked like shore. It was steep and sandy, with the fine river sand rising to at least fifteen feet, atop which, from the water, we could see a thin layer of green. In the distance, trees and huts were visible. There on the river's edge a woman clad in colourful sari with four young children stood waiting with a bundle under one arm. No one said anything as Abu Said cut the engine and we drifted ashore. We started walking up towards the woman and her children, who were still wordlessly staring in our direction. Someone, probably Raju, asked her the name of the place. It was a river island called Char Boira. The woman and her kids fell in step with us, and showed us the way past fields of paddy to a cluster of houses made from tin roofing sheets. It was a village complete with a village tea shop in which a group of men with long beards sat watching a Bengali comedy film on a mobile phone. Between episodic laughter the tea was served. It was not the good old chai; it was teabags. I spotted a solar panel. The place, like most river islands on the Brahmaputra, had no electricity connection, but to imagine it is cut off from the currents of life in the wider world outside would be a mistake.

Morning life at the ghat is especially busy. It is the time the night's fish catch is auctioned. Poltu had complained, like good Bengalis everywhere, about rising fish prices. The prices he cited for rohu and katla in Sirajganj were indeed astronomical. 'There is no river fish below 500 taka a kilo,' he said. 'You may get pond rohu-katla for 250 a kilo.' The river fish is apparently more tasty, and hence more prized. I enquired whether the river fish is twice as tasty, since it costs twice as much, to which he laughed.

Sirajganj ghat also has boat-makers and repairers, and like other river people they too start their days early. The skeletal frame of a new boat under construction, its wooden ribs showing, lay on its side. Next to it, a big old boat with a typical blackened wooden hull was being repaired. It looked like it would be rugged, sleek and fast in the water. Here on land it had been pushed so it stood with its hull off the ground at an angle of around forty-five degrees. It was pegged into this unstable position by a frame of long bamboos driven into the ground that had been tied together into a scaffolding. Its body showed evidence of work in good progress; planks of fresh, unpainted wood had replaced several of the old ones from the prow and stern. The rest of the boat was left unchanged. It reminded me of the story of the Ship of Theseus.

The Ship of Theseus was said to be a ship in which the ancient hero of Greek legend, Theseus, had sailed from Crete to Athens. Its tale was recounted in Plutarch's *Lives* which was written around AD 120 and it presented a philosophical paradox that has intrigued people through the ages. Plutarch wrote: 'The ship wherein Theseus and the youth of Athens returned had thirty oars, and was preserved by the Athenians down even to the time of Demetrius Phalereus, for they took away the old planks as they decayed, putting in new and stronger timber in their place, insomuch that this ship became a standing example among the philosophers, for the logical question of things that grow; one side holding that the ship remained the same, and the other contending that it was not the same.' If all the planks of the boat were to be changed over time, would it still be the same boat?

The ways of boat-building are probably not greatly changed in the villages along the Brahmaputra from the times of Plutarch. There are now the odd metal boats but the old ways to making them by hand from various kinds of wood still survive. Many types, sizes and shapes exist, each with its own name and special characteristics. They are all called 'nauka,' the generic term for boat, and the particular names are mostly forgotten, except for a couple of popular ones such as the tiny dinghy, dingi or dinga and the fabled and extinct mayurpankhi (meaning wings of the peacock), both of which could be found further upriver in Assam as well.

The boats are built by hand, by a master carpenter and his assistants. A carpenter was at work on an upturned frame of a boat that morning on Siraj ghat. He was working at it with a hammer and chisel. The larger planks had been perfectly nailed together to give it the typical lean, elongated shape. How the curvature of the planks had been achieved was a mystery to me, and one that the carpenter, absorbed in his work, had no time or inclination to explain.

I moved on to board the *Sajib*, the same boat that we had taken the previous day. Abu Said greeted me with a wide smile and without much ado set about poling the boat out into midstream with a bamboo pole. I waved my goodbyes to Poltu, little Saurav, Salim and Kalam who had all come down in a delegation to see me off. We had gone barely a few hundred metres when suddenly he turned the craft back towards land, muttering all the while into his mobile phone. 'What happened?' I asked him in Bengali. 'Two people are better than one,' he replied.

This was to be the last time that Abu Said would speak to me in Bengali.

After his assistant Shahadat Hossain had joined the crew, and we had resumed our journey, I went up to Abu Said to ask how boatmen on the beautiful, treacherous river piloted purely by instinct and sight. He replied volubly – in Chinese English with a few random words of Bengali thrown in. I was flummoxed; why was a Bangladeshi boatman from Sirajganj talking in Chinese English? '*Apni Bangla bolen* (Please speak in Bengali),' I suggested. He ignored my request and carried right on in a language that was his alone. I understood not a word of it. Abu Said sensed my incomprehension, and finally uttered a sentence I got. 'Brother!' he exclaimed. 'You lookalooka!'

Conversation was pointless. Picking up my camera, I went off to lookalooka.

The scenes around were idyllic, postcard-like. Winter had set in, and out in the sun on the water it was pleasantly warm. The expanse of the river was dotted with little fishing boats and their ragtag crews of twos and threes. The shoreline was clearly visible on one side. On the other, what appeared to be shore near at hand was really a giant river island, or char. It was indistinguishable from the shore, except in one detail: the shore near Sirajganj town had structures for defence against floods.

We passed a nearly thirty-foot high embankment lined with concrete blocks jutting into the river on the Sirajganj side. On seeing it, Abu Said immediately got animated. He left the rudder to Shahadat and came up to me. The story, which he told in his Bangladeshi version of Chinese English, was one that I managed to piece together from a few stray words that I subsequently checked with Shahadat.

Abu Said had worked on ferrying the engineers who had constructed these embankments. They were Chinese engineers; these structures had been built by a Chinese company. He had been in their service for a couple of years. The memory of the experience, and the language of communication – to my regret – had stayed with him.

The Koreans have also been building things on the river in these parts, albeit without Abu Said's assistance. A short distance out of Sirajganj, we came to a great bridge spanning the river. This is the Jamuna Setu, a 5.63-km bridge which, when completed in 1998, was Bangladesh's first bridge across the river. It was built by Hyundai.

Our first halt was at a sandbar in the middle of the river downriver from the Jamuna Setu. It stood barely a few feet above the water line, its fine sand gleaming white in the sun. Two little canoes were pulled up at its edge, and five men were busy pulling furrows in the sand. This was free land, newly born of the river, on which they had staked a tenuous claim. They were planting peanuts. They gave us a handful of the raw, fresh nuts to eat.

We resumed our journey. The sound of the boat's engine was loud in the silence that stretched all around us. There was only water, with the sun glinting off the surface, and the faraway shapes of occasional fishing boats. In the distance, we could see edges of protruding land. Sometimes an occasional human silhouette would be visible.

A few of the boats that we passed were overloaded passenger boats going to or from the chars. Feeding the animals is a big part of the work for the villagers on the chars. It is also a considerable part of the river traffic. All along the river, there are boats big and small ferrying fresh grass and bales of hay to the river islands. The produce from the islands, in the form of vegetables, milk and animals for meat flows out to the surrounding river ports on the mainland.

I was hungry. It was well past lunchtime, and the little food I had packed for my journey was over. A picnic on the river would have been great, but what would really hit the spot would be a cooked meal ... especially one that featured the legendary Goalando chicken curry. 'Can we stop somewhere for lunch?' I asked Abu Said, looking hopefully towards what appeared to be a big river island with evidence of human habitation that we were racing past. This time he said something I understood bits of. 'There many peoples!' he said. And then: 'Dakat.' Dacoits. Abu Said turned around and began to show me the back of his head, close to his neck. There was a scar from an old wound. It stretched across his scalp.

It transpired that when he was working with the Chinese, they had once been held up by pirates somewhere in these waters after dark. Abu Said had been lucky to survive; he had been hacked with a machete. Two or three inches lower and he would have lost his head.

I looked at the idyllic scene of tree-lined shore and country boats drawn up on white sand with new eyes. Pirates had been a danger to river traffic even in Mughal and British times, and apparently, they were still around. I was glad when we left the island, with its alleged population of pirates, safely behind.

The river grew calmer. The water was a deeper green. We crossed more villages, in easy view. Once I saw a woman in a colourful sari walking down to the river's edge with a pot to fill water. It was a scene that could have been from this century or any of the twenty that preceded it.

I had been following this river for a thousand kilometres by now. In so many places along the length, I had seen signs of a timeless flow of life. It was there in the annual ebb and flow of flood waters, in the annual migrations of the animals of Kaziranga, in the seasonal struggles of the paddy farmers planting their crops, and the daily struggles of fishermen casting their nets in the great river, as their ancestors had done for generations before. It was there in the form of wandering holy men at the places of worship along the river's banks. It was there in the theatrical lives of satras in Majuli and the quotidian details of nondescript, ramshackle shops on peripatetic ghats.

The river grew wider. It was evening, and a deepening golden glow covered its surface, stretching into the distance. There was a boat on the horizon. In the last light of the day, I saw a dark silhouette of a man standing on a sandbar with the vast river around him.

Minutes later, the river opened up into what looked like ocean. There were large ships about. Ferries and boats bustled busily about, tooting their horns now and then. It was Goalando ... or what had become of it. We had reached the confluence of the Brahmaputra and the Ganga.

The celebrated ghat is no longer where it used to be. 'Goalando has the wandering habits of the prodigal son and constantly evinces a strong desire to escape from doing its duty in that state of life to which it has pleased an imperious trade to call it,' the nameless writer of *From the Hooghly to the Himalayas* published by the Eastern Bengal State Railway in 1913 had noted. 'It is the unstable water which has misled it, as it has misled many another Eastern towns into these ways.'

There is still a bustling ghat near Goalando. Daulatdia, like Goalando of yore, is a place where rivers and people meet. Ferries busily cross back and forth between the banks. There are the usual ramshackle stalls selling food and tea, and a surprising number selling cheap clothes. Long lines of trucks stay lined up entire nights waiting their turn to cross the river.

Barely a sign remains of the famed ghat of British times. The currents – of rivers, of people and of time – have swept the physical past away. There is only the continuity in 'imperious trade' at the spot. Most other businesses here have shrunk since the glory days of the ghat, but the oldest profession in the world has done well. Daulatdia is now the biggest red-light area in Bangladesh. In the narrow lanes of closely packed tin shacks, a couple of thousand prostitutes, many of them underage girls, ply their trade. Rough men, many of them truckers, swarm the place. Occasionally, one catches a glimpse of a woman with cheap, too-bright clothes, usually sari or salwar kameez, and too much make-up.

Abu Said and Shahadat had a mumbled conversation shortly after we pulled into Daulatdia, and then went ashore for what they said would be an hour. I was left alone on the boat in the dark and busy waters. Suddenly there was a rattling from the river side – as opposed to land side – of the boat. It was two men in a canoe, their heads and faces obscured by shawls. They shone a torch in my direction; I could barely see them. 'What have you brought?' one of the men demanded.

'Er ... brought? We have come ... passengers,' I said.

'Where from?'

'Sirajganj.'

They flashed the torch around the dark interiors of the boat that looked like a pleasure boat.

'Where are the others?' they asked.

'Gone ashore,' I replied.

'For picnic?'

It took me a moment to understand what they meant.

'Yes,' I said.

It was the right answer. They demanded Rs 100, supposedly tax, and rowed off into the darkness.[51]

It is perhaps fitting that the oldest profession in the world holds sway at this spot over what must surely be the second oldest. Priests and maulanas have little business at this confluence of the two greatest rivers of the Indian subcontinent; this seedy, friendly yet darkly sinister spot is about the changing and changeless aspects of life in this world, not any other.

Epilogue

IT WAS BITTERLY COLD, a kind of clammy cold that makes its insidious way through layers of clothing and flesh to touch the very bone. A light morning fog covered the narrow channel of river, not even 100 m wide. On both sides, the low mangrove forest stretched into the indeterminate distance. This was the Sundarbans, the greatest riverine delta in the world, where the Brahmaputra and Ganga, in their final avatar as Meghna, meet the waters of the sea, losing themselves through myriad braids into the Bay of Bengal. The name Sundarban in Bengali means 'beautiful forest'. It is not classically beautiful. There is to it only the raw beauty of a landscape that may be destroyed, but cannot be tamed.

I had felt that cold before, in other places. I remembered it well from Goalando, where I had spent a sleepless night on the boat. We had docked in the little dockyard next to the ferry ghat, but parking space in that ghat was at a premium. A local fisherman whose regular parking spot we had apparently taken set the boat, with me in it, adrift before realizing I did not know how to handle the craft. He only just managed to drag it back with a pole and left me hanging on to it for dear life. It was untethered and unanchored, and only my hand prevented it from drifting off.

The night had been bitterly, bone-chillingly cold, disturbed with many comings and goings. The river at night is a busy place in the dense darkness that sight cannot penetrate. Only the sounds, of engines and of softly splashing oars, and sometimes, of a shout across the water, tells of traffic. Occasionally there's the light of a hurricane lamp. Once, we had leapt up with a start because a massive ferry, its huge, blinding light shining in our faces, bore down on us. Our little boat rocked in the waves that rolled off its bow. Abu Said shouted at the top of his voice and waved his arms about. The ferry, as large as a two-storey building, stopped perhaps ten feet from us. After that, Abu Said again poled us out of that spot, and we went looking in the middle of the night for a safer parking spot.

The idyll of the riverine space hides the many currents of danger that lurk beneath its literal and metaphorical surface. It is a place where there are snags hidden in the water that can rip the bottoms out of boats. Where an invisible sandbar can ground a large steamer or ferry so that it is unable to move, after which, if the incident happens to be in the deltaic space of tidal rise and fall of water, its back may break with the falling water and the boat, snapping in two, will sink. There are accounts of such incidents from the long years when steamer communication was the main mode of transport connecting the Brahmaputra Valley to the outside world. In those years, the route from Calcutta to Dibrugarh ran through the mangrove maze of the Sundarbans delta. That is where, in the entire length of the river, the most boats sank.

The Sundarbans are a landscape of ebb and flow. You can see it painted on the entire forest, where everything above the high tide mark is green, and everything below it the colour of clay. It is a water-world ... And I had seen something like it before, at the birth of the river more than 1000 km upstream where the braids of the Siang meet those of the Dibang and Lohit.

The place where the Brahmaputra is formed is inexact. It had not been easy to find the river itself, gigantic though it is, because I had been looking for a reality that reflected the neatness and order of lines on a map. I was looking for three streams of water called Siang, Lohit and Dibang meeting at one point, after which there would be one big stream, Siang plus Lohit plus Dibang, called the Brahmaputra. It was of course stupidity. There is no such point. The Brahmaputra is not a single big stream made up of three smaller streams.

A river is not a canal. It is a living, organic entity. It changes with the seasons. It ebbs and flows. The word for the river's rise is 'jwar', and its fall is called 'bhata', and these words are inscribed into the geographies and cultures of the riverine lands. Its ebb and flow are the life pulsating through the land. In the rains, up in the green forested hills of Northeast India, the earth rejoices in songs of water. Its gurgling, splashing sounds, as it makes its way down towards the Brahmaputra, soft but insistent, are everywhere – and every little trickle there is, in a sense, the Brahmaputra. It is a time of rejuvenation and rebirth – a time etched into the human geography of the land as fertility rites, such as the Ambabuchi Mela at Kamakhya that celebrates the menstruation of the goddess.

Fluidity is the very essence of water. It is the nature of the river to be fluid; it has no fixed name, no address, no unchanging course. You can call it the Tsangpo in Tibet and the Siang in the hills of Arunachal, the Dihang in the plains, the Brahmaputra after, the Jamuna in Bangladesh, the Padma after it merges with the Ganga, and the Meghna at the end before it loses itself in the Bay of Bengal. You can call it what you will – because those are but mere local names, and they have no fixity. I can show you a Yamuna in north

India too, that was once a river like the Jamuna in Bangladesh. They are names on maps, a human invention that came into being scant centuries ago after the river that is older than the Himalayas had lived, in one form or another, for a few million years.

The map is never the territory. Somewhere in the vague recesses of my memory there is a story, perhaps read ages ago, of a man who wants to draw the greatest map of all time, the most detailed ever. He eventually draws a map as large as the earth itself.

Even that map would be inexact, for it would be in two dimensions, not three. To accurately model the earth in all its detail would need another earth.

'This is China,' we say, 'and this is India, and downriver from here is Bangladesh.' The river doesn't know, and it doesn't care. When an earthquake causes a landslide to muddy the waters of the Tsangpo in eastern Tibet, the fishermen in Goalpara lament their falling fish catch. When China and India plan dams and river diversion or interlinking projects, farmers and fisherfolk in Bangladesh anticipate devastation.

The devastation of flood visits the riverine lands every year. There are floods in the floodplains of the Brahmaputra in Assam and further downriver in Bangladesh. A company called The East India Company, naturally interested, like all companies, in maximizing revenues, had marked some of these lands near the river as 'wastelands', and eventually put them to use for paddy and jute cultivation. It was great for the economy, but the river doesn't know or care that there are now 'permanent' human settlements on the lands that are part of its annual monsoon home. Of course, we are powerful, we can dam the river. We just don't fully know what harm that will eventually do to the cycle of life in the lands through which it flows, and to the ocean into which it flows.

To see the river in its entirety is to see the connectedness of nature and love the intricate workings of the cycle of life – that cycle which pulses with the seasons, and the movement of water from sea to mountain and back to sea. We may dam the river on land, but if we wish to survive as organic beings, we cannot dam the great river in the sky that flows with the monsoon clouds. From the Himalaya to the Bay of Bengal it is all one unity, and the smallest fish that spawns in a wetland of the Kaziranga in the Brahmaputra's seasonal floods is as much a part of it as the largest elephants that head up the Karbi Hills to escape the rising waters. The Brahmaputra is not a canal. It does not flow between two neat banks. Its untidy braids, channels of history and commerce, witness to the ebb and flow of empires, are the architects of the surrounding landscape of nature and of humans.

Waters, peoples, languages and cultures have flowed into one another along the entire length of the river for thousands of years. Many streams of humanity have flowed in to become braids in the cultural mainstreams of the riverine lands by the Siang, Brahmaputra and Jamuna. Industries that shaped the economy have emerged from global interactions along its banks; Assam tea became Assam tea with the contributions of forgotten Singpho chieftains, Chinese growers, British planters, men and women of the tea tribes, and Calcutta merchants. Time and movement have added variety even to the river itself. Take the water hyacinth, for example. No sight is more emblematic of the river's flow than a clump of this plant bobbing downriver with the current. It seems an ageless sight, a part of the Brahmaputra's landscape. It is a plant from South America that came to India with ships in the British colonial period, and survived all attempts to exterminate it. Like its South American cousin, the potato, and the chilli plant from Mexico, it has flowed in, across space and over time, and become ancient in its new home.

'*Mahabahu Brahmaputra*' is, as Bhupen Hazarika sang, the pilgrimage of great confluences. You cannot know the river without knowing flow.

Notes

1   D.N. Wadia, *The Himalaya Mountains: Their Age, Origin and Sub-Crustal Relations*, National Institute of Sciences of India, 1964

2   James Rennell, *Memoir of a Map of Hindoostan, or The Mogul Empire*, W. Bulmer & Co., 1788

3   Franklin B. Wickwire and Mary B. Wickwire, *Cornwallis: The Imperial Years*, UNC Press, 1980

4   Ronald Kaulback, '*The Assam Border of Tibet*', *The Geographical Journal* 83, no. 3, 1934

5   A style of architecture that developed and became widespread in undivided Assam during the British colonial period. The frame was made of wood. The walls used to be made from bamboo and ikra reed, and covered with a plaster of mud and dung. Sloping tin roofs sat on top.

6   Frank Owen, *The Campaign in Burma*, His Majesty's Stationery Office, 1946

7   Ashwini Machey, 'Society, Family, Village and Housing Pattern: A Study of the Singphos of North East India', *International Journal of Social Science and Economic Research*, 1 January 2018

8   'Special drive against illegal poppy cultivation in Changlang', 15 February 2020; https://changlang.nic.in/illegal-poppy-cultivations-destroyed-in-changlang/

9   Edward Gait, *A History of Assam*, Thacker, Spink & Co., 1906

10 Opium through History, Central Bureau of Narcotics; http://cbn.nic.in/
html/opiumhistory1.htm

11 Draft minutes of the 31st meeting of the Expert Appraisal Committee
for river valley and Hydroelectric Projects held on 5 March 2020;
https://environmentclearance.nic.in/writereaddata/Form-1A/
Minutes/200320206F8JBC6N31.pdf

12 'Rapid Ecological Assessment of Impacts of Lower Demwe Hydro-Electric
Project on Wildlife Values', Wildlife Institute of India, August 2018

13 Mohit Bhalla and Saloni Shukla, 'Navayuga, Sikkim Power bid for
Arunachal Pradesh's stressed power project', *The Economic Times*, 25 June
2018; https://economictimes.indiatimes.com/ industry/energy/power/
navayuga-sikkim-power-bid-for-arunachal-pradeshs-stressed-power-
project/articleshow/64724447.cms?from=mdr

14 Proceedings of the Forest Advisory Committee meeting held on 29th and
30th April 2014, Ministry of Environment, Forest and Climate Change,
Government of India

15 NHPC Limited; http://www.nhpcindia.com/Default.aspx?id=186&lg=
eng&CatId=7&ProjectId=15

16 Subhayan Chakraborty, 'Rejected by experts, Dibang hydro project gets
green nod', *Business Standard*, 24 June 2015; https://www.business-
standard.com/article/economy-policy/rejected-by-experts-dibang-hydro-
project-gets-green-nod-115062400037_1.html

17 Parag Jyoti Saikia, 'Six Years After PM Laying the Foundation Stone: No
Clearance, No Work for 3000 MW Dibang Dam', SANDRP, 31 January
2014; https://sandrp.in/tag/dibang-hydropower-projects/

18 'Makeshift Arunachal assembly runs from a hotel', *India Today*,
17 December 2015; https://www.indiatoday.in/india/arunachal-
pradesh/story/speakerless-arunachal-pradesh-assembly-runs-from-a-
hotel-277774-2015-12-17

19 'Kalikho Pul, Ex-Arunachal Chief Minister, Found Dead, Left Note in
Diary', 9 August 2016; https://www.ndtv.com/india-news/kalikho-pul-
ex-arunachal-chief-minister-and-congress-rebel-found-hanging-1441971

20 'Full Text of Kalikho Pul's 60-Page Secret Note', The Wire; *https://thewire.
in/politics/kalikho-pul-note-full-text*

21 Bismee Taskin, 'Ex-Arunachal CM Pul's son found dead in UK', The
Print, 11 February 2020; https://theprint.in/india/ex-arunachal-cm-
kalikho-puls-son-found-dead-in-uk-family-says-showed-no-signs-of-
depression/363589/

22 Nilanthi Samaranayake, Satu Limaye and Joel Wuthnow, *Raging Waters:
China, India, Bangladesh and Brahmaputra River Politics*, CNA and
Marine Corps University Press, 2018

23 Nilanjan Ghosh, 'China Cannot Rob Us of Brahmaputra', *The Hindu Business Line*, 27 November 2017; https://www.thehindubusinessline. com/opinion/china-cannot-rob-us-of-brahmaputra/article9974000.ece

24 Col. Vinayak Bhat (Retd), 'Images show China may be using secret tunnel to divert Brahmaputra water into desert', The Print, 13 December 2017; https://theprint.in/report/first-evidence-of-complete-brahmaputra-by-china/21694/

25 This tale is recounted in James C. Scott's *The Art of Not Being Governed*, Yale University Press, 2009

26 For details, see Shiv Kunal Verma's *1962: The War That Wasn't*, Aleph Book Company, 2016

27 Leslie Waterfield Shakespear, *History of Upper Assam, Upper Burmah and North-Eastern Frontier*, Macmillan, 1914

28 J.N. Phukan, 'Relations of the Ahom Kings of Assam with those of Mong Mao (in Yunnan, China) and of Mong Kwang (Mogaung in Myanmar)', *Proceedings of the Indian History Congress*, Vol. 52, 1991, via JSTOR

29 For further details, see Harakanta Barua Sadar-Amin's *Assam Buranji, or A History of Assam*, ed. S.K. Bhuyan, Department of Historical and Antiquarian Studies, 1930

30 Rahul Karmakar, 'Book re-unites Chinese de-Indianized by 1962 war', 13 April 2010; https://www.hindustantimes.com/ india/book-reunites-chinese-de-indianized-by-1962-war/story-e0SNTIPn5BViQJM61xfvvM.html

31 Pankaj Kumar Sarma and Sambit Saha, 'ULFA chief acquitted in Surrendra Paul case', *The Telegraph*, 24 May 2012; https://www.telegraphindia.com/ india/ulfa-chief-acquitted-in-surrendra-paul-case/cid/420449

32 Swapan Dasgupta, with Avirook Sen and V. Shankar Aiyar, 'Assam government mounts pressure on Tata Tea to come clean on its alleged funding of ULFA', *India Today*, 20 October 1997

33 'Tata Tea are difficult customers', Rediff, October 1997; https://www. rediff.com/news/oct/13assam.htm

34 Swapan Dasgupta, 'Assam govt mounts pressure on Tata Tea to come clean on its alleged funding of ULFA', *India Today*, 20 October, 1997; https://www.indiatoday.in/magazine/cover-story/story/19971020-assam-govt-mounts-pressure-on-tata-tea-to-come-clean-on-its-alleged-funding-of-ulfa-832785-1997-10-20

35 Ritu Sarin, 'I said please do something...I won't tell a soul about it', *The Indian Express*, 5 October 1997; https://web.archive.org/web/ 19971023074806; http://www.expressindia.com:80/ie/daily/19971006/ 27950853.html

36   George M. Barker, *A Tea-Planter's Life in Assam*, Thacker, Spink & Co. 1884

37   Edward Gait, *A History of Assam*, Thacker, Spink & Co., 1906

38   Avirook Sen, 'Sanjoy Ghose killing: All leads point to a well-thought-out plan by ULFA', *India Today*, 22 September, 1997; https://www.indiatoday.in/magazine/crime/story/19970922-sanjoy-ghose-killing-all-leads-point-to-a-well-thought-out-plan-by-ulfa-830579-1997-09-22

39   Smita Bhattacharyya, 'ULFA admits Sanjay "mistake"', *The Telegraph*, 30 May 2011; https://www.telegraphindia.com/india/ulfa-admits-sanjay-mistake/cid/392566

40   Anil Yadav, *Is That Even a Country Sir!*, trans. Anurag Basnet, Speaking Tiger, 2017

41   Mrinal Talukdar, Utpal Borpujari and Kaushik Deka, *Secret Killings of Assam*, Nanda Talukdar Foundation and Human Rights Law Network, 2009

42   This section first appeared in an article in *Mint Lounge*

43   The Asiatic Journal and Monthly Register for British and Foreign India, China and Australasia, May–Aug 1838

44   The Census of Bengal, Henry Beverley, Journal of the Statistical Society of London, March 1874

45   J.B. Bhattacharjee, 'Reaction of people of the Surma Valley to transfer to the Valley of Assam' (1874), Proceedings of North East India History Association, 1989

46   J.B. Bhattacharjee, *The First Partition of Bengal (1874)*, Proceedings of the Indian History Congress, Vol. 66 (2005-06), via JSTOR

47   Himanta Biswa Sarma, 'Assam government rejects present NRC, wants to be part of national NRC', *India Today*, 20 November 2019

48   Imran Hussain, *The Water Spirit and Other Stories*, trans. Mitali Goswami, HarperCollins India, 2015

49   Arunabh Saikia, 'Interview: No one will be classified as superior, says top Assam citizens register official', Scroll.in, 5 January 2018; https://scroll.in/article/863831/interview-everyone-will-be-the-same-level-of-citizen-says-the-state-coordinator-in-assam

50   Sanjoy Hazarika, *Rites of Passage*, Penguin, 2000

51   Part of this section was first published in *National Geographic Traveller*

Index

Aamay bhashaili rey, 357–58
Abe, Shinjo, 329
Abedin, Joynal, 24
Abor Hills, Abors, 88–90, 155
'Act East' foreign policy initiative, 305
Adis, 75, 87, 88, 90, 98–105, 106–8, 143, 155–56, 173, 289
Agarwala, Jyoti Prasad, 254
Agnigarh, 255
Ahmed, Abbasuddin, 357–58
Ahoms, Ahom kingdom, 10, 76, 79, 80, 162, 182, 184, 186, 188, 205, 211–12, 225–26, 248, 254, 285–87, 291, 320, 325, 322–23
   capitals, 214–21, 310–11
   and the Mughals, Battle of Saraighat, 1671, 226, 284–85, 287–89
Aikyo, 205
Aings (outsiders), 106–7

Aisung chapori, 173–76
Ajan Fakir (Shah Miran), Pir from Baghdad, 222–24
Akash Ganga, 23
Akha (houseboat), 165–69
Aksai Chin, 115, 126
Alamgir, 357
Ali, Syed Mujtaba, 362–63
All Assam Gana Sangram Parishad (AAGSP), 327
All Assam Students' Union (AASU), 18, 327, 328
All Idu Mishmi Students' Union (AIMSU), 73
All Tai Ahom Students' Union, 205
Allied campaign in Burma, 48
Ambika, Ahom Queen, 213
androgyny, 234
Anglo Abor wars, 103
Anglo-Burmese war, 1826, 189, 260
animal keepers, 271–75

387

Apang, Gegong, 98
apong, 53–54, 102, 104, 109, 110, 244
Arimatta, Chutiya King, 248
Aruna chapori, 242–44
Arunachal Pradesh (formerly North East Frontier Agency), 12, 14, 39, 40, 43, 45, 67–68, 131, 173, 326
 Chinese push into. See China and India border dispute
 Inner Line Permit (ILP) for, 41, 42–46, 50, 140, 141, 149
 life, 106–8, 109–11
 Reserve Forests, 71
 Restricted Area Permit, 42
Ashoka, Mauryan Emperor, 52
Asom Gana Parishad (AGP), 191, 229
Assam Accord, 327–28, 353
Assam Agitation, 327
Assam Company, 336
Assam earthquake, 1950, 90, 163, 180
Assam Frontier Tea Company, 190
Assam Match Factory, Dhubri, 52
Assam Rifles, 15, 115, 125, 127
Assamese
 culture, 18, 32, 176, 186, 220, 254, 301, 305, 319
 identity, 169, 184, 319
 language, 37, 153, 157, 170, 178, 182, 185–86, 206, 208–9, 210, 213, 215, 216, 232–33, 246, 253–54, 257, 277, 318–21, 322–23, 330, 353
 people, 23, 38, 131, 155, 163–64, 170, 172, 181–82, 184–86, 189, 195, 204, 208,

239, 262, 278, 288–89, 318–19, 324, 351–52
asura kings, 253, 307, 314
Athena Demwe Power Ltd, 60
Aurangzeb, Mughal Emperor, 217, 286–87, 289, 292, 343–44
Austroasiatic language, 298

Baan Theatre, Tezpur, Assam, 254
Baganiyas (tea tribes), 182, 262, 338, 348, 361
Bahadurabad, 365
Bailey, F.M., 66
Bali chapori, 169, 170–71
Balijan, 177
Balipara Frontier Tract, 43
Banabhatta, 309
Banasur, 247, 253–55, 314
Bangladesh, 4, 55, 123, 182, 202, 233, 252, 259–60, 285, 287, 294–95, 296, 303, 329, 333–34, 355, 357–63, 364–66, 372, 375, 379–80
 Awami League, 197
 birth of, 1971, 289, 352, 357–58, 365
 illegal immigrants from, 46, 195, 261–62, 327–38, 340–41, 347–49, 352–53
 Mukti Bahini, 365
 ULFA insurgency, 195, 197, 240
Bangladeshis, 278–79, 289, 328, 330, 347, 349, 353, 371–72
Baptist Missionaries, 324–25
Barak Valley, Assam, 43, 326, 362
Barisal, Bangladesh, 360
Barker, George, 198, 202, 317, 338, 339, 361–62
Barman, Rathin, 271–75

Barpeta, Assam, 250, 302, 315–16, 317
Barua, Gunabhiram, 324
Barua, Hemchandra, 324
Barua, Parbati, 354
Barua, Prabhat Chandra, 318, 354
Barua, Pramathesh Chandra (P.C.), 318, 354
Barua, Pratap Chandra, 354
Barua, Pratima Pandey, 318, 354
Baruah, Manju, 277–80
Baruah, Paresh, 186, 189–90, 192–93, 195, 197, 240
Baruas, 184, 318
Basumatary, Panjit, 268–69, 270, 273–75
Bay of Bengal, 4, 377, 379, 381
Beda, 239–41
Beki river, 317
Bengal Atlas, 9–10, 358–59
Bengal Eastern Frontier Regulations, 1873, 43
Bengal Presidency, 323, 325
Bengali, Bengalis, 181–82, 305, 326, 362, 369
Beverley, Henry, 323
Bezbaroa, Lakshminath, 254
Bezbaruahs, 184
Bhagavata Purana, 247
Bhakra dam, Punjab, 137
bhaona, the folk theatre, 232, 234–35
Bharat and Hindustan, political concepts, 9
Bharatiya Janata Party (BJP), 51, 93, 99, 157, 200, 229, 284, 322, 328–29
Bhaskar Varman, King, 298
Bhati, bhatiyali, 357
Bhattacharjee, Krishnaram, 301
Bhattacharjee, Pinaki, 328

Bhattacharya, Samujjal, 328
'bhawaiya' songs, 357
Bheladuar satra, Cooch Behar, 316
Bhismaknagar, Arunachal Pradesh, 67–68
Bhootnath, 301–2
Bhutan, 126, 197, 239, 259, 286, 295, 312, 314, 315
bhut-bhuti, 24, 177, 242–43, 249
Bhuyan, S.K., 182
Biharis, 170, 305
Bihu, 213, 308
Bishing, Yingkiong, Arunachal Pradesh, 139, 155
Bistirno parore, 291
Biswanath Chariali, Assam, 246, 247–50, 251
Biswasingha, Koch King, 297
black magic, 343–46, 356
Black Savages (Lalo or Laklo-Nagpo), 13
Bodo, Bodos, 87, 288, 308, 329
    militants, 192
Bodo Security Force, 191–93
Bodoland Autonomous Council, 87
Bodoland Liberation Tigers, 87
Bodoland Territorial Region, 87
Bodoland, movement for, 326
Bogibeel Ghat, 84
Bomdila, Arunachal Pradesh, 127
Bora, Bhaben, 166–68, 170–71, 173, 174
Boras, 182, 184
Borbaruas, 183
Border Roads Organisation, 86, 141, 144, 145
Bordoloi, Bolin, 192–93
Bordoloi, Gopinath, 192
Bordumsa, Changlang, Arunachal Pradesh, 49–51

borgeet, 232
Borgohains, 184
Borpatrogohains, 184
Borphukan, Lachit, 188, 226, 284, 287–88
Borphukans, 183
Bose, Subhash Chandra, 180
Brahma Kund, 8, 37, 40, 41
Brahmaputra, a very old river, 6–14
Brahminical
    caste system, 105
    Brahmins, 169, 210
Brajabuli, 232, 320
Brame, Alfred, 334–38
bride price, 99
British
    administrative reorganization of
        states, 1874, 260, 325–26, 348
    annexation of former Ahom
        kingdom's territories, 1826, 225, 260
Bronson. Miles, 324–25
Brown, Nathan, 320, 324–25
Bruce, Charles Alexander, 162, 201
Bruce, Robert, 181
Buddha, 52, 53, 119, 312–14
Buddhism, Buddhists, 40, 115, 129, 333
buffer states between India and
    China, 125
bungalows' architectural style in tea
    estates, 199–200
Bura Buri Than temple, Sadiya,
    Tinsukia, Assam, 75–79
Buragohain, Atul, the Ahom
    chauvinist, 179–86, 189
Buragohains, 184
bureaucracy, 41, 105, 324
Burma. *See* Myanmar

Bylakuppe, Karnataka, 143–44

Cachar, Barak Valley, Assam, 43, 325, 326, 360
Calcutta to Allahabad travel
    by boat, 335
    by steamer, 334–38
Cape buffalo, 31
Carr, Tagore & Co., 336
Carr, William, 336
cartography, 9, 38, 116
caste, gender and age, hierarchies, 200
Centre for Wildlife Rehabilitation
    and Conservation (CWRC), 268, 271–77
Chabua, Dibrugarh, Assam, 162, 178
Chadha, Ponty, 280
Chakradhwaj Singha (Chakradhar),
    Ahom King, 287, 345–46
Chandra Sekhar, 191
Chandpur, Cachar, Assam, 360, 363
Chandravanshis, 210
Chang Tan plateau, 7
Changlang, Arunachal Pradesh, 50–51
Chaolung Siu Ka Pha, founder of
    the Ahom dynasty, 214
Charaideo, the first Ahom capital, 214–17
Charlton, Captain, 181
chars and chaporis, 167–68, 170–78, 242, 244, 278
Che-Rai-Doi, 215
Chiang Kai Shek, 48, 125
Chilarai, Koch General, 188, 217, 297, 312
chillies, 176–77
Chilmari ghat, 353, 358–59, 364

Chin Sha Chiang, Ta (Great) and
    Hsiao (Small), 88–89
China, 12–13, 42, 48–49, 51, 85,
    88, 94, 97, 108, 111, 116, 134,
    180, 182–83, 186, 189, 240,
    298, 315. *See also* Tibet
    People's Liberation Army, 125,
        189
    Three Gorges Dam on Yangtze
        river, 74
    Tibetan Autonomous Region,
        67
    Yellow River civilization, 9
China and India
    war, 1962, 14, 39, 100, 115,
        118, 126–27, 156, 189, 306
Chiring, 183
Chou En Lai, 126
Choudhury, Sagar Poltu, 364–71
Choudhury, Surja, 364–65
Christians, 40, 51, 105, 146, 315, 329
Chutiya kingdom, Chutiyas, 67,
    168–69, 216, 248
Citizenship Amendment Act (CAA),
    319, 322–33, 353
Citizenship Amendment Bill (CAB),
    329–30
citizenship tensions, 319, 322–33,
    349, 350–56. *See also* National
    Register of Citizens (NRC)
climate change, 175
Coke Studio Pakistan, 357
colonialism, 320–21
communal politics, 348–49
Congress, 93, 98, 192, 196, 200 ,
    229, 261
Cornwallis, Lord, 16–17
corruption, 92–93, 174–75
Cretaceous period of the Mesozoic
    era, 6–7

culture shocks, 129–33
culture wars to National Register of
    Citizens (NRC) and Citizenship
    Amendment Act (CAA), 322–33
Curzon, Lord, 13
Cutter, O.T., 320, 324

Dadan Hill, Goalpara, Assam, 333
Dai' community of China, 186
Daimary, Ranjan, 192
Dalai Lama, 14, 115, 125–26, 129,
    315
Dalai river, 39
Dalton, Colonel, 78, 79, 312–13
Dam Dama Sahib, 344
dams and environmental concerns,
    59–61, 71–74, 96–105, 258,
    380–81
    Chinese dams on Brahmaputra,
        38, 120–24
Darrang, Assam, 43, 286, 319
Das, Atul, 171, 172
Das, Rajib, 240
Datta, Tapan, 190
Daulatdia, Bangladesh, 375
Dehong Dai, 186
Deka, Pranati, 194
Demwe dam, 59–60
Deopahar, Numaligarh, Upper
    Assam, 80
Deori, Juganta, 166–69, 176
Deoris, 169
Devdas, 318
development, 103, 156–57, 230,
    240, 245, 303, 304–9, 337, 342,
    359
Dhanpur, Bangladesh, 344–45
Dhansiri river, 284
Dharma Narayan (Bali Narayan),
    King of Darrang, 286

Dhekeri, 321
Dhekiakhowa Bor Namghor, Jorhat, 227
Dhemaji, 84–85, 99
Dhodar Ali, 220
Dhola-Sadiya Bridge, 69
Dhubri, 218, 285, 334, 338–39, 340–49, 350, 354, 359, 361, 363, 365
Dibang, 3–5, 26, 38, 65–74, 115, 126, 156, 233, 379
Dibang Multipurpose project, 71–74
Dibaru river, 161–62
Dibru Sadiya Rail, 205
Dibru Saikhowa National Park, Assam, 19, 21, 24, 26, 29–30, 40, 91
Dibrugarh, Assam, 15–19, 21, 26, 42, 45–46, 50, 83, 90, 107, 140, 148, 158, 161–64, 165, 180, 187, 189, 202, 210, 360, 361, 363
Digboi, Assam, 47, 205
Dighili Pukhri, 290
Dihing river, 123, 205, 209
Dikhow river, 223
Dikkorbasini river, 294–95
Dikshu river, 233
Dimasa Cacharis, 326
Dimasa language, 161
Dispur, Assam, 284
Dogra, S.S., 193, 194
Donyi Polo faith, 94, 98–99, 105, 157–58
Donyi Polo Vidya Niketan, 94
Doom Dooma, 191, 199
Doom Dooma India, 190
Dorje, Lonchen Shatre Paljor, 14
Doss & Co, Jorhat, 226, 227
Dravida Munnetra Kazhagam (DMK), 196
Dri Valley, 39

Durjaya, Pala King, 307
Dutta, Amrit, 240
Dutta, J.C., 80

East Bengal Railway, 338
East Himalayan Biodiversity, 71–72
East India Company, 10, 11, 162, 180, 260, 318, 323, 335, 359, 380
   annexation of Assam, 189
East Pakistan, 348
   genocide by Pakistan military, 327, 363, 364
Eastern Bengal State Railways, 360, 374
Elephant Path, 22–23
Environmental Impact Assessment (EIA), 71–72, 74
ethnic conflicts, 288–89. *See also* Saraighat Battle
ethnic organizations, 205–6
Euphrates, 9

fashion, 110–11
fauna and fish, 72–73
ferries, ferry rides, 84–85, 306, 364–76
Fertile Crescent, civilizations, 9
flooding, 60, 65, 70, 74, 92, 199, 230, 243, 245, 263–64, 268–69, 271, 277–78, 286, 317–18, 358–59, 372
Forbidden City, Peking, China, 88
Forest Advisory Committee, 72
From the Hooghly to the Himalayas, 360–61, 374

Gadadhar Singha, Ahom King, 291
Gait, Edward, 51, 211–12, 216, 285–86
Gallongs, 155

Gam, Bessa, 181
Gam, Danny, 240
Ganakkuchi, 315
Gandhi, M.K., 309, 339
Gandhi, Rajiv, 196
Ganga, Ganges, 4, 10, 23, 40, 99,
    258–59, 334, 336–38, 360–62,
    374, 377, 379
    and Brahmaputra, confluence,
    4, 374–76, 381
Gao, Oyar, 98–99, 103
Garhgaon, 217–20, 222, 286
Garo Hills, Meghalaya, 43, 287,
    317, 325, 326, 340, 355, 358,
    366
Garos, 305, 318
Gaurinath Singha, Ahom King, 225
Gauripur, 353–54
'gayan bayan', 232, 234
Gelling, Arunachal Pradesh,
    134–36, 138–42, 144, 156
gender stereotypes, 200, 234
Ghatak, Kirata King, 307
Ghazipur, Uttar Pradesh, 16–17
Ghiyasuddin Auliya, Sufi pir, 311
Ghosh, Sanjoy, 238–40
Goalpara, Assam, 10, 286, 317–19,
    325–26, 328, 330–33, 334, 340,
    348–49, 380
Goalpariyas, 208, 318, 330
Goalundo ghat (presently in
    Bangladesh), 202, 338, 359–63,
    373–75, 377
Gobuk, Yingkiong, Arunachal
    Pradesh, 155
Gogoi, Brojen, 192–94
Gogoi, Nitul Kumar, 183
Gogoi, Pradip, 190
Gogoi, Ranjan, 328, 352
Gogoi, Satya, 76–77
Gogoi, Saurav, 190

Gogoi, Tarun (Chief Minister of
    Assam), 261
Gogoi, Tarun, 270–75
Golaghat, Assam, 209
Gopal, 131–32, 134, 146
Goriyas, 216, 349
Goswami, Khagen, 234–36
Government of India Act, 1919,
    319
government's inefficiency and
    corruption, 92–94, 132–33
Grand Trunk Road, 334
Great Game, 12, 13
Great Trigonometric Survey, 11
Gregorson, Dr., 89–90
Griffith, Major, 162
Gujral, I.K., 196
Gupta, Atulchandra, 338–39, 362
Gupta, Indrajit, 196
Gurung, Kamal, 165
Guwahati, 4, 20, 21, 74, 156, 161,
    180, 195, 204, 221, 227, 240,
    284, 286–87, 290–95, 296–99,
    303, 304–7, 314, 327, 329, 337,
    346–47, 352, 363
Gyala Sindong, 90

Hajela, Prateek, 350–52
Hajo, 285–86, 310–13, 317, 354
Hajong, 318, 329
Hamilton, Angus, 99–100
Han River, 121
Harman, H.J., 66
Harsha, Thanesar King, 309
Hasina, Sheikh, 197
Hastings, Warren, 182
Hayagriva Madhava temple, Hajo,
    314–16
Hayuliang, 39
Hazarika, Bagh alias Ismail
    Siddique, 288

Hazarika, Bhupen, 37, 220, 291, 381

Hazarika, Chitrabon, 194

Hazarika, Millie, 15–16, 42, 44, 49, 83, 179, 185, 188, 387–88

Hazarika, Mridul, 240

Hazarika, Sanjoy, 165–66, 353

Hazarikas, 182, 182, 184

hilsa, 362

Himalayas, 6, 7, 11, 66–67, 71, 74, 83, 115, 123, 125–26, 180, 259, 295, 317, 380–81

Hindi–Hindu–Hindustan, 322

Hindu nationalism and Indian secularism, political contest, 185

Hindu Rajputs, 16, 288

Hindu tradition myths about Brahmaputra, 8

Hinduism, 105, 185, 209, 234, 322 polytheistic traditions, 301

Hindus, 40, 185, 210, 292, 326

Hindustan Lever Limited, 190

Hiuen Tsang, 298, 313, 314

holy waters in faiths, 40

Hostir kanya, 318

Hu Zhiyong, 124

Hudum puja, worship of the Hudu god, 333

Hukawng Valley, Burma, 48

human sacrifices, 78–79, 115

hunting, 19, 53, 57, 101, 148

Husain Shah, the Nawab of Gaur, Bengal, 354

Hussain, Rockybul, 261

hydropower exploitation, 120–22

Ice Age, 8–9

iconography, 80, 129, 314

identity conflicts, identities politics, 185, 323–26

language and identity, 184, 289, 317–21

Idol worship in Hinduism, 333

India General Navigation and Railway Company, 361

India General Steam Navigation Company Ltd, 334, 336–38, 361

Indra, 182–83

Indus Valley civilization, 9

Industrial Revolution, 335

insurgency and militancy, 24, 85, 87, 189–93, 302–3, 308. *See also* United Liberation Front of Asom (ULFA)

Intelligence Bureau (IB), 114–15, 117, 130–31, 134, 135–36, 149, 150, 151, 195

International Fund for Animal Welfare, 271

Iraq, 9, 311

Irrawaddy, 89

Islam in Assam, 222–24, 297, 329

Islam Khan, Nawab of Dacca, 285

Ivan Chen, 14

Jagannathganj ghat, 365

Jai Singh, Mirza Raza of Ambar (Jaipur), 343

Jaintia Hills, 43, 299, 325, 326

Jaintias, 288 Kachari and Ahom kings, conflicts, 285–86

Jaitley, Arun, 195, 196

Jalan, Manoj, 203

Jamuguri Hat, 251

Jamuna, 4, 365–66, 372, 380

Janata Dal, 191

Jasa Manik, Jaintia King, 285

Jasimuddin, 357–58

Jayadhwaj Singha, Ahom King, 218, 286–87

Jaypee, 98, 103
Jehangir, Mughal Emperor, 285–86
Jenkins, Francis, 180–81
Jethmalani, Ram, 195, 196
Jews, 40, 330
Jia Bhoroli River (Kameng in
     Arunachal Pradesh), 258
Jingpo Autonomous Prefecture,
     China, 49, 186
Johnston, Reginald, 13, 88–89
Jonai, Assam, 86–87
Jordan River, Israel, 40
Jorhat, Upper Assam, 209, 214,
     225–37, 243, 259, 299, 353
     Marwari business community,
     226
Joya nai, 254
Joymoti, 254
Jumla, Mir, 217–18, 286–87, 289,
     343–44
Jurassic period, 7
justice system in rural Arunachal
     Pradesh, 104

Kacharis, 183, 288, 293, 320
     and Ahoms, conflict, 285
Kachins, 48, 49, 192, 216
Kaho, Anjaw, Arunachal Pradesh, 39
Kailash, Mount, 3, 8, 83
Kalapahar, 297
Kalia Bhomora Bridge, 256–57
Kalika Purana, 55, 296
Kalitas, 318
Kamakhya temple, 284, 293, 295,
     296–303
     symbolism of blood, 299
Kamalabari Satra, 231–34
Kameng, 258
Kamlang Wildlife Sanctuary, 59
Kamrup, Kamrupa, Lower Assam,
     43, 55, 80, 115, 217, 283–86,

294–95, 296–98, 307, 309,
     313–16, 319–21, 325, 343,
     345–46, 348
Kamarupa Anusandhan Samiti, 354
Kamrupi
     language and identity, 318–21
     Prakrit, 184, 233
     Vaishnava tradition, 233
Karakoram mountain range, 126
Karanjawala, Rajan, 195
Karatoya river, 233, 252, 294
Karbi Anglong, Assam, 209, 263
Karbi Hills, 249, 381
Karbi state, demand for, 326
Karko, Jengging, Arunachal Pradesh,
     155
Karnaphuli, 258
Karunanidhi, K., 196
Kathing, Major Bob, 125–26
Kaulback, Ronald, 38
Kaziranga National Park, Assam,
     249, 261–69, 271–72, 275–76
Kebang, 89–90, 104, 157. *See also*
     Abor Hills
Kechai-Khaiti temple, Sadiya, 79,
     295
Keramat Bhai, 353
Khambas (Khampas), 126, 155, 156
Khamjang, 216
Khampatis, 52, 53, 162, 183, 324
khap panchayats, 104
Kharghuli Hills, 304
Khasi Hills, Meghalaya, 43, 325,
     326
Khasis, 298, 305
khorika, 176
Khyamanondo, 346
Kibithoo, Anjaw, Arunachal
     Pradesh, 39
Kinthup, 12, 90
Kipling, Rudyard, 12

Koch Behar (or Cooch Behar), 217, 285–86, 316, 319, 320
Koch kingdom, Kochs, 217, 285–86, 318–19, 323; civil war, 292
Koch Hajo, 285–86, 310–13, 317, 321
Koch Rajbongshis, 326
Kokot, 106–8, 158
Kombo, 118–19, 128, 134, 147, 149
Komsing, 90, 101
Kongjogiri mountain, 295
Kopili, 26
Krishna Kumar, R.K., 194, 196
Kumar Bhaskar Varman, Kamrup King, 309
Kundil. *See* Sadiya
Kurigram, 358

Ladakh, 126
Lake of No Return, 15, 49, 138
Lake, W.L., 47
Lakhimpur, Assam, 43, 162
Lakhya, 295
Lakshmi Narayan, King of Koch Behar, 285
Lakshminarayan, 316
land and water, elemental war, 168
landslides and earthquakes, 71, 74, 124, 137, 292, 358, 380
Assam earthquake of 1950, 90, 163, 180, 293
language and identity, linguistic identities, 184, 289, 317–21
Lauhitya, 8
Lhasa, the Forbidden City, 11, 13, 126
Liberation Tigers of Tamil Eelam, 196
Likabali, 80

Line of Actual Control (LAC), 128
linguistic reorganization of states, 349
Lisu tribe, 53
logging, 19, 175
Lohit (Red river), 3–5, 26, 37–41, 52, 55–56, 59–60, 66–67, 379
Lu Kang, 124
Lushai Hills, Mizoram, 43, 325–26

Madan Kamdev temple, Guwahati, Assam, 297
Madhab, 22, 29, 32
Madhava Kandali, 320
Madhavadeva, Madhavdev, 227–28, 315–16, 320
Magadhi Apabhramsa, 319
Magadhi Prakrit, 232–33
Mahabahu Brahmaputra, 381
Mahabharata, 9, 67, 247, 253, 285, 307
Mahadeb, 270–72
Mahamanikya, a Kachari King, 320
Mahanta, Jugal Kishore, 190
Mahanta, Prafulla Kumar, 18, 191, 194–96
Mahavidyas, 300, 301
Mahendraganj, Garo Hills, Meghalaya, 366
Mahendravarman (Surendravarman), Varman King of Kamarupa, 297–98
Maithili, 232, 320
Majuli island, Assam, 229, 242–43, 245, 353, 374
development, 230
tourism, 240–41
ULFA militancy, 238–40
Vaishnava tradition, 228, 231–37
Makum, Assam, 17–18, 188–89

Malinithan temple, Likabali, Sadiya, Arunachal Pradesh, 80
Mallya, Vijay, 279
Man Singh, Rajput King, 285
Manas river, 26, 317
Manekshaw, Sam, 194
Mangaldoi (Mangladahi), 285–86, 321
Manikut Hill, 313
Mao Tse Tung, 48, 189
Mao Zedong, 125
mapping and surveying, modern techniques, 9–12, 66, 359
Mardana, 344–45
Margherita, Tinsukia, Assam, 47, 205
Martin, Robert Montgomery, 295, 346
Marwaris, 105, 163, 226, 302, 305
Masood, 15–20, 42, 44, 49, 83, 179, 201, 387–88
Matiabag Palace, 354
Mauryan Empire, 9, 333
Mayo, Lord, 325
Mayudia, Assam, 69
McMahon Line, 14, 66–67, 118, 126, 139, 142
Meghalaya, 43, 287, 298–99, 326
Meghna, 258, 377, 379
Meghwal, Arjun Ram, 124
Mein, Chow Chali, 52–53
Mein, Chowna, 53
Membas, 113–14, 155–56
Mercator, Gerardus, 9
Meyor (Zakhring), 39
Middle Pleistocene (780,000–126,000 years ago), 7
Migging, Siang, Arunachal Pradesh, 148
Mills, A.J. Moffat, 324–25
Minyongs, 97, 155

Mipi, Dibang valley, Arunachal Pradesh, 66
Miri tribes, Miris, 173, 183
Mishing Autonomous Council, 86
Mishings, 75, 86–87, 173–74, 242, 245, 278
Mishmi (Idu) tribe, 39–40, 66, 68, 73
Mission Indradhanush (a national vaccination programme), 167
Miyas. See Muslims
Mizoram, 43, 326
Moamaria rebellion, 188, 212, 225
Modi, Narendra, 157, 328
Mohilary, Hagrama, 87
Molai Kathoni (forest), 243
Mong Mao, the old Tai kingdom, Yunnan, 215
Montgomerie, T,G., 11
Morans, 183
Morshead, Henry, 66
Motok kingdom, Motoks, 162, 188, 225, 323, 325
Mountain Strike Corps, 128
Mountbatten, Luis, 48
Mughal empire, Mughals
    administration system, 321
    and Ahoms, conflicts, 226, 284–89
    invasion of Assam, 289, 292, 343
    invaded Koch Hajo, 285–86, 321
    succession war, 217–18, 286
Munawwar Khan, 288
Mundas, 202, 262
Mung-ri-mung-ram and Mung-khu-mung-jai kingdoms, 183
Muslims, 40, 223, 289, 315, 318, 324, 329, 353. See also Bangladesh, illegal immigrants from

Goriyas and Moriyas, 349
Miyas, Bengali Muslims in
    Assam, 259–60, 279,
    327–28, 331, 341, 348–49,
    350–51
Muttock, 162
Myanmar (formerly Burma), 15, 39,
    49, 51–52, 89, 138, 182–83,
    186, 197, 204, 206, 216–17,
    239, 303
    fell to Japanese, 48
Mymensingh, Bangladesh, 259–60,
    348, 358

Nag Shankar temple, Jamuguri Hat,
    251–52
Naga tribes, Nagas, 48, 155, 183,
    186, 216, 223, 289, 305
    militant groups, 15, 51
Naga Hills, Nagaland, 43, 180, 220,
    324–26
Nagamese, 186
Nagaon, Assam, 233, 320
Nagasankara, a legendary King, 252
Nain Singh, 12
Nam Ka Chu, 127
Namami Brahmaputra Festival, 305
Namcha Barwa peak, Himalayas, 83
Namdang, 225
Namdapha National Park,
    Arunachal Pradesh, 53
Nanak, Guru, 344–45
Nanchao, Tai kingdom, 208
Narakasura, 307, 314
Naranarayan, Koch King, 217, 297,
    299, 312, 316, 320
Narayanganj, Dhaka, 360, 363
Nariman, R.F., 352
National Board for Wildlife, 60
National Democratic Front of
    Bodoland, 192

National Green Tribunal, 60, 262,
    268
National Productivity Council,
    Guwahati, 74
National Register of Citizens
    (NRC), 279, 319, 322–33, 349,
    350–51
Needham, J.F., 37
Needham-ghat (Nizamghat), 70
Nehru, Jawaharlal, 126, 189, 200
Nellie, 327
Nepali language, 157, 261, 329
Nepalis, 68, 75, 76, 92, 96, 97, 102,
    132
Netai Dhobani, 345–47
Netai Dhobani ghat, 356
NHPC Limited, 71, 73
Nilachal Hills, 293, 296–97,
    300–1
Nile Valley civilization, Egypt, 9
Nimati Ghat, Jorhat, Assam,
    228–29
North East Frontier Agency
    (NEFA). *See* Arunachal Pradesh
North East Frontier Tracts, 43
North-West Frontier Province, 323,
    325
Nowgong, Assam, 43, 319, 325
Numaligarh Refinery, 268
Nyigma Buddhist monastery,
    Tuting, Siang, Arunachal
    Pradesh, 129–30

O ki gariyal bhai, 358
Operation Bajrang, 191, 196
Operation Golden Bird, 197
Operation Searchlight, 327
opium business in India, 18–19
opium consumption in Arunachal
    Pradesh, 51–52
Oraons, 202, 262

orientation of life in Northeast
India, 304–9
Orunodoi, 324

Padams, 155
Padma, 4, 360, 362, 379
Padmanabhaiah, K., 194
Padmasambhava, a Bodhisattva
Guru, 7–8, 115, 314
Paganini, Roberto, 47, 205
paiks, 184
Pakistan
Army, 363, 365
and India wars, 1965 and 1971,
363, 366
Pal, Radhabinod, 24–25, 28–31
Pala dynasty of Kamrupa, 80, 297,
307, 307
Panbari mosque, Rangamati Hill,
353–54
Pandu, 180, 284, 286, 306–7
Panghis, 155
Panging, Arunachal Pradesh, 97–98
Pangsau Pass, 15, 216
Parikshit Narayan, Koch King,
285–86, 321
Parlung Tsangpo, 123
Parshuram Kund, 37, 40, 41, 46,
47–54, 55–61, 175
Parshurama, sage, 8
Partition of Bengal (1905), 354
Partition refugees, 327
Pasighat, Arunachal Pradesh, 68, 83,
87, 88–95, 102, 112, 131, 136,
139, 150, 156, 158, 165
Patkai Hills, 183, 215–16
Paul, Surrendra, 190
Payeng, Jadav, 242–43
Payeng, Malbuk, 243
Pegu, Bhobon, 87
Pemako, 12, 115, 136, 148

Persian language and culture, 311,
322–23
Pervez, Fariha, 357
Phalereus, Demetrius, 370
Phukan, Anandaram Dhekial, 324
Phukan, Bhrigu, 18
Phukans, 184
Phulesvari, Ahom Queen, 211–13
Plains Miris, 173
plantation labour, 182, 262, 338,
348, 359, 361
Plutarch, 370
Poa Mecca Dargah, Hajo, 311–12,
315
Polo, Marco, 48
popular culture in Arunachal
Pradesh, 94
poverty, illiteracy, alcoholism, 203
Pramatta Singha, Ahom King, 220,
294
Pratap Narayan, Kachari King,
285–86
Pratap Singha, Ahom King, 183–84,
285
proselytization, 105
Pu Yi, Chinese emperor, 13, 88
Pudda, 338
Pul, Dangwimsai, 93
Pul, Kalikho, 93
Pul, Shubhanso, 93
Puranas, 9, 314

Rabha, Bishnu Prasad, 254
Rabhas, 318
racism in the British Indian
administration, 16–17
Raghudeva, Koch Rajbongshi King,
312, 316
rail infrastructure, railways, 336–37,
359
Raj and Runtun, 199–200, 205

Rajbongshis, 312, 318, 326
Rajeswar Singha, Ahom king, 218
Rajkhowa, Arabinda, 190, 197, 239
Rajkhowas, 184
Ram Singh, King of Jaipur, 226, 287–89, 343–46
Ramayana, 235, 320
Rang Ghar, 220, 222–23
Rangamati Hill, 353–54
Rangpur, 219, 294, 319
Rashtriya Swayamsevak Sangh (RSS), 105
Raunak Cinema, Calcutta, 254
Rehman, Sheikh Mujibur, 365
religion, spirituality and magic in Jorhat, 225–37
Rennell, James, 9–10, 317, 358, 359
Rhinos, 261–69, 270–72
Rijiju, Kiran, 68
River Dog, 277
River ferry pilots, 364–76
River Steam Navigation Company, 338, 361, 363
roads and infrastructure in Northeast India, 18, 41, 47–50, 54, 55–56, 61, 65, 67–70, 75, 84–86, 90–92, 96–100, 112–14
Rohingyas, 217. *See also* Bangladesh, illegal immigrants
Roing, Arunachal Pradesh, 67–69
Rowmari ghat, 358
Royal Bhutan Army, 197
Rudra Singha, Ahom King, 301

Sadiya, 37–38, 75, 78–79, 89, 115, 295, 307, 324, 335
    British garrison, 162
        Dibru Sadiya Rail, 205
        Kundil Nagar of Mahabharata, 67, 169

Sadiya Frontier Tract, 43
Said, Abu, 367–68, 371–73, 375, 378
Saikia, Ankush, 256
Saikia, Arunabh, 350
Saikia, Hiteshwar, 192, 196
Saikia, Parag Jyoti, 73–74
Saikia, Rohini, 268
Saikias, 182, 184
Samaguri Satra, 234
Sanaullah, 328
Sankardev, Sankardeva, 227–28, 231–37, 309, 315, 320, 344
Sanskritization and gentrification, 333
Santhals, 202, 262
Saraighat, Battle of, 1671, 226, 284–85, 287–90
Saraighat Bridge, 306
Sarbananda Singha, Motok king, 188
Sarma, Hemanta Biswa, 328, 329
Sarma, Phani, 254
Satrajit, 299
schools' infrastructure and conditions, Pasighat, Arunachal Pradesh, 92–93
Shah, Amit, 329
Shah Ismail Ghazi, 354
Shah Jahan, Mughal Emperor, 217, 286, 312
Shakespear, Leslie Waterfield, 78, 89, 155, 181
Shakta tradition of Hinduism, 211–12, 298, 301
Shakti peeths of Hinduism, 80
Shan hills, Myanmar, 182
Shand, Mark, 142, 277
Shankaracharya, 105
Shillong, Meghalaya, 58, 303, 305, 360

Shimong, 155–56
Shitalakhya, 295
Shiva temple, Biswanath Ghat, 247–48
Shuja, Shah Muhammad, 217, 312
Siam, 206, 208
Siang (Dihang), 3–5, 26, 37–40, 65–66, 83–87, 112, 114, 118, 137, 150, 155–56, 173, 379, 381
and China-India relations, 120–28
dams, 96–105
Pasighat, 88–95, 136, 139
Siang People's Forum, 98
Sib Singh, Ahom monarch, 211–12
Sikhs, 39, 40, 329, 343–45
Silapathar, 85–86, 143, 145
Silchar, Cachar, Assam, 361
Silghat, Nagaon, Assam, 299
silk in Assam, 307–9
Simen Chapori, 87
Singh, V.P., 191
Singpho tribe, Singphos, 49–51, 162, 180–81, 324
Sirajganj, Bangladesh, 364–72, 375
Siu Ka Pha (Sukapha), 182–83, 197, 215–16
Sivasagar, Upper Assam, 43, 210–13, 214, 220–21, 222, 225, 286, 311, 320, 324, 350, 353
smuggling, illegal logging, 18–20, 49, 72, 173–75
Sobro, L.V., 144–45
Sonowal, Sarbananda, 230, 240–41
Sorabjee, Soli, 196
South-North Water Diversion Project, 121–22
sports in Arunachal Pradesh, 94–95
steamer business, 180, 202, 334–38, 359, 361–63

Stilwell, Joseph, 48, 180
Stilwell Road (Ledo to Kunming), 15, 48, 138, 180
Storm, John, 336
Straits Settlements, 336
Sualkuchi, Guwahati, village of Assamese silk, 307–9, 310
Subansiri, 26, 245
Suez Canal, 201–2
Suhunmung, Ahom king, 217
Suklenmung, Ahom king, 217
Sukreswar Temple, 249, 294
Sunaridiya satra, 316
Sundarbans delta, 338, 377–79
Surendravarman. See Mahendravarman
Surya Pahar, 333
Suryavanshis, 208, 210
Sutaphaa (Gadadhar Singha), Ahom king, 220
Sutiya kingdom, Sutiyas, 75, 76, 79
Sylhet, Bangladesh, 325–26, 335, 360
Sylheti, a dialect of Bengali, 185
Sylheti Hindus, 348
Syria, 9, 14

Tagore, Dwarkanath, 336
Tai Ahoms, Tais, 185–86, 204, 208, 209, 210
language, 205, 210, 322
Tai Aiton, 209
Tai Khampti, 52, 209
Tai Khamyang, 209
Tai Phake, 209
Tai Turung, 209
Taimur, Syeda Anwara, 328
Taklamakan desert, China, 124
Talish, Shihabuddin, 217–19, 343–44, 345

Tamasari Mai, 78–79
Tamreswari Mai, Sadiya, Tinsukia,
    Assam, 115
Tantric Buddhism
    and Tantric Hinduism, 300, 314
    Vajrayana tradition, 298
Tata Tea, 191–95
Tata, Ratan, 194–95
Tawang, Arunachal Pradesh, 67–68,
    125–27, 156, 189
tea industry, Assam, 161–63, 177,
    198–204, 229, 249, 317, 325,
    336–38, 381
    discovery of tea in Assam,
        180–81
    labour unrest, 200–1
    tea tribes, Baganiyas, 182, 262,
        338, 348, 361
    and United Liberation Front of
        Asom (ULFA)'s insurgency,
        187–97, 201
Teesta, 26, 123, 233, 358
Tegh Bahadur, Guru and the
    sorceress, 340–49, 356
Tekseng, 154–58
Telanga tribe, 202, 262
temples in Sadiya, Tinsukia, Assam,
    75–80, 295
Tengapani, Arunachal Pradesh, 52
Teram, Vijay, 103–5
territorial boundaries, 155, 298
Tethys, 6
Tezpur, Sonitpur, Assam, 127, 247,
    251–54, 256–59, 261, 314
Thailand, Thais, 204, 206, 208
Thapa, Tulobai, 102, 110
Three Gorges Dam on the Yangtze
    river, China, 74
Tibet, Tibetan plateau, 6, 11–14,
    38–39, 66–67, 83, 99, 155,
    312–15, 379–80

Chinese push into, India-China
    border dispute, 13–14, 66,
    88–89, 115, 118, 120–21,
    123–28, 142, 186, 332
Tibetan Buddhism, 129, 136,
    143, 155, 298, 312–14
tribes "Lalo" (i.e. savages) and
    Chingmi, 13
Tibetan Autonomous Region of
    China, 67
Tigris, 9
timber mafia, 18–20, 174–75
Tinsukia, 21, 163, 165, 187, 189,
    227
travel on rivers, 24–25, 306, 310,
    334–39, 359–60
tribal folk practices, 333
Tsangpo, 3, 4, 6–8, 10, 12–13,
    37–39, 66, 83, 88–89, 120,
    122–24, 379–80
Tuki, Nabam, 93
Turbak Khan, 216
Tuting, Arunachal Pradesh, 112–16,
    117–19, 128–33, 134, 137, 144,
    147, 150

Umananda island, 291–93
Umatumoni island, 248
United Front, 196
United Liberation Front of Asom
    (ULFA), 24, 186, 238–40,
    302–3, 304
    and tea industry of Assam,
        187–97
    Surrendered ULFA (SULFA),
        196–97
    ULFA (Independent), 240
Uzan Bazar, Guwahati, 291

Vaishnavism, Vaishnav satras, 212,
    227–37, 308, 315–16

Mayamaras, 188
Victoria, Queen, 354
Vidarbha kingdom, 67, 80
Vidyapati, 232, 320

Waddell, Lawrence, 12–13, 312–14
Wadia, Nusli, 194
Walong, 39
Wang Shucheng, 122
Ward, Frank Kingdon, 38
Welsh, Thomas, 225
White, Major, 162
Wilcox, R., 37
wild babies, 270–80
Wild Grass, Kaziranga, 262, 267, 277–80
wildlife and riverine life, impact of dams and development projects, 38, 59–61, 71–74, 96–105, 120–24, 156–57, 230, 240, 258, 304–9, 342, 380–81
Wildlife Institute of India, 60
Wildlife Trust of India, 271
Williamson, Noel, 38, 89–90, 101
Wilson, H.H., 314

World War I, 14, 361
World War II, 48, 179–80, 191

Xihu (Ganges River Dolphin), 258–59
Xinjiang, 125–26
Xishuangbanna Dai Autonomous Prefecture, China, 186

Yahya Khan, 363
Yamuna, 379
Yangtze, 74, 121
Yarlung Tsangpo, 3, 120, 122, 123
Yellow River civilization, China, 9, 121
Yingkiong, Arunachal Pradesh, 97, 99, 101–2, 109–10, 112–13, 147–49, 150–52, 153–56
Yogini Tantra, 233
Younghusband, Francis, 13

Zahaz Ghat, 255
Zamzam River, Mecca, 40
Zangmu dam, Tibet, 120
Zayul Chu, 38–39

Acknowledgments

THIS BOOK IS A result of serendipity. The first serendipitous encounter that got me writing it was with the former publisher Preeti Gill, who had then recently set up her own literary agency. Preeti was looking for a writer to write a book on the Brahmaputra. We bumped into each other at a conference, and she asked me if I would like to take on the task. So thanks, Preeti, for thinking I could be the right person, and getting me started on this epic journey.

I don't know what kind of journey it would have been without the company and conversation of my old friend and fellow traveller, the photographer Akshay Mahajan, but I do know that the journey would be a lot less fun. Akshay is a genuine traveller, with a deep curiosity and a keen eye, and travelling with him on this long and often arduous path was a joy. Thanks, Akshay, for being there on this trip of a lifetime.

Our first hosts, Millie Hazarika and Masood Khan in Dibrugarh, were the ones who gave us the comfort and security of home in a strange place. They also gave us our first insights into the place. Over long dinner-time conversations, with Masood regaling us from his inexhaustible store of Upper Assam lore, I learnt a lot about Assam, some of which has gone into this book. Thanks, Masood, and thanks, Millie, for the friendship.

For the first serendipitous encounter with Preeti, I have to thank Sanjoy Hazarika, author, journalist, activist and academic, who had invited me for a conference. He also subsequently helped us to get a place on the Akha as it sailed on its char and chapori hopping duties. Thank you, Sanjoyda, for making that trip possible.

The crew of the Akha are a treasure. I would like to thank them all, and especially the two doctors, Dr Bhaben Bora and Dr Juganta Deori, who render a valuable service in a remote place. My salute to them.

Thanks to Raj and Runtun Chowdhury who graciously hosted us in their bungalow on a tea estate, and to Mrigayanka Roy Chowdhury, a gracious host herself, for making that possible.

In Guwahati, research and travel became much more pleasant thanks to my friends Mary Therese Kurkalang, Nishat Ahmed and Avik Paul, who opened their homes to me. The story of our ride to Hajo is told in the book. What is not mentioned is that Nishat was a new driver, which probably added some urgency and devotion to our prayers to the gods of various faiths.

In Bangladesh, I would like to thank my friend Zafar Sobhan, editor of the *Dhaka Tribune*, and his friend Morshed Ali Khan. Morshedbhai told me much about the river in Bangladesh, and worked the phone to introduce me to river pilot Sagar 'Poltu' Choudhury, about whom I have written in the book. My thanks to Choudhury for hosting me in Sirajganj, and to my old friend Saleem Samad for hosting me in Dhaka.

The writing of a book is a whole epic and meandering journey in itself. I would like to thank Aienla Ozukum, who offered critical feedback on the first draft of the manuscript, and Simar Puneet, who edited it. The text is much improved thanks to them. I would also like to thank the book's first 'civilian' reader, Silayan Cajucom, whose keen eye for detail has been of valuable help.

Last but certainly not least, my thanks to Siddhesh Inamdar and Krishan Chopra at HarperCollins for believing in this book, to Tanima Saha for taking it through to publication, and to my old friend and former boss, the editor and author Aditya Sinha, for pointing me in their direction.

For a non-academic such as me, who lacks institutional backing, accessing research material is often a problem. I am deeply grateful to JSTOR, the Open Library and Internet Archive, which made it possible for me to study original texts and documents to which I would otherwise have no access. I would also like to thank the Chevening Fellowship. Although I was in London as a journalism fellow at the University of Westminster, I took the opportunity to spend some happy afternoons reading history and looking through maps in that most wonderful of places, the British Library.

I have spent a few years on the travelling and the writing of this work. I grew to love the river and the lands through which it flows. I have tried my best to tell something of its stories along the way, but it can only ever be a partial and incomplete effort. The braided river is too vast to fit between the covers of a book. My homage to Mahabahu Brahmaputra, and to the lands through which it flows.

About the Author

Samrat Choudhury is a columnist and author. Somewhat like the river, he has been known by different names during the course of his life – as Samrat, sans surname, and also as Samrat X, by which name he is known on social media. An engineer by training, he is a former editor of the Mumbai edition of *The Asian Age*, the Delhi edition of *The Sunday Hindustan Times* and the Bengaluru edition of *The New Indian Express*. He has published widely in India, South Asia and around the world. His first novel, *The Urban Jungle*, was published by Penguin Books, and some of his essays and short stories have appeared in translation in Spanish, Portuguese, German and Italian. He was an Asian Leadership Fellow at the International House of Japan, Tokyo, in 2018, and a Chevening Fellow at the University of Westminster, London, in 2019. His current interests, apart from the Brahmaputra and Northeast India, include Partition. Samrat is co-founder and executive editor of the *Partition Studies Quarterly*.